GHOST SHIP

GH🛳OST
SHIP

THE MYSTERIOUS TRUE STORY OF
THE *MARY CELESTE* AND HER MISSING CREW

Brian Hicks

BALLANTINE BOOKS / NEW YORK

A Ballantine Book
Published by The Random House Publishing Group

Copyright © 2004 by Brian Hicks

www.ballantinebooks.com

LIBRARY OF CONGRESS CATALOGING-IN-PUBLICATION DATA
Hicks, Brian, 1966-
Ghost Ship : the mysterious true story of the *Mary Celeste*
and her missing crew / Brian Hicks.
p. cm.
Includes bibliographical references.
ISBN 0-345-46391-9
1. Mary Celeste (Brig) I. Title.

G530.M3H53 2004
910'.9163'3—dc22
2004043698

Manufactured in the United States of America

First Edition: June 2004

3 5 7 9 8 6 4 2

Book design by Casey Hampton

In memory of Rhoda Mae Coleman

Acknowledgments

It would have been impossible to conjure the spirit of the Ghost Ship without the help of dozens of people around the country who took the time and care to make sure I stayed on course.

At Ballantine Books, my editor, Zachary Schisgal, guided this project with a steady hand and keen eye, while Gina Centrello took the time to pass along suggestions that made the book much better. Many thanks also to the rest of the crew at Ballantine, especially Deirdre Lanning and Casey Hampton.

In Marion, Massachusetts, I'd like to thank Pete Smith of the Sippican Historical Society for showing me around his wonderful town; Judith D. Kleven and the staff at the Elizabeth Taber Library, which provided a good amount of the source material used in the writing of this book; and Neale Birdsall, for giving me an advance peek at his outstanding model of the *Mary Celeste*.

At the National Archives, Sally Kuisel and Milton Gustafson patiently walked me through the intricacies of State Department documents. The staffs at a half dozen outstanding museums and libraries also were most gracious and helpful to a sometimes-lost researcher.

Thanks especially to Christine Michelini at the Peabody Essex Museum in Salem; Michael Lapides at the New Bedford Whaling Museum; Louisa Alger Watrous and Leah Prescott at Mystic Seaport and its G. W. Blunt White Library; and the staffs at the New Bedford Public Library, the Buffalo and Erie County Public Library, and the New York Public Library.

At the South Street Seaport Museum in New York, Marine Historian Norman J. Brouwer took particular time to chat about the city's harbor and waterfront in the nineteenth century, and put me on the trail of several good leads (any errors in describing the scene in those days are my mistakes, not his). Sharon Desrosiers at the *Standard-Times* of New Bedford pointed me in the right direction a couple of times as well. From one reporter to another, thanks. Barb Thompson, manager and curator of the Cumberland County Museum and Archives in Amherst, Nova Scotia, supplied the wonderful photo of the *Mary Celeste* on the cover, while my friend and coconspirator Gill Guerry provided the great maps for this book.

As usual, Clive Cussler was superb. His Authorship was gracious with his time and eager to recount the National Underwater & Marine Agency's trip to Haiti in search of the bones of the *Mary Celeste*. NUMA proves time and again to be a wonderful agency filled with great people who care about the work they are doing. Thanks also to Mike Fletcher for sharing his story, and to the entire team at Eco-Nova. A special nod goes to Carole Bartholomeaux at NUMA for setting it all up.

At Atlantic Mutual, MaryBeth Iannaccone and Theodore R. Henke offered help, hospitality, and a great tour while I was in New Jersey. And for explaining all the properties of alcohol, offering his general expertise and invaluable historical knowledge, thanks to Chris Morris, master distiller with Brown-Forman in Kentucky. I also appreciate Ellen Nelson in Nashville and Michael J. Davis in Norfolk for all their sober guidance.

At the *Post and Courier,* several editors offered their encouragement for my extracurricular activities, only occasionally asking if I was done yet. Many thanks to John C. Huff, Larry Tarleton, Steve

Mullins, Marsha Guerard, Barbara Williams, Dan Conover, and my own personal editor and good friend, Steve Knickmeyer. I also appreciate the continued support of the guys in the *P&C* chapel: Fred, Tom, Bryce, Schuyler, Robert, Mic, Tony, and especially Arlie—you guys are better than the NEA.

I am grateful to my family for their continued support, especially my mother, Judy Hicks, who first introduced me to the *Mary Celeste* nearly thirty years ago; my father, Larry Hicks; and my brother, Todd, who makes sure my books are clearly visible in every bookstore he visits. Thanks as well to Alan and Donna Spears, Mary Ellen Spears, and particularly the late William D. Spears. He was a good friend, grandfather, and inspiration who offered sound advice on this project before his passing. He is greatly missed.

As always, this book could not have been written without the support, patience, and assistance of Beth Hicks, who not only reads the rough drafts but also manages the rest of the world—and Cole Hicks—while I stay locked away for months at a time. Thanks for everything.

Finally, a special nod to my friend Tracy Brown, who suggested this.

Brian Hicks
Charleston, South Carolina
November 2, 2003

Down dropt the breeze, the sails dropt down,
'Twas sad as sad could be;
And we did speak only to break
The silence of the sea!

—Samuel Taylor Coleridge,
The Rime of the Ancient Mariner

Is the ship accursed? Was there ever a voyage which began so fairly
and which changed so disastrously?

—Arthur Conan Doyle,
"J. Habakuk Jephson's Statement"

Dramatis personae

John Johnson   Seaman
Charles Lund   Seaman
Unknown
Unknown

The Briggs Family of Sippican Village

Nathan Briggs m. Sophia Cobb 1830
Maria Briggs   b. 1831
Nathan H. Briggs   b. 1834
Benjamin Spooner Briggs   b. 1835
Oliver Everson Briggs   b. 1837
James C. Briggs   b. 1839
Zenas Briggs   b. 1844

Joshua Dewis—builder of *Amazon,* later renamed *Mary Celeste*

Robert McLellan—*Amazon*'s first captain

George Spicer—a young sailor from Fundy

James Henry Winchester—New York shipping agent, majority shareholder of *Mary Celeste*

Horatio Jones Sprague—American consul at Gibraltar

Frederick Solly Flood—queen's advocate and proctor, attorney general of Gibraltar

Hon. James Cochrane—Judge of the Vice Admiralty Court of Gibraltar

Henry Pisani—attorney for the *Dei Gratia* crew

John Austin—surveyor at Gibraltar

R. W. Shufeldt—U.S. Navy commander and investigator

Arthur Conan Doyle—author of some note, wrote "J. Habakuk Jephson's Statement"

Gilman C. Parker—final captain of the *Mary Celeste*

Oliver Cobb—cousin of Benjamin Spooner Briggs, family biographer

Arthur Briggs—orphaned son of Benjamin S. and Sarah Briggs

Clive Cussler—author of some note, founder of National Underwater Marine Agency

Mike Fletcher—Eco-Nova diver, Nova Scotia

GHOST SHIP

December 4, 1872

The ship drifted restlessly through the whitecaps, like a lost soul wandering among tombstones. There was no hurry or purpose in its movement, no discernible momentum urging it along. Its circuitous path through the North Atlantic suggested nothing beyond mindless, random motion.

It had appeared out of nowhere, very much like the ghost ship sighted by Samuel Taylor Coleridge's wayward sailor in "The Rime of the Ancient Mariner." In the epic poem, the skeletal vessel that haunted the mariner first emerged from the mist as "a little speck" on the horizon, a ship that "plunged and tacked and veered" with only a hint of sail hanging from its masts. Coleridge hardly could have described the scene better had he been there on that colorless December day when the men of the Nova Scotia freighter *Dei Gratia* first spotted the ship destined to haunt them forever. The only difference was that, unlike the mariner, the sailors who discovered this wayfaring vessel detected no hint of malevolence—at least not initially.

The men had watched this curious sight from a distance all afternoon, hypnotized by its awkward, almost primitive, rhythm. At first glance, they thought little of the anonymous ship, but later changed course to intercept it when they finally decided it must be in some sort of distress. Something about its gait seemed, well, unnatural.

At the wheel of the *Dei Gratia,* seaman John Johnson most likely did not know the similarities between the approaching vessel and the ship of doom described in Coleridge's verse, which by 1872 was already a classic. But then Johnson, a Russian Lutheran, could barely speak the King's English, much less read it. His knowledge of seafaring lore was limited to whatever his fellow sailors related to him on long, cold deck watches. That afternoon, however, Johnson would join that mythology as he played a small role in an incident destined to become one of the ultimate stories of the sea; for on that day, December 4, 1872, the crew of the *Dei Gratia* sailed into maritime history after a chance encounter with a small merchant ship called the *Mary Celeste.*

For nearly an hour after first spying her, the men watched the ship yawing erratically as it lumbered along with only a few sails flying. The *Dei Gratia's* captain attempted to signal her crew several times, but received no reply. A cautious man, he could not shake the feeling that something was wrong, and knew he must lend whatever assistance he could—that was the unwritten law of the sea. So, when the two ships passed within a quarter mile of one another, the captain sent three of his men, including Johnson, to investigate.

The sailors rowed over in a small lifeboat and climbed aboard the vessel, where they stumbled onto a chilling scene: an empty deck, a tattered sail hanging from the foremast, the ship's wheel spinning untended. More than 400 miles from the coast of Portugal, the *Mary Celeste* was sailing without a soul on board.

Perhaps the oddest thing was that, for the most part, she appeared to be in fine shape—almost eerily so. The *Dei Gratia* crew found no serious weather damage, no trace of a struggle, or any other sign of trouble that would have made veteran sailors abandon ship in the middle of the ocean. Stranger still, the crew had left behind foul-weather gear, personal belongings, even their pipes—things they almost certainly would have taken, or would have been wearing during a storm.

There were other things that seemed more than a little peculiar: The form of a sleeping child was imprinted in the wet mattress of one bunk, a few barrels of alcohol had broken open or leaked in the hold, and there was a decorative sword in the captain's cabin, its blade peppered with a reddish stain. The last entry in the *Mary Celeste*'s logbook was an innocuous notation made ten days earlier that suggested nothing but a routine passage—and placed the ship more than 300 miles west of its current position. The men of the *Dei Gratia* could not imagine how the ship had traveled so far sailing under so little canvas, nor could they explain where its crew had gone or, just as confounding, *why*. The brigantine's captain and crew had simply vanished into the cold salt air.

More than a century later, many sailors and historians still consider the story of the *Mary Celeste* the greatest maritime mystery of all time. It is a tale that evokes man's most primordial fears of the sea, of simply vanishing without a trace beneath the waves. It has become one of the most appropriated stories in nautical history, but its legend also resonates with elements of literature written decades before it sailed—not only Coleridge's "Mariner," but also Edgar Allan Poe's *Narrative of Arthur Gordon Pym*. But in the case of the *Mary Celeste*, the truth is undeniably stranger than fiction.

The *Mary Celeste* shares a certain kinship with the *Flying Dutchman* as well; both vessels are routinely called "ghost ships." When the *Mary Celeste* sailed in the mid-nineteenth century, fantastic tales of the *Dutchman*—an apparition said to appear in the stormy waters off Africa's Cape of Good Hope—were already more than 200 years old. It is said that the *Dutchman*, hopelessly searching for safe harbor, is doomed to forever haunt the cape, where it was lost during a storm in the fifteenth century.

For the *Mary Celeste*, the label of ghost ship has a somewhat less supernatural, but arguably as suspenseful, definition. "Ghost ship" is an old mariner's term for any vessel found sailing without her crew.

Abandoning a ship in the middle of the ocean was not an uncommon occurrence in the nineteenth century; every year dozens of vessels were found unoccupied just in the Atlantic. There was almost always a reasonable explanation. Men prematurely left ships they thought were sinking, either taking to lifeboats or flagging down a passing vessel to rescue them. Often an entire crew could be swept overboard in a storm, but the ship they left behind sported enough damage to make their fate obvious. Sometimes, sailors who came upon an abandoned vessel might even find a note or logbook telling why the crew was gone.

On occasion, the disappearance of a ship's crew could be attributed to violence, not from the sea, but brought on by other men. Mutiny and piracy were still of some concern in the nineteenth century. In those days, entire crews could be shanghaied—abducted and forced to work on other ships. But by the latter years of the century those were, mercifully, relatively rare events.

More than 130 years after the *Mary Celeste* sailed, no one can say for certain what happened to the ten people who sailed on her. There were a half dozen theories offered in the months after the ship was discovered derelict, and there have been a dozen more advanced since, but there has never been a clear consensus on any one scenario. It is a mystery that has tormented countless people, including the families of the lost sailors and hundreds of others who have tried in vain to solve the riddle. The Ghost Ship may be the best example of the old proverb that the sea never gives up its secrets.

The *Mary Celeste* sailed at the height of the Industrial Age, a time when men felt they were on the verge of conquering nature. Great advances in science and engineering were opening new worlds to people. Even the ocean seemed less forbidding, as the invention of steamships had made passage from one port to the next easier and quicker—no longer were men at the mercy of the wind. In the wake of this blossoming age of mechanization and discovery, people were slowly abandoning their old superstitions, sometimes with an almost arrogant swagger. Sailors, among the most superstitious of all, were becoming less likely to attribute accidents at sea to unknown evils lurking beneath the waves. But the strange disappearance of the *Mary Celeste*'s passengers and crew reminded men that the ocean was still a dangerous place.

The historian George S. Bryan said the story of the enigmatic derelict captured America's imagination because it gave the New World a nautical mythology of its own. Bryan, a biographer of Abraham Lincoln, called the *Mary Celeste* the most famous ship since the *Mayflower,* and said that she "took rank alongside that of the Old World's phantom craft eternally sailing but never making port." For some time, it became arguably the most *infamous* ship in the world, inspiring countless stories, radio plays and, eventually, movies. It has taken its place alongside the legend of the *Flying Dutchman,* but ultimately a comparison of the two ghost ships is not a fair measure: the saga of the *Mary Celeste* is infinitely more frightening because there is no question that this legend is true.

At the time it sailed, the *Mary Celeste* was just another anonymous brigantine, one in a fleet of thousands of merchant ships plying the Atlantic. There was nothing remarkable about her; she was small for her day, and carried only a modest amount of cargo. At the time, the brigantine was in danger of being supplanted by the growing number of steamships, which crossed the ocean in much better time than two-masted sailing vessels. As such, running the *Mary Celeste* was not a particularly profitable way to make a living. Mostly, small firms hired the ship, which was one of a dozen owned by a major New York shipping company.

The *Mary Celeste*'s captain, Benjamin Spooner Briggs, had just taken command of the ship—it was his first voyage on her. He was hired to deliver a load of alcohol to Italy, carrying a crew of experienced Americans and for-hire foreign sailors. It was supposed to be a routine cruise, nothing out of the ordinary. When the *Mary Celeste* sailed from New York in November of 1872, Briggs thought it safe enough to take along his wife and two-year-old daughter.

The disappearance of the *Mary Celeste*'s crew a month later became an international scandal. Captain Briggs was a respectable, veteran sailor—certainly not the sort of man who would panic and recklessly abandon a seaworthy ship, particularly while traveling with his family. But it appeared that was just what had happened, and many people saw a frightening pattern of destiny in his fate. Briggs hailed from a long line of respected sailors, many of whom had been lost at sea, some in similarly bizarre mishaps. The *Mary Celeste* incident was only the latest in a long series of tragedies to befall the family, and not even the last one of that winter.

On both sides of the Atlantic, the story prompted speculation of foul play, and soon the men of the *Dei Gratia* grew to regret their decision to salvage the derelict. At the mercy of an overzealous, conspiracy-minded bureaucrat, the sailors very nearly found themselves on trial for the murder of Briggs and the *Mary Celeste*'s crew. As it was, it took several months for the crew of the *Dei Gratia* to escape the jurisdiction of the Gibraltar Vice Admiralty Court, and the taint of scandal followed them forever.

For a while, new theories of the crew's fate were promoted almost monthly, sensationalized by newspapers in America and Europe in a fashion that foreshadowed the tabloid journalism that would proliferate in the next century. Some people believed pirates had abducted the *Mary Celeste*'s crew and forced them to walk the plank. Others suspected the increasingly common ploy of insurance fraud, as several policies paid off, yet the owners retained the ship. For a while, mutiny was a popular theory, one even endorsed by the ship's owners. Although there was a maddening lack of evidence to support any of the wild theories, nothing could quell the speculation.

In 1884 the ship became forever cemented in the lore of the sea when a young man named Arthur Conan Doyle tackled the case of the *Mary Celeste* in one of his first published short stories. The story, which appeared just three years before Doyle introduced the world to a master of deduction named Sherlock Holmes, had an immeasurable impact on the legend of the *Mary Celeste*. More than a few people thought the unbylined piece of fiction was a true confession, and it sparked investigations by the U.S. and British governments. Soon, clever elements of Doyle's story—untouched lifeboats, a spool of thread still balanced on a table—became part of the ship's legend, and survive to this day in many variations of the tale. Later stories, picking up where Doyle left off, claimed there was even a hot meal found on the galley table.

As is often the case with unsolved mysteries, the infamous story was later dredged up by a string of hoaxers, some of whom claimed they had been aboard the ship on that mysterious cruise or knew someone who had survived. In one twenty-year span of the last century, newspapers breathlessly chronicled the elaborate and far-fetched tales of no less than three imposters.

At one point or another, nearly every popular maritime legend has been linked to the Ghost Ship, especially those with some connection to the occult. A few have insisted a giant squid ate the *Mary Celeste's* crew, while others point to alien abduction. In the days following the *Titanic* disaster some folks even believed the *Mary Celeste's* crew abandoned ship fearing they were about to hit an iceberg. In the mid-twentieth century, the Ghost Ship helped to establish the Bermuda Triangle legend, even though it sailed nowhere near those waters on its most famous voyage. The particulars mattered little to most storytellers. In a vacuum of answers, some people were willing to believe almost anything.

One of the most exhaustive investigations of the ship and its lost crew was conducted by Charles Edey Fay, an executive with the Atlantic Mutual Insurance Company (Atlantic held a policy on the ship's cargo at the time of the crew's disappearance). Fay released his findings and opinions in Mary Celeste: *Odyssey of an Abandoned Ship*, published in 1942 by the Peabody Essex Museum in Salem, Massachusetts. In his fine work of scholarship, Fay collected all the information on the ship that had been uncovered in seventy years, and offered a handful of solutions to the mystery. Since that time, new details of the ship, the people on board and the circumstances leading up to their disappearance have emerged. Fay worked from an incomplete transcript of the Gibraltar salvage hearing, and suspected that something was amiss. In his text he laments the fact that neither the ship's owner nor the captain of the *Dei Gratia* testified at the hearing—a curiosity that also perplexed members of the Briggs family for years. In fact, both men did testify, but their words were lost for nearly a century.

In the 1960s, a more complete transcript of the December 1872 "Judge's notes on evidence, Vice Admiralty Court of Gibraltar" was discovered in Europe by Mrs. Parker Converse, who had the manuscript published in a limited edition by the Sippican Historical Society. The find has an immeasurable impact on the story of the Ghost Ship. Captain David Reed Morehouse's testimony, in which he recalls encountering the *Mary Celeste* at sea, is even more chilling than his crew's account, and reveals for the first time what drew the men to the strange vessel on the horizon. The observations of James H. Winchester, majority shareholder of the ship, fill in some of the blanks in the ship's background. While neither man delivers the smoking gun that solves the mystery, their testimony adds depth to the story, clears up some misconceptions and answers a few of the seemingly endless nagging questions. Their words add weight and suspense to the story, but also help steer it toward a single, logical explanation.

In the midst of increasingly outlandish theories, there have been various serious attempts to explain the mystery of the *Mary Celeste* over the years. The most plausible solutions—including water spouts, disappearing islands and problems with the ship's cargo of alcohol—offer explanations which might clear up the mystery save for the fact that they all depend on extraordinary circumstances; each includes a modicum of freak occurrence to fit the theory into the known facts. The truth is most likely much simpler. Using various elements of these theories, along with details of the case that have come to light only in recent decades, it appears that the loss of the *Mary Celeste*'s crew was the result of a short series of unfortunate accidents and mistakes. While no one will ever be able to say for certain exactly what happened on board the *Mary Celeste* in the fall of 1872, it now appears safe to say that the crew's disappearance was the result of bad luck, poor timing and an unspeakable accident.

One of the most unsettling aspects of the story of the *Mary Celeste* is that the disappearance of Briggs and his crew is only one chapter in its long, strange history. Built in Nova Scotia in 1861, the ship was originally christened *Amazon*. After a series of bizarre mishaps on its maiden voyage, it sailed for a half dozen years before it ran aground in a storm and was thought lost forever. Then it turned up in New York, where Briggs bought his interest in her and set a course for his destiny.

For more than a decade after Briggs and his crew went missing, bad luck followed anyone who had the misfortune to buy shares in her or sail aboard her. Many sailors refused to take a job on the ship. One man, interested in buying a bargain freighter, allegedly ran screaming from a New York City dock when he saw the name on her stern. After its discovery in December of 1872, the *Mary Celeste* passed from one owner to the next in what the British author Macdonald Hastings called "the sad way of orphans." It consistently lost money for another decade before finally disappearing in yet another scandal.

Over the course of twenty-four years, the Ghost Ship drifted into and out of the lives of dozens of people, leaving bad luck, financial ruin and death in its wake. More than a century later, it remains man's fear of the sea personified. It is a compelling and unsettling legacy for a modest merchant ship that began this bizarre journey into infamy and the occult on a desolate beach in Nova Scotia more than 140 years ago.

PART I

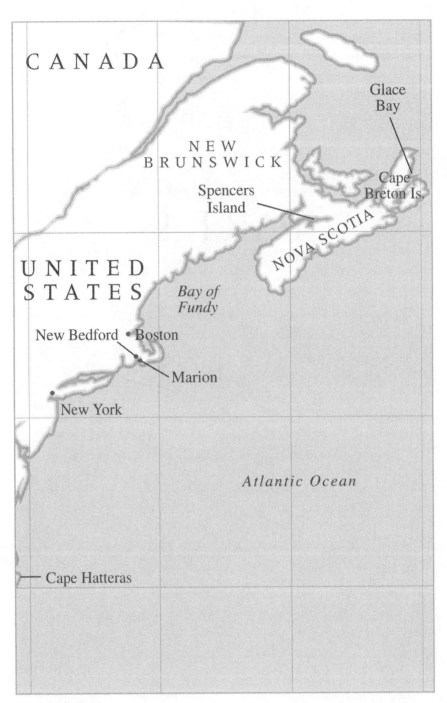

CANADA

NEW
BRUNSWICK

Glace
Bay

Spencers
Island

Cape
Breton Is.

NOVA SCOTIA

UNITED
STATES

Bay of
Fundy

New Bedford • Boston

Marion

New York

Atlantic Ocean

Cape Hatteras

Map by Gill Guerry

ONE

A Simple, Handsome Ship

For as long as he lived, George Spicer was haunted by the sight of a worried young woman running along the Nova Scotia shore.

It was a summer morning in June of 1861, when Spicer was just a teenager with dreams of going to sea. He had been aboard a skiff sailing into Economy, a small fishing village shrouded by Acadian pines on the Minas Channel. In the town, locals watched the world's most powerful tides rise and fall as much as fifty-three feet in a matter of hours—a surge that impressed upon them a healthy respect for the sea. The ocean provided a life for many of them, and they knew it could just as easily take one away. And as the tide often did, on that morning George Spicer was carrying bad news.

Mary Ann McLellan had noticed the small boat approaching and, as it drew closer, thought she recognized the boys on board as crew from her husband's ship. A week earlier, Robert McLellan had sailed as captain of the newly christened *Amazon,* a cargo ship built by a group of businessmen forty miles down the coast. The *Amazon* was bound for London hauling a load of timber cut at nearby Five Islands.

From there, the ship was to take on more cargo and sail south to Lisbon. They were supposed to be gone for months, probably through the end of the year. Now, oddly, they had returned. The sight of the boys in the boat alarmed Mrs. McLellan. She knew that something was wrong.

She never could have imagined, though, how the approaching boat would impact her life. For on that morning, Spicer and his friends had been assigned the sad and unfortunate task of delivering Captain McLellan's body to his hometown, and his new bride.

It had all happened so quickly. McLellan took ill almost immediately after setting foot onboard the *Amazon*. Admittedly, he had been suffering from a cold while the crew loaded the ship, but the captain insisted a good dose of salt air was all he needed—a trusted antidote among sailors. McLellan was eager to set out on the vessel's first run, and most likely no one thought anything of it at the time. Calling in sick wasn't a consideration in the nineteenth century.

As the *Amazon* made its way into the Bay of Fundy, McLellan's cold quickly escalated into pneumonia. He grew weaker by the hour, and the crew soon realized the ocean air would do their captain no good. Fearing McLellan would not survive a 3,000-mile trip across the Atlantic, they turned back. On its maiden voyage, the *Amazon* had barely made it to New Brunswick.

It took scarcely a day to circle back to Spencers Island, where the captain was taken to the home of Jacob Spicer—George's father and a shareholder in *Amazon*. There, Captain McLellan lingered for two days before quietly dying.

Although he was just fourteen at the time, George Spicer later remembered thinking that McLellan seemed so *young*—not so much older than himself; certainly not old enough to die. Spicer had planned to be aboard the *Amazon* for its first sail, but took ill while the ship was being loaded and returned home, not sharing the captain's confidence in the healing powers of salt air. After McLellan died, Spicer offered to help take his body to Economy. Along with some hands from the *Amazon*'s crew, he wrapped the captain's body in a blanket and carefully loaded it on the small boat.

In his long life, George Spicer would see much of the world as mate and master of several oceangoing vessels. But as a retired sea captain in the 1930s, he still counted the trip in that skiff as one of his most memorable because he could not forget the moment Mary Ann McLellan met him on the beach. Years later, he would tell people he could still see that widow, who did not yet know she was a widow, in the moment before her heart was broken.

"I remember," he recalled, "his young wife came down to the shore to see what was in the boat."

Thus began the voyages of the ship that would one day be known as the *Mary Celeste*. It was built with indigenous wood and local labor at Spencers Island, a rural community in northwestern Nova Scotia on the northern shore of the Minas Channel. The basin is the eastern arm of the Bay of Fundy, and it bisects the Nova Scotia countryside with a mighty tidal surge that has carved a craggy coastline into the mountainous region. In the nineteenth century, the area was home to miners, farmers and sailors descended from British Loyalists, many of whom had come north a century earlier when the American colonies declared their independence. There they raised cattle, harvested clams and tended farms of sturdy timber to earn a living. Although technically connected to mainland New Brunswick by an isthmus nearly twenty miles wide, Nova Scotia is in all practical ways an island. And like islanders around the world, Nova Scotians of the day made their living from the sea, either working in fisheries, on fishing boats, or by hiring out as sailors on local freighters. Their ships still flew British flags when the *Amazon* was launched in 1861, six years before Nova Scotia joined a young band of provinces called Canada.

With the *Amazon*, Joshua Dewis was attempting not only to build a profitable cargo ship but also to establish a new shipyard. He had been building boats on a smaller scale most of his life. When he was a teenager living in Economy, he designed and constructed rowboats, yawls and skiffs that he sold to local farmers. By the time he was thirty, in 1845, he had built his first schooner. Not long after that, he moved west to a farm at Advocate Harbor that overlooked the wide expanse of the Bay of Fundy. There, at the gateway to the world's busiest ocean, Dewis grew serious about becoming a shipwright.

It was a good time to get into the business, for Nova Scotia's maritime industry was booming. The embryonic stages of a global economy created a great demand for cargo ships, and the American Civil War would soon cause a shortage in the market. Nova Scotia, which had long envied the success of New England's shipping and whaling industries, was more than happy to fill that void. In the nineteenth century, communities in northwestern Nova Scotia alone launched more than 200 ships. The coast was littered with shipyards as a result, any one of which Dewis could have gone to with his plans for a wooden sailing ship. Instead, he chose to start his own.

Most likely, a combination of financial and family interests had spurred Dewis to build his ship (and shipyard) on the crescent-shaped beach of Spencers Island. Two local brothers, Jacob and Isaac Spicer, were shareholders in the ship, which may have been payment for the use of wood from their 2,500-acre timber farm in its construction. Dewis had several ties to the Spicer family: Jacob Spicer was married to Dewis's sister-in-law Mary (they were George Spicer's parents), and Dewis's son was sweet on Isaac Spicer's daughter. It was, in several ways, a very cozy business arrangement.

Construction began in the fall of 1860 on the beach near the town mill. Using Dewis's plans, workers laid the keel for a brigantine, a two-masted sailing ship that would be one hundred feet long. Building a wooden ship was—and still is—more art than science. The men had to select the heartiest timbers, but timbers that also could be carefully contorted into the feminine shapes of a sailing vessel. It was tedious, backbreaking work, but slowly the elegant outline of a ship's hull was formed. By the time harsh weather forced them to retreat indoors, Dewis's crew had finished the ship's frame. Through the winter, the skeleton of *Amazon,* giant ribs sprouting from its keel, lay on the beach like a whale carcass.

The crew resumed work in the spring, piecing together a smooth hull along the ribs of the ship and raising two masts that were nearly as tall as the ship was long. They bought the materials for the rigging—miles of line, blocks and chain—from a new general store that probably opened as a direct result of the ship's economic impact on the area. The benefits of the shipyard, for the rest of the century, would go well beyond employment opportunities for Spencers Island residents.

By early May, just as the Nova Scotia spring turned pleasant, Dewis finished his ship. Its final measurement put it just inches shy of one hundred feet long. It had a beam of twenty-five feet and a draft of nearly twelve feet. It had been built from the various types of available timber—spruce, pine, birch, beech—and had rock salt packed between its boards to help prevent rot. The craftsmanship was evident in its smooth, hydrodynamic hull, preferable to the overlapping planks common on some ships. It had a squared-off stern and a single deck. The sole nod to ornamentation was a billeted bowsprit arching out above the bow. It was a simple but handsome sailing ship.

Aside from spare quarters for the captain and crew on deck, the brig's interior looked unfinished, its walls made of unpainted, coarse wood. As most of the cubic footage was reserved for cargo there was no reason to spend time or money making its innards attractive. In almost every way, the ship was built for one purpose: to make money. It had a gross tonnage of about 200 tons, a figure that referred to the total amount of space on board (net tonnage referred to the actual space for cargo, but that statistic for the ship was never recorded). Little of that area was reserved for the crew. The more cargo and fewer sailors a ship's owners squeezed into that space often meant the difference between profit and loss.

Even the decision to build a brigantine as opposed to a barkentine or schooner—fast becoming the most popular type of sailing ship—was a nod to economy. The brig straddled two eras: Its foremast was square-rigged, like the sailing ships of Captain Cook and Christopher Columbus, while its mainmast carried triangular fore-and-aft sails, like a schooner. By taking advantage of both types of rigging, the ship could carry a smaller crew, as schooner sails were easier to manage than those of a square-rigger. Maritime registries classified Dewis's ship as a hermaphrodite brig or half brig, because the majority opinion of the day was that a "true" brigantine was meant to carry at least one square sail, if not a full complement, on its mainmast. Dewis rigged the ship's mainmast to carry only fore-and-aft sails, not bothering to add even a square topsail, most likely because he didn't see the need. In truth, most brigantines plying the waters of the mid-nineteenth century used the same sail arrangement that Dewis employed on the *Amazon*. There was nothing unusual or spectacular about it.

Dewis financed the ship by selling shares in it, a common arrangement of the day meant to dilute costs. He kept sixteen of sixty-four shares, retaining 25 percent ownership. The Spicer brothers together held another quarter. Five local businessmen and Robert McLellan, who would be the ship's captain, owned the rest. The profits of the ship would be divided according to shares.

Although there were only nine shareholders, the entire community felt some sense of pride and ownership in the first major ship built in their little town (and would later resent any notion that it was cursed from the beginning). Many of those people, and some from neighboring communities, gathered at the beach on May 18, 1861, to watch as the ship was slid down greased rails, or ways, and floated in the Minas Channel. The ceremony launched the era of shipbuilding at Spencers Island; more than two dozen sailing vessels would follow before the turn of the century. Dewis christened his ship the *Amazon*, but no one could ever recall what had prompted that decidedly generic name.

Later, its launch would come to be mired in controversy—like almost everything else concerning the ship—because of conflicting stories and recollections. After the *Mary Celeste* made international headlines more than a decade later, various newspapers and magazines reported that the ship got stuck on the ways when shipyard workers first attempted to float it. Some even claimed it stubbornly refused to budge for days, a dozen men straining to pry the ship from its perch. Several newspapers repeated the legend on the basis of comments from Dewis's own son, John.

"This craft seemed possessed of the devil to begin with, but where she got it I don't know. I am sure it couldn't have been from any of our good people," he said.

It was easy to attribute such ominous beginnings to the ship in retrospect. Such foreboding tales were common in Nova Scotia, which—like most seafaring communities—generated its share of maritime legend. More than a century before *Amazon* was built, a similar brigantine had haunted Fundy waters. In December of 1735, residents of Chebogue awoke one morning to find a silent ship anchored in their harbor. For nearly the entire day, townsfolk stood on the shore watching for signs of life aboard the brig. By that afternoon, when a small boat was launched to investigate, locals were already speculating on the supernatural powers that had steered the empty vessel into their harbor. The ship was called the *Baltimore,* and the men in the skiff soon discovered evidence to fuel their superstitious notions: the ship's deck was awash with blood.

The men found no one onboard until they reached the barricaded door of the captain's cabin. There, they discovered a frightened woman who claimed to be the wife of the ship's owner. She told them the crew had put into port for fresh water, but were attacked and killed by local Indians; she survived only by hiding. The locals were skeptical; they had seen or heard nothing unusual, but nevertheless allowed the woman to stay. The *Baltimore* soon came to be known as the "Death Ship." No one wanted to buy it, sail it, or even go aboard. For seven years it swung at anchor in Chebogue Harbor, until Yarmouth County officials finally ordered it towed to sea and burned. Later, locals learned that the *Baltimore* was actually a prisoner ship that had sailed from Ireland. The inmates had broken loose, killed the captain and crew, and then each other. Out of sixty inmates, only ten survived. Nine of the men escaped into the Nova Scotia countryside, and the tenth was the woman found in the captain's cabin. By the time the mystery was unraveled, however, the woman had disappeared.

In the *Amazon's* home county, near Parrsboro, locals were wary of "Maiden's Cave," a hollow in the rocky shoreline where some people believed they could hear the moaning of a long-dead British girl. According to legend, the young woman had been sailing on her father's ship when pirates raided it. The pirates, led by an Italian swashbuckler named Deno, forced the captain and crew to walk the plank, but spared the girl. Deno was smitten. Showing uncharacteristic pirate chivalry, he tried without luck to win the girl by conventional methods.

Deno kept the young woman prisoner until a storm drove the pirate ship into the Bay of Fundy. After the gale died, the crew gazed with amazement at the Nova Scotia coast, which sparkled in the morning sun. The pirates went ashore, where they found a beach littered with valuable amethyst, and a cave. There, Deno gave his prisoner-maiden her final choice: marry him or face banishment in the cave. She chose imprisonment over the man who killed her father, and Deno made good on his threat. Years later, when the wind was right, locals swore they could still hear the cries of that imprisoned girl.

As superstitious as they were, Spencers Island residents for decades refuted any suggestion that the launch of *Amazon* deserved a place among these strange tales. George Spicer, who was there when the ship was launched, was among its staunchest defenders. He claimed that everything went smoothly on that pleasant spring day.

Within a few weeks of *Amazon*'s launch, Dewis had the ship registered at Parrsboro and contracted to haul a load of timber to England. And then Captain McLellan died. The ship remained docked with its cargo onboard until Dewis hired Jack Parker from Walton—a town across the channel—as its new master. Parker soon had ship and sailors ready to depart. Even though George Spicer was feeling better after his return from the somber trip to Economy, he chose not to rejoin the crew. He had been sailing local ships across the Bay of Fundy for two years and wanted nothing more than to go to sea, but Spicer nevertheless delayed his first transatlantic voyage for a while longer. He never said why.

Even though Spicer later dismissed such notions, to some people it seemed that the new ship was already plagued with bad luck. Robert Dewis, another of Joshua's sons, said the *Amazon* stopped in Eastport, Maine, on that first trip and, on its way out of the harbor, hit a row of weirs—stakes set in the water used to help catch fish. It reportedly took several days to repair the damage.

Robert Dewis also claimed that shortly after delivering its load of timber to London, the *Amazon* rammed another brig in the Strait of Dover, the waterway connecting the English Channel and the North Sea. The collision was serious enough that the other ship sank almost immediately. According to Dewis, the *Amazon*'s crew had to rescue the sailors from the other ship and limp into port at Dover, England. There, for the second time in two months, the brig was delayed for weeks as it underwent repairs. No one ever explained what caused the two ships to collide or whether the accident cost any lives.

It was a shakedown cruise of the worst kind, but that incident seemed to mark the end of the *Amazon*'s run of bad luck. The rest of its first voyage was routine, and the ship soon settled into the day-to-day grind of merchant sailing. A few months later, while still in Europe, Captain Parker commissioned the only contemporary painting of the ship. Dated November 1861 in Marseille, it depicts a proud new vessel carrying more than a dozen billowing sails from its two masts. The hull is dark, shown gliding across calm water, and the bowsprit stands proud, but there are few other details. It is an idealized image that conjures nothing but the most benign notions of life at sea. Certainly, it suggests nothing malevolent about the *Amazon*. She appears to be just another graceful but plain sailing ship.

The *Amazon* traveled the busiest trade routes in the world through the mid-1860s, crossing in shipping lanes between New England and Europe, sailing up the Mediterranean and down to the Caribbean, carrying coal, corn, fruit and lumber in its belly. The ship was not particularly fast or profitable, but its owners got a fair return on their investment. There were few complaints from Dewis and his partners, at least initially.

A couple of years later, George Spicer finally joined the crew of the *Amazon*. He was a tall, wiry young man and an enthusiastic, hard worker who was quickly promoted to second mate. During his early days before the mast, Spicer caught his first glimpses of much of the world, of places much different from the red mudflats of his home-land. One day in the spring of 1865, while the ship was in port at Pro-greso, Mexico, on the Yucatán peninsula, Spicer first heard the news that the American president, Abraham Lincoln, had been assassinated.

For Spicer, who had grown up working on the family farm, his two years aboard the *Amazon* were enjoyable but uneventful, an ap-prenticeship that began a long life aboard sailing ships. A few years later he would become the master of a larger brig, the *Globe,* and he ultimately commanded four other vessels over a career that spanned nearly five decades. Still, as a retired sea captain living near the old family farm at Spencers Island, Spicer spent his final days telling visi-tors about his short time on board the *Amazon,* and defending her from charges that she was cursed.

"There was nothing unusual about the ship, she went along very well," he said.

Joshua Dewis and his partners kept the *Amazon* at sea almost con-stantly for nearly seven years. After more than two years as captain, Jack Parker left to become master of another ship and William Thompson, one of the original shareholders, took his place. In the fall of 1867, however, Dewis and the other owners had a falling out with Thompson, perhaps over dwindling profits. The shareholders decided Thompson should be replaced. Dewis sent a new skipper to Halifax, where the *Amazon* was unloading a shipment of corn from Baltimore.

It was there that George Spicer left the *Amazon.* He had been sail-ing aboard her for more than two years and decided that was enough. He quit the crew in Halifax and struck out across land for home, never to sail on the ship again. His timing could not have been better.

When Dewis's new captain arrived in the Nova Scotia capital, the *Amazon* had already departed. After its cargo was unloaded, Thomp-son had taken the empty *Amazon* to the easternmost reaches of Nova Scotia. At Cape Breton Island, the ship stopped in Big Glace Bay near modern-day Port Morien, an inlet with minimal protection from the harsh nor'easters that regularly sweep through the uppermost reaches of the Atlantic in the fall and winter. The area was considered so dan-gerous for sailing ships that most insurance companies in the nineteenth century refused to cover damages sustained there after a certain time of the year. November was unquestionably past that cutoff date.

Thompson said he was going to pick up a load of coal to sell farther down the coast, perhaps in New York. But in early November 1867, a gale came barreling up the Gulf Stream and into the North Atlantic, blowing the *Amazon* onto the rocky shore of Big Glace Bay. Robert Dewis, still a mate on the ship, reported to his father that the ship ran aground near the site of a dock being built by an American company. The crew survived the crash and left the ship stranded on the rocks.

It looked like the end for the *Amazon*. The damage to the ship was so bad, or reportedly so, that Dewis and his partners could not afford to have it repaired. It was never clear whether she sustained heavy hull damage or the owners just thought it would cost more than the ship was worth to get it off the rocks. Either way, with little hope of salvage, Dewis sold the *Amazon* to a Cape Breton Island man. Almost immediately, the new owner sold it again.

Years afterward, some people claimed the paperwork surrounding these sales suggested some foul play in the wreck of the *Amazon*. A new registry was issued for the ship on November 9, 1867, and registries weren't supposed to be issued until a ship was deemed seaworthy. That meant Thompson had either exaggerated the damage or someone had issued an improper or fraudulent registry on a wrecked ship. Some speculated that Thompson, knowing he was going to be replaced, sold out his partners. Whatever happened, the result was the same: Dewis and the Spicer brothers lost the *Amazon*. Although his shipyard launched another thirty vessels before shutting down, Dewis himself would never build another ship.

The *Amazon* essentially disappeared for a year following its change in registry. There was most likely nothing sinister about it. Paperwork was sporadic in those days, notations often lost. More than likely, its new owners spent a good part of that time making the ship seaworthy enough to sell again. But they didn't do a very good job. A year later, in November 1868, the *Amazon* resurfaced in New York. It went up for public auction but seemed so rickety that it didn't attract many bidders. Richard W. Haines bought it for a mere $1,750—about one third what the ship had been valued at when she was launched in 1861.

With his bargain brig, Haines had his work cut out for him. He had to replace the *Amazon*'s stern, keel—in fact, its entire bottom. He ordered new spars, rigging and sails. Altogether, he spent more than $9,000 on the ship, only to lose it less than a year later when he couldn't pay off the loans he'd taken out to do the work. It's not clear how many trips—if any—Haines was able to make with the ship before it was seized. In October 1869, his creditors sold the ship at auction to J. H. Winchester & Co., Ship Owners & Commission Merchants, of New York City.

Although he owned it for only a brief time, Haines made his own indelible mark on the ship. Before he lost the *Amazon,* Haines obtained a questionable registry from a customhouse broker and changed its name. He reflagged the ship as an American vessel and, without giving any particular reason, rechristened it the *Mary Celeste.*

More than seventy years later, when its name was known throughout the world, James Franklin Briggs—a nephew of the ship's doomed captain—said the little half brig had been misnamed. Instead of *Mary Celeste,* which meant "Heavenly Mary," Briggs suggested they should have called her *Mary Diablesse,* or "Mary the She-Devil."

"For she brought disaster on every man that put his trust in her," he said.

TWO

The Seafaring Life

Benjamin Spooner Briggs was not a superstitious man.

If he knew anything of his new ship's troubled past, he said nothing of it. A practical, deeply religious New Englander, hushed stories of dying captains and bizarre accidents would have meant little to him. In twenty years of sailing, Briggs had heard it all: mermaids, sea monsters, the *Flying Dutchman*. To be sure, nineteenth-century sailors could dream up some dandies. They passed these stories amongst themselves like gossiping schoolgirls in ports around the world—myths born of equal parts boredom, genuine wonder at the might and vastness of the ocean, and a fear of drowning (an amazing number of sailors in those days could not swim).

There certainly were peculiar things in the ocean, but Briggs had grown accustomed to life at sea—he was a confident, able sailor who felt he could handle anything. His fears were more solidly grounded in reality. Presently, Briggs was most concerned with how well his new command, a modest brigantine, would ride in the water after a major overhaul. He was right to worry, as he had invested a lot of money in her.

No, superstition was clearly not in Captain Benjamin Briggs's nature, for if it were he never would have set foot onboard a sailing vessel. Not after the great number of tragedies his family had suffered at the mercy of the sea. In thirty years, Briggs had lost two brothers, his only sister and an uncle to the ocean, all in separate incidents. The family had seen more than its share of hardship, even for the times. Just two years earlier, its patriarch—the respected Captain Nathan Briggs—had died in a fluke accident. Oddly enough, the most experienced sailor among them was the only one to die on dry land. The sea was so cruel to the Briggses that soon people around their hometown would begin to whisper of a curse on the family. But Benjamin Briggs knew all too well these misfortunes were just the way of the seafaring life.

Still, on Saturday, October 19, 1872, Briggs awoke to a morning he had been dreading for weeks because it was time to go back to sea. That day he was scheduled to leave for New York, where he would supervise the loading of his new ship in preparation for a transatlantic voyage. In a few weeks, Briggs and his crew would set out on the first leg of a European trip that might eventually take them halfway around the world. He had not sailed with these men before, nor on board this ship, which was called the *Mary Celeste*.

The dread that Briggs felt, however, had nothing to do with the trip, the crew or the ship. He had just returned from his previous voyage, and simply hated to leave again so soon. He hated to say good-bye.

It was a crisp fall morning at Rose Cottage, the Briggs family home on the outskirts of Marion, Massachusetts. A faint trace of saltwater hung in the air and a light breeze off the harbor rustled the few golden, dying leaves remaining on the trees surrounding the house. It was a picture-perfect New England day—a scene from Currier & Ives—and Benjamin Briggs wanted nothing more than to spend it with his family. He didn't know when he might see them again. Briggs was due in Genoa, Italy, in early December. From there, the *Mary Celeste* would take on more cargo for a quick run to Messina, in Sicily. Then he would most likely pick up another load for the voyage back to America—that is, if he didn't find another charter to deliver elsewhere. The owners wanted to squeeze as much profit as possible out of every trip and, truth be told, that only meant more money for Briggs, too. But the captain could count days—sometimes he did little else—and figured he would be gone until spring at least. By then, new leaves would be growing on the trees around Rose Cottage.

Briggs did not complain about his lot; it was not his style. And while his deadline ate at him, he still managed to enjoy a few weeks in Marion, sitting with his mother and playing with his son Arthur, who was growing up so quickly. There had been a bit of sadness on this visit—it seemed there always was. Benjamin's younger brother, James, had just lost his wife, Rebecca. Her death came not long after the couple had buried a child. If the death of his sister-in-law didn't weigh on him more heavily, it was only because Benjamin Briggs had become numb to it all. It was just another in a long line of family funerals he had to attend.

While he was home, Briggs had visited many of his neighbors and other townsfolk, most of whom he seemed to catch up with only a couple of times a year. He enjoyed attending church regularly for a while, even getting up to give testimony once. Like his wife, Sarah, Benjamin valued both fellowship and socializing—it was a luxury he went without for months at a time. But then, even sleeping in his own bed in his small home next door to Rose Cottage was a treat.

Mostly, though, he liked spending afternoons with his extended family. There was always something happening with the large clan of Briggses and Cobbs in the area, always some fresh gossip: one of the cousins had a new beau, or a nephew had gotten work on a freighter. He particularly enjoyed the company of his younger brother, Oliver, who was the family jokester. The two brothers could not have been more different (Benjamin was famously serious) or closer. Ben rarely got to see Oli, however, because like most Briggs men, he too was a sea captain. The Briggs family claimed a respectable share of the few sailors still in Marion by 1872.

With its strategic location on Buzzards Bay, Marion had once supported a healthy maritime industry, home to at least a dozen shipyards and salt mills, as well as a sizeable whaling fleet. Benjamin Briggs had grown up immersed in the sailor's life—the sounds, the smells, the adventurous stories. He heard fantastic tales of exotic ports not only from his father but from just about everyone in town. In those days, an amazing number of Marion men earned their living from the sea—and they were quite proficient at the work: One statistic had it that for every four Marion men who sailed, three of them became captains. At one point, nearly a hundred skippers lived in the small village of just a few hundred souls. Twenty years earlier, in fact, sea captains had exerted so much influence over the community that they had Sippican Village renamed in honor of the South Carolina Revolutionary War hero Francis Marion. The Swamp Fox had no local ties to the area, but for some reason was almost universally admired by the captains, many of whom sailed into Charleston regularly. When the village broke off from Rochester, it adopted the new name.

Now the little town was a seaport in decline. Briggs had noticed the harbor seemed particularly empty these days. The great maritime industry of the early half of the century had passed by Marion and its shallow harbor. These days, ships were being built bigger to haul more cargo, and Marion's little inlet off Buzzards Bay couldn't support their deeper drafts. There were only three shipyards left in town and the entire whaling fleet was gone. Even nearby New Bedford, which had replaced Nantucket as America's whaling capital, saw fewer ships going out every year. Men had discovered oil in Pennsylvania that did the trick just as well as the sea's own liquid gold, and it was much easier and cheaper to harvest than whale oil.

The only new development in Marion was a yacht club that foreshadowed the town's future. Soon, many of the grand houses with sweeping porches built by ship captains would be owned by summer residents, and the village would become largely a resort town. By the end of the century, Marion would be a retreat for President Grover Cleveland's family and the Victorian illustrator Charles Dana Gibson, and host luminaries such as Mark Twain and Henry James.

Briggs did not especially miss the maritime industry in Marion, for he enjoyed escaping the business when he was home. The truth was that he was somewhat envious the town had broken from its mold. He, too, wanted to give up the sea. Briggs had sailed full-time for more than half his thirty-seven years and thought that was enough. He had his reasons. His mother was getting old and she had no one anymore—save for his younger brother James—to look after her. Also, his own young family was growing. Sophia, his daughter, would be two in a couple of weeks and Arthur was seven and had started school. Benjamin Briggs was raised with his father gone most of the time and remembered what that was like. He wanted better for his son.

For years, Briggs had taken Sarah and Arthur with him on the occasional trip, but now that his son was in school it was no longer feasible. The boy couldn't be away for months at a time. As a result, Briggs now made most of his transatlantic runs alone. That may have been the harshest blow, the time away from Arthur. By his count, every ocean voyage cost him nearly half a year in his son's life.

What Benjamin Briggs really wanted was to start a business of his own. To read the *New Bedford Evening Standard,* its front page littered with advertisements for companies offering newfangled tonics that boasted of miraculous health benefits, "imported tobacco and segars" and "new fall styles" of clothing, it appeared the real money was on the other end of the shipping business. Briggs dreamed of owning a store he could lock up and leave behind at night. He had come close to doing that just months earlier, but at the last moment decided against it. The sailing life was all he knew, the one way he was certain to make enough money to support his family. Benjamin Briggs was a man who learned from others' mistakes, and he had seen his father try to quit the sea once with disastrous results.

It had left an impression on him, as many things had in his eventful life.

Benjamin Spooner Briggs was born in Wareham, Massachusetts, on April 24, 1835, the third child, and second son, of Nathan and Sophia Briggs. The future mariner counted Revolutionary War soldiers and passengers of the *Mayflower* among his ancestors. The Briggs family had, in fact, migrated no farther than twenty miles from Plymouth

Rock in 250 years, Wareham being a trading post on the north shore of Buzzards Bay. As much as anything, geography steered Briggs men to the sea.

Benjamin's father, the son of a sailor, had been entranced by the ocean from an early age. As a boy, Nathan Briggs watched ships sail into and out of Wareham until he was old enough to join them. At fifteen, he became a deckhand on a cargo ship, beginning his maritime career the way many New England boys did. He took to life aboard a ship well, enjoyed the work, and soon had enough experience to become a mate. By the time he was twenty-one, he was a ship captain making trips up and down the eastern seaboard.

It was in his twenty-first year that the course of Nathan Briggs's life was set. After the death of his father, the young sailor was taken in by William Cobb, a harness maker and sailor who lived in nearby Sippican Village. The Cobbs were a large, happy and devout family, with as many ministers among their ranks as there were sailors in the Briggs family. Nathan enjoyed visiting their home, where he found new brothers to socialize with and met two sisters who equally infatuated him—Maria and Sophia.

Although in many ways already a crusty sailor, Nathan Briggs was also an unlikely romantic, a dreamer at heart. Perhaps inspired by the majesty of the sea, he wrote poetry in a journal he kept, some of the verses odes to people and places, others more introspective. In 1824, while sailing to Marseille, the young captain penned a Valentine poem to the two Cobb sisters that suggested he could not decide which of them he wanted to court the most. The twenty-four-line verse pondered the origins of the Valentine holiday and included Nathan Briggs's untraditional solution to his dilemma.

> *If this be all, to custom I adhere*
> *And choose me two for the succeeding year.*

A few years later Briggs finally made his choice. On August 14, 1827, he married Maria Cobb, establishing the first of several links between the two families.

Nathan and Maria made a happy couple, but they did not have much time together. Shortly after their honeymoon, the captain left his bride at home with her parents and went back to sea, where he passed the time composing more verse for his expecting wife. Some of these lines hinted at his desires to give up sailing, emotions Briggs's son would inherit years later.

On September 4, 1828, Maria gave birth to Nathan Briggs's first son. It had been a hard pregnancy, and the child was unhealthy from the start. Despite the constant attention of the local physician, the baby died within a month. Nathan had not recovered from that blow before he was hit with a loss that was even worse. Four days after the death of their son, Maria also passed away. In less than a week's time, Nathan Briggs had lost his entire family.

Refusing to stay home and be pitied, Briggs tried to escape his sorrow on the deck of a ship. The ocean became a comforting refuge. He sailed out of Massachusetts on one trip after another, crisscrossing the globe, along the way becoming a master mariner. But the life he had dreamed of as a young boy was of little solace to him. The verse he composed in his journal turned dark and melancholy. The world, of which he was now seeing so much, no longer seemed such a beautiful place.

Two years later, Nathan Briggs got a second chance. In grief he had turned to his second Valentine—now his sister-in-law—Sophia. The two shared much in common, more than just grief, and soon Nathan began courting her. In 1830, Nathan and Sophia were wed. A year after they married, the couple had a beautiful, healthy daughter. They named her Maria.

For the next few years, the Briggs family prospered. Nathan suddenly was in great demand as a ship captain and he gladly took the work, leaving Sophia behind with her parents. The couple had another child, a son named after his father. The family's joy was tempered only by the death of Nathan's mother. In his journal, Captain Briggs composed a long, loving tribute to her.

In 1835, when the future master of the *Mary Celeste* was born, his parents named him for two other sailing Briggs men. Benjamin had

been the name of Nathan's father and Spooner was his only brother
to survive childhood (Spooner was also Nathan's middle name, and
his mother's maiden name). For many years, the Briggses would consider it a worthy tradition to honor relatives with the names of their
children. Benjamin never knew his grandfather and would have little
or no memory of his uncle: Spooner Briggs was lost at sea somewhere
off Block Island, Rhode Island, in 1839, when Benjamin was just four.

By the time Benjamin was born, Nathan Briggs had decided to
become a businessman. The captain invested the money he'd made
sailing in a Wareham company and, for the first time as an adult, settled into a life on land. Initially, it seemed he had made the right decision. As a direct result of his regular presence at home, the family
kept growing. Two more sons, Oliver and James, soon crowded the
Briggs house.

The Briggs family lived a simple New England life, growing their
own food, wearing homespun clothes. All the children worked from a
young age, shoveling snow off the walk or tending to the animals.
They weren't coddled by any means, but neither did they want for
anything. Nathan Briggs subscribed to the *Youth's Companion,* a popular magazine for children in its day, teaching morality, responsibility
and citizenship. The only true luxury item the family indulged in was
one of the first stoves in town.

Within five years, their prosperity withered. Nathan Briggs was
broke. The captain had to admit that he had made a mistake, that he
knew much more about running a ship than a business. But it was too
late. When the company failed, it cost Briggs his fortune and eventually his home. Nathan sent Sophia and their five children to live with
her parents once again while he returned to the sea. It was his only
choice.

Nathan Briggs took only five years to recoup what he had lost.
He sailed various ships for a number of companies—including J. H.
Winchester in New York—while his income steadily grew. In 1844,
shortly after the birth of his sixth child, Zenas, Nathan Briggs built the
family a grand home on the outskirts of old Sippican Village (a few
years before it was renamed Marion). It was a tall, white clapboard

house with a steep roof, piazzas and black shutters. The home was nestled on a wooded lot fronting Pleasant Street a few blocks inland from the harbor, and had a sweeping carriage driveway that circled the house. The entire yard boasted ornate landscaping that Nathan and Sophia designed themselves. They planted so many roses that the house came to be called "Rose Cottage." Briggs was clearly proud to rejoin the ranks of prosperous sea captains. The craggy-faced sailor delighted in carrying his ship terminology onshore, calling his front porch the "quarterdeck," and referring to the upstairs bedrooms as being "aloft." The children loved the new home, particularly nine-year-old Benjamin, who enjoyed climbing on the stone wall that ran along the street.

The captain raised Benjamin and his brothers to go to sea. Benjamin Briggs served as a deckhand while a teenager, and by the time he was twenty had made his all-important first trip around Cape Horn—still a rite of passage among seafaring men today. On that voyage, he served as a mate on the *Hope,* a ship commanded by Nathan Briggs. Although it was perhaps the most uninterrupted time he had ever spent with his father, Benjamin enjoyed no special status as the captain's son. In fact, he was barely acknowledged by the captain while on deck. He took his turn aloft, worked the rotten shifts and did the most hated jobs just like every other sailor on board. Benjamin most likely was complimented by this—his father treated him like a sailor.

At sea, Benjamin Briggs quickly grew into a sturdy young man. He had dark, wavy hair, salt-toughened skin and—like his father—icy, wolflike eyes that belied his gentle nature. He was soft-spoken and reticent, a serious and intelligent fellow. Without intervention by the captain, Benjamin garnered respect beyond his years on the high seas. In more ways than one, he was following in his father's wake.

After his apprenticeship aboard the *Hope,* Benjamin sailed on a brig called the *Sea Foam,* and soon became its captain. Sailors in the nineteenth century worked their way up through the ranks, and once they had their master's certificate moved from one ship to the next every few years. Benjamin Briggs stayed that course. Soon he traded

As a young man, Benjamin Spooner Briggs followed family tradition and became a sailor. By the time he was twenty, he had
made his first trip around Cape Horn. Within a few years, he
would be a ship's captain. *Photograph Courtesy Peabody Essex Museum*

up to a larger ship, the three-masted schooner *Forest King,* which he
sailed across the Atlantic and back on commercial runs for several
years.

In 1862, Benjamin returned home just long enough to marry his
childhood sweetheart, Sarah Elizabeth Cobb. Sarah was his first
cousin—the daughter of his mother's brother—and seven years his ju-
nior. They had seen each other often growing up and, gone for
months at a time, Benjamin found that he missed her terribly. They
were soul mates, friends and relatives recalled, the sort of lovers that as

a couple almost meld into one entity. On September 9, 1862, they were married in the Congregational Church of Marion by Sarah's father, the Reverend Leander Cobb. After that, the only thing that would keep them apart for the rest of their lives was the sea.

Often, even the Atlantic couldn't separate them. The couple honeymooned aboard the *Forest King* on a sail through the Mediterranean that they must have found agreeable for, after that, Sarah often accompanied Benjamin on his voyages. She did not relish living aboard a ship with a bunch of sailors, but both Sarah and Benjamin believed it better than the alternative. For years, it had been considered bad luck to carry a woman on a sailing ship, but that was one old superstition that had been abandoned by the mid-nineteenth century. In the merchant marine, anyway, many captains' wives accompanied their husbands on voyages. Even Benjamin's mother had traveled with his father on a few trips, before it was all that common.

For Sarah, joining Benjamin at sea was certainly more exciting than living in the quiet confines of Marion. Not only did the young couple see the world together at a time when many people never traveled more than a hundred miles from their home, but they also occasionally stumbled upon history. Less than a year after they were married, they found themselves civilians on the front lines of the Civil War, watching naval maneuvers from the deck of the *Forest King*. In May 1863, while anchored off Galveston alongside ships in the Gulf Coast Blockading Squadron, Benjamin wrote to Sarah's brother, William Cobb, that they had been delighted to see the Yankee ships take target practice during a lull in the fighting.

"We had a fine chance to watch the effect as they were near us and fired across the bow," he wrote with a measure of excitement.

Even though Benjamin was only a merchant-ship captain, he was welcomed as a brother sailor by the Union Navy. He and Sarah spent several days visiting various ships off Galveston, where the *Forest King* was making a routine cargo run. While touring the Union gunboat *Sciota,* Benjamin and Sarah saw more action—and from an even closer vantage point. Shortly after going aboard, one of the lookouts spotted an unidentified vessel and the *Sciota* gave chase. It turned out to be a friendly ship, but Briggs was thrilled by the short drama. Later, he saw another gunboat chase a blockade-runner ashore and burn it.

The Civil War was transforming the nation into a much more complex place and Benjamin Briggs was torn by the prospects of it all. In some ways he felt it was his duty to join the navy, as many of his friends and acquaintances had, but he felt no desire to do so. Some later said he regretted not serving, but if Briggs felt this way it didn't show. The exciting scenes off Texas did little to change his mind. Briggs's ideals and opinions were heavily influenced by his father, a Democrat solidly against the war. Nathan Briggs was a pacifist who believed fighting to be a waste of money and human life. The differences between the two sides should be settled diplomatically, he often said in conversations around town, once suggesting that the federal government might buy the freedom of slaves as a compromise. One of the most often told tales of wartime Marion was that some men suspected the elder Briggs might be a Southern sympathizer and set out to test his allegiance to the United States. One night a mob carried an American flag to Rose Cottage to make Nathan Briggs salute and kiss it. The men felt a wrath that years earlier had been reserved for the slackest deck hands.

"Gentlemen, I have carried that flag to many parts of the world," Briggs told them. "I have had it saluted and have saluted it gladly and willingly many times, but under compulsion, never!"

And with that he slammed the door. It was the last time anyone questioned Nathan Briggs about anything.

Benjamin had to hear the colorful stories of his family and life in Marion almost exclusively from letters. Whether traveling with Sarah or alone, he stayed at sea nearly all the time. He regularly corresponded with his brother-in-law, parents and, of course, his wife when she wasn't with him. To his father he wrote mostly about business, sailing and the like. To Sarah, he composed loving notes detailing how much he missed her. His mother received his most philosophical letters, in which he shared his deepest thoughts on family and life in general. Although he was in all ways his father's son, Benjamin was by far closer to his mother. Mother Briggs, daughter of a minister, had instilled in her son a strong sense of puritanical values.

In 1865, Briggs returned to Rose Cottage following the birth of his son. The boy was named for Briggs's latest command, a three-masted barkentine christened the *Arthur.* Although no one in the family ever mentioned it, the child's name could have been homage to the location of his conception. As soon as Arthur was old enough to travel, the family sailed together in the captain's quarters on his namesake ship. For Benjamin, it was a joy to have Sarah and the baby so close, but it was only a temporary arrangement. They could not live at sea full-time. More often than not, Sarah stayed behind in Marion with little Arthur when Benjamin shipped out.

As much as he tried to do differently, Briggs found his life and his career mirroring his father's almost exactly. He was away so often that his son had a hard time recognizing him. When the family went with him on a trip to the Caribbean in 1868, three-year-old Arthur sometimes mistook his father for Oliver.

"[He] called him Oli most all the time, but will say Papa once in a while. I was very much pleased that he got acquainted so readily," Sarah wrote to her brother from the *Arthur.* "His Papa had a little watch and chain and whistle for him and soon won his heart by playing with him."

Having to constantly renew his relationship with his own son pained Benjamin Briggs, and may have stirred feelings similar to those that had driven his father ashore years ago. There is some evidence that Sarah lost a child, perhaps even two, around this time—something that only would have added to Briggs's misery. In a wistful note to his mother a few months later, Benjamin reminisced about his childhood; about ripping his pants while sliding down the huge rock across the street from Rose Cottage.

"What a trial I must have been to you in my younger years with 'I don't want to do this or that.' I don't think you gave me any hard whippings, at any rate I don't feel any stings and can't see any streaks on my legs after I've done washing," he wrote. "I can't help laughing now when I think how I might have bawled out sometimes when I wasn't much hurt."

Writing from somewhere off the west coast of Cuba, Benjamin Briggs ended the note to his mother with lyrics from a popular song of the day, "the dearest spot on Earth to me is Home Sweet Home."

His longing was only going to grow more intense. Two years later, on October 31. 1870, Sarah gave birth to a daughter they named Sophia Matilda. She had her father's eyes.

It was a traumatic time for Benjamin Briggs. Just months before his daughter was born, his father died. He and his brothers had met in Marion to settle the affairs of their father's estate, appointing James— the only one who didn't sail—to manage business matters and make sure their mother was provided for. So much was changing in his life that Benjamin felt he should be in Marion. His letters home arrived with increasing frequency. Now, he even wrote to Arthur.

"Dear Arthur," one of the notes began. "I wish I could see you and that cunning little sister, you must tell her all about Papa, so she will know me when I come home, and if she is a good little girl you may kiss her every night for me, you can tell her what funny pictures fa- ther makes for you and when she gets to be a big girl and goes to school perhaps he'll make some for her. I should like to have a ride on your sled, Don't you wish I could. See if you can tell what all my pic- tures are. Good night, Father."

On the back of the letter, Benjamin Briggs sketched a horse, chicken, duck, dog, ox and cat. He drew a detailed picture of Rose Cottage with people sledding in front of it—his own version of a Currier & Ives print. Below that, Briggs reproduced a scene he was most familiar with: a sailboat towing a dinghy toward a lighthouse on a distant shore.

Although family considerations were his chief concern, Briggs may have had other reasons fueling his growing desire to retire from sailing. He knew the dangers of the life and had always accepted the risk one took, the price one paid, to earn a living from the sea. Accidents were unavoidable. In the days surrounding Briggs's departure for New York and the *Mary Celeste,* the *New Bedford Evening Standard* reported the loss of at least three merchant ships: the *Guatemala,* the *Cairo,* and the *Umpire.* Every week there were dispatches about some captain who had been swept overboard during a storm or a ship that sank, dragging its crew to the bottom of the ocean.

As common as these disasters were, it seemed the sea had exacted an especially steep price on the Briggs family. In 1855, Nathan H. Briggs—Benjamin's oldest brother—sailed out of Galveston as mate on a ship. Three days from land, he died of the yellow fever and his body was dropped overboard. The family did not even have a funeral for him.

A year after the death of his oldest son, in 1856, Captain Nathan Briggs retired to Rose Cottage, arriving just in time to attend the wedding of his only daughter. At twenty-five, a ripe old age for a maiden in those days, some had thought Maria might be doomed to life as a spinster. But she had fallen in love with a man who was, unsurprisingly, a sea captain. Joseph D. Gibbs was a friend of the family from a nearby town, and a sailor familiar to the Briggs men. As Sarah Briggs would do some years later, Maria often sailed with Joseph on his travels, leaving their newborn son behind with Mother Briggs at Rose Cottage. On one such trip in November 1859, Gibbs's ship collided with a steamer off Cape Fear. Some of the crew survived, but Joseph and Maria were swept overboard and lost in the accident. Their orphaned son died in Marion less than a year later.

Oliver Briggs had narrowly avoided death on two separate occasions. Once, while sailing a Winchester schooner back from Beaufort, North Carolina, Oliver was caught in a deadly blow. His ship, the *Thomas Jefferson,* lost its rudder in a storm off Cape Hatteras near the Graveyard of the Atlantic. The cargo was ruined, and the damage to the ship was so bad it was a total loss. Not long after that, he took command of the *Royal Charles* as a favor to a friend. Returning from Rotterdam, the *Charles* hit an iceberg and sank off Halifax. The crew launched the ship's lifeboat and luckily managed to make the Nova Scotia coast.

Oliver eventually bought his own ship, the brig *Julia A. Hallock*. It was not as fine a command as he wanted, but it earned him a decent living. For some time, Zenas—the youngest Briggs boy—sailed with him as a mate. But shortly before the ship arrived at Southport, North Carolina, in October of 1870, Zenas died onboard, also of yellow fever. While they were in port, Oliver Briggs buried his younger brother.

The most crippling blow to the Briggs family, however, came with the strange death of its patriarch earlier that same year. Nathan Briggs and his wife were alone at Rose Cottage when a summer storm blew into Marion on June 28, 1870. Thunder shook the house in short intervals and lightning charged the air. One flash followed by a clap of thunder startled the old captain, who told his wife the bolt might have hit the town schoolhouse. Briggs got up for a look and while standing in the doorway another jolt of lightning struck the door casing. He died instantly. Sophia Briggs heard her husband fall to the floor and, running in from the parlor, found him lying in the hall. She sat with the body until the storm passed and she was able to call for help.

Following this long series of family tragedies, only Benjamin and Oliver were still sailing (James was never a sailor; he worked at the local post office and later went into business in New Bedford). No one would have blamed the last two seagoing Briggs men had they chosen to retire from the sea, but they probably gave little thought to the notion—later perpetuated in the press—that the family was cursed. More likely, they wanted to give up sailing for the same reason their father had years earlier. Although they were mariners first and foremost, they were also homebodies, which was obvious from their ship preferences. The Briggs men lived on the doorstep of the world's largest whaling industry, but none of them would ever sail on a whaler, most likely because those ships were sometimes gone for up to two or three years at a time.

Even four-month voyages on merchant ships were becoming too long for the brothers, both approaching middle age. The ideal situation, Benjamin and Oliver decided, would be to go into business together. A year earlier, in 1871, they had considered buying a hardware store in New Bedford, but their father's failure in business—coupled with a shaky postwar economy—made them tentative and they lost their chance. Someone else bought the store before they made a decision.

Oliver seemed even more determined to relinquish his command than Benjamin, as he had his own growing family to consider. Taller and thinner than most of the Briggs men, the quick-witted Oliver was also more resolute. As his older brother made plans to join the *Mary Celeste* in New York, Oliver told their mother that his next trip aboard the *Julia A. Hallock* would be his last. He would sell the ship and find a job somewhere around Marion. He had bought a lot next to Rose Cottage where he would build his new house. Already, he had marked off his territory with a stone wall along Pleasant Street that would stand for more than a century. But Benjamin felt he couldn't make such a commitment until he had some other means to make a living. Oliver, in that sense at least, was braver than his older brother.

Around that time, in the fall of 1872, Benjamin Briggs bought a one-third interest in the *Mary Celeste*. He financed the purchase through a loan from Simpson Hart, a New Bedford businessman. The majority shareholder of Briggs's new ship was J. H. Winchester, the owner of a major shipping company in New York, and a friend of the family. Nathan Briggs had sailed Winchester ships—even their flagship, the *Winchester*—and both Benjamin and Oliver, who also had sailed for them, were well known and respected in the company. Winchester sold Benjamin Briggs eight of twenty-four shares in the brigantine on the condition that he also take over as captain.

The *Mary Celeste* was not as large a ship as others Briggs had commanded, and would not earn near the profits, but he may have been enticed to invest in her because of modifications Winchester had recently made. The brig had been built with a single deck, but now another had been added. Winchester designed the additional room with the idea that he would sail the *Mary Celeste* as captain and take his family along. But his wife wouldn't go because her mother had taken ill, forcing her husband to make other arrangements. Winchester had as little desire as Briggs to leave his family behind.

Briggs may have seen the *Mary Celeste* as a temporary solution to his dilemma. Running a smaller ship than he was accustomed to would be easy work and the extra cabin space made it possible to take Sarah and their baby daughter, Sophy, with him. He would have taken Arthur as well, but the boy had just started school in Marion. He was a smart child and needed to keep up with his lessons, something that would have been all but impossible with the distractions on a sailing ship. It was soon settled: Arthur would stay behind at Rose Cottage, under the supervision of his grandmother and his uncle James. Benjamin made arrangements for James to pay their mother room and board for the boy, an acceptable way for her to take money from her sons.

Knowing that Sarah and Sophy would follow in a week was the only thing that tempered Briggs's unhappy farewell to Marion on October 19, 1872. The family would celebrate Sophy's birthday in the big city and with any luck see Oliver, who was due in New York just before the *Mary Celeste* was scheduled to sail.

And so Benjamin Spooner Briggs left Marion for the last time. On the daylong trip to New York, Briggs had plenty of time to reflect on his new situation. He probably didn't consider the danger of taking his family to sea with him; he'd been doing it for years. If he happened to think about his lost siblings, it might have occurred to him that in twenty years he had not encountered even the slightest problem at sea. He was the only sailing Briggs who could claim such a feat. It would have been a comforting statistic for Benjamin Spooner Briggs if he knew anything of the bizarre history of the *Mary Celeste*.

That is, had he been a superstitious man.

THREE

The New World

New York's waterfront was as busy as a tall ship's rigging.

From the harbor, the masts of nearly 300 wooden sailing vessels obscured the great metropolis growing out of lower Manhattan. Piers and warehouses crowded the seawall, interrupted only by the occasional ferry terminal offering passage to Brooklyn. Smoke belching from steamships filled the air and the smell of dead fish wafted on the breeze. The sounds of the port were an endless cacophony echoing through the canyons of city streets, the maze of docks a nation unto themselves—an overpopulated world of longshoremen, shipping merchants and wharf rats.

A year earlier, in 1871, this waterfront jungle had impressed a young French sculptor named Frédéric-Auguste Bartholdi, who sailed into the city to scout locations for the statue he dreamed of building—a monument to liberty that would be a gift to America. In language more suited to a French poet than a sculptor, Bartholdi recorded his thoughts:

The picture that is presented to the view when one arrives in New York is marvelous, when, after some days of voyaging, in the pearly radiance of a

beautiful morning is revealed the magnificent spectacle of those immense
cities, of those rivers extending as far as the eye can reach, festooned with
masts and flags; when one awakes, so to speak, in the midst of that inte-
rior sea covered with vessels . . . it is thrilling. It is, indeed, the New
World, which appears in its majestic expanse, with the ardor of its grow-
ing life.

By the fall of 1872, when Benjamin Briggs arrived to take command of the *Mary Celeste,* the Port of New York was at the apex of
its growth. It had surpassed Philadelphia as the nation's largest port
seventy-five years earlier and since that time had grown even more
quickly. When the Erie Canal opened in the 1820s, it flooded the city
with a constant flow of produce and products from the Midwest.
Later, new rail lines converged in the area adding to that supply. As a
result, Lower East Side warehouses were stuffed with merchandise
waiting to be shipped to foreign ports or distributed throughout the
country. The East River docks could no longer handle the demand, so
a good portion of the surplus had already begun to move to the Hud-
son River. New York had irrevocably established itself as the hub of
commerce in the New World.

Briggs transported more than his share of those goods, and he nav-
igated this cityscape like a native. No sea captain working in the re-
constructed United States could avoid New York and, like every other
sailor in the merchant marine, Briggs went where the work was. In
some ways, a trip to the city was another sort of homecoming for
him. On October 20, 1872, as he made his way through the South
Street scene, Briggs likely ran into old acquaintances, former shipmates and merchants he'd known for years. He would have stopped to
chat—he was a friendly man—but he did not dally. He had business
to attend to, and she was at Pier 44, just north of Rutgers Street.

She was a beauty.

That was what Benjamin Spooner Briggs thought when he saw
the *Mary Celeste* for the first time. He had been expecting a much
more modest vessel and was struck by her clean lines, her smooth

hull. The ship was sleek and dark, with a flared stern and a striking bowsprit. She was more aerodynamic than many freighters, wonderfully simple in her design. If such a word had existed in the nineteenth century, he might have called her sporty.

On this morning, men moved about the ship with purpose, in the normal flurry of activity that preceded a voyage. They loaded supplies into the stern and prepared the ship for a jog across the river to Hunter's Point, where they would pick up a portion of the cargo for this trip. Briggs paid little attention to the men; he was focused on the ship. *His* ship now—for he owned a third of her. Even though she was smaller than most of his previous commands, and he had worried about that, the captain was nonetheless pleased.

Recalling this sight in the last letter he wrote to his mother, Benjamin Briggs declared the *Mary Celeste* "in beautiful trim."

At the very least, she cleaned up nice. In the past two months, the *Mary Celeste* had undergone such extensive renovations that she barely resembled the simple vessel built on a quiet Nova Scotia beach a decade earlier. The work clearly had been needed, as months earlier she was showing her age—and her mileage. Between wrecks and neglect, the *Mary Celeste's* previous owners had allowed her to deteriorate, ignoring the harsh effects of saltwater on the rigging and hull. The rock salt originally packed into her joints had not been enough to hold off rotting and some of the boards were unsalvageable. In some places the ship had to be stripped down to the waterline, rebuilt and recaulked.

At the time, New York was a major shipbuilding center and the *Mary Celeste* benefited from having its refit done there. The job was handled with an eye toward quality and, at the direction of James H. Winchester, speed: this major overhaul took less than two months. The results were striking. The brigantine Briggs saw before him was an elegant lady that offered no hint of the banged-up derelict towed into New York nearly four years earlier. It was very nearly a new ship.

Metal sheathing had been attached to the ship's underside to prevent marine growth from eating through the wooden hull. The copper gleamed in the water, complementing a deck so clean that it very

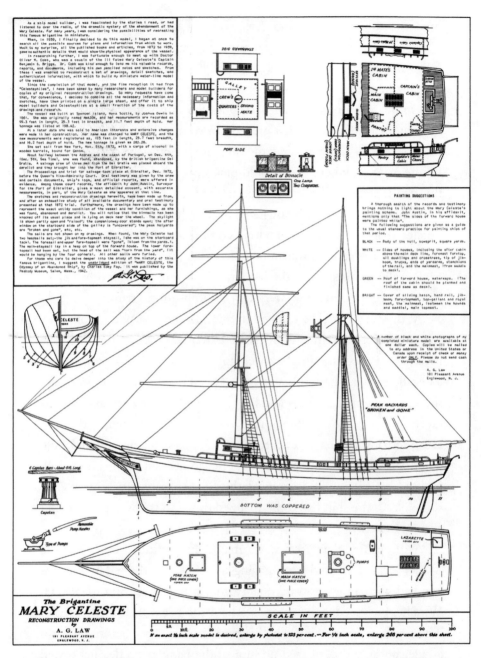

This diagram showing the sail plan, deck and cabin layout of the *Mary Celeste* just before her November 1872 voyage was made by a New Jersey modeler named Alexander G. Law. Law's model based on these drawings is on display at the Mystic Seaport Museum in Connecticut.

nearly shined. The two masts, towering more than seventy-five feet above the deck, rocked gently in the wakes of passing ships. Five yardarms were balanced along the foremast while a huge boom nearly forty feet long swung from the mainmast. Two cabins peeked out of the deck, the larger of which—tucked snugly under the boom—included quarters for the captain and first officer. The forward deckhouse included space for the remainder of the crew and the galley. The *Mary Celeste*'s main hatch to the cargo hold lay just aft of the forward deckhouse, and the wheel was mounted near the stern. Much of the ship was completely redesigned, including the addition of the fifth yardarm on the foremast. The changes were so extensive that some of the ship's original windows had been filled in and new ones cut.

The renovations weren't purely cosmetic. Besides enlarging the cabins, the size of the hold had been increased to allow for another seventy-five tons of cargo. The ship's hull was very nearly hollow. In one trade publication, an advertisement for J. H. Winchester & Co. boasted that the *Mary Celeste* could now haul up to 3,500 barrels. To add this extra cargo space, Winchester had been forced to change the dimensions of the ship. The *Mary Celeste* was lengthened by four feet and had four feet added to its draft. A storage area for the crew's food and supplies—a lazaret—was built on the stern. The modifications cost more than twice as much as it took to build the ship originally, but the work had been done well and it pleased Briggs, who was as optimistic as he could be.

"I hope we shall have a fine passage, but as I have never been in her before can't say how she'll sail," Briggs wrote to his mother.

The *Mary Celeste*'s refit came only after a grueling year of short trips up and down the East Coast. Winchester had pushed the ship hard before he invested in a refit—he intended to make money off her. In the past year, the brigantine had called on Morehead City, North Carolina, and sailed up the Satilla River, near Brunswick, Georgia. Much of its time was spent on the West Indies route, stopping in Barbados, Martinique, Jamaica and Cuba. Its last voyage before Briggs took command included a brush with its troubled past. A few months earlier, the *Mary Celeste* had hauled a load of coal from Cow Bay, Nova Scotia, where it had run aground five years earlier while sailing as the *Amazon*.

Soon after settling into the city, Briggs met with James H. Winchester. The two men had known each other for years and got along fine; the family business connections between them went back decades. Briggs's father, Captain Nathan Briggs, had sailed the *Winchester,* and Oliver had once commanded the company's *Thomas Jefferson,* the ship lost off the Outer Banks. Winchester had never employed Benjamin Briggs, but had little doubt that he'd make a fine captain for the *Mary Celeste*. By reputation, Benjamin was considered one of the better sailors among the Briggs men.

Winchester was anxious to reregister the ship to reflect Briggs's one-third interest in her. Not only would that speed up the *Mary Celeste*'s departure once she was loaded, but it also gave Winchester peace of mind. The troublesome little brig had caused him a fair amount of inconvenience recently. Earlier in the year, a government surveyor had showed up at Winchester's office and claimed the ship was fraudulently registered. The surveyor told Winchester that since it wasn't his fault they could perhaps work something out if he was willing to pay a fine. The thrifty Winchester bristled at the word *fine* and felt he was being blackmailed, or at the very least solicited for a bribe. He told the bureaucrat if the government wanted the ship, they could have it. He wasn't paying anyone.

When the *Mary Celeste* arrived from the Caribbean a few weeks later, the government seized it. But as soon as the case went to trial, Winchester was cleared of the charges, the matter dropped. The surveyor had been correct. Winchester was not at fault.

After that, Winchester had been inspired to patch up his ship, which was suffering from several years without an overhaul. Winchester chose to personally supervise the *Mary Celeste*'s refit because he was a man closely involved with his business. Not only did he manage the fleet himself, keeping his ships running smoothly and—best he could influence it—on time, but he also stayed in close contact with his captains. Every day one of his ships was in port, Winchester walked from his office at 52 South Street to the docks just to make an appearance, or to make sure they were working.

When Winchester visited the *Mary Celeste* with Benjamin Briggs on October 20 or 21, he must have been encouraged by the sight of a crew of stevedores loading supplies at the direction of first mate Albert G. Richardson. The ship had been chartered by German merchants in New York—Meissner, Ackersman, and Company—to haul 1,700 barrels of alcohol to Genoa, and Richardson and Briggs would take the brig across the river to pick up much of that cargo in the coming week. Richardson figured they could move nearly 300 casks a day. Winchester thought that a respectable pace, but pushed them to move a little faster. The sooner the ship sailed, the sooner it would be back, ready to take on another charter.

In the stories that followed, some claimed the *Mary Celeste*'s longboat was damaged during loading when a barrel of alcohol fell on it. The accident left the crew with only one lifeboat for the trip—a smaller and less seaworthy yawl. Later, Winchester told friends a different story. He said that he had pointed out the dilapidated condition of the larger of the ship's two boats to Briggs, declaring it too unsafe to use with the captain's wife and child making the trip.

"I will order another boat to be put on board before you leave," Winchester said.

There is no evidence a new longboat arrived before the *Mary Celeste* sailed from New York or that the ship carried three lifeboats, as Winchester claimed. There is some proof that suggests Briggs left port with only one lifeboat on board, a small yawl, and it may have been the shoddy boat he and Winchester had discussed replacing.

Such an appearance of caring from the owner, however, made Briggs feel better about his situation. Winchester had delivered on all of his promises, the ship had been refit nicely, and there was room for his family to accompany him. The cabin was a little cramped but at least Sarah and Sophy had a little room to stretch out. He felt confident that the ship was safe. He probably didn't give much thought to an extra lifeboat.

A Civil War veteran, Albert G. Richardson was well known
and respected by Captain Benjamin Briggs, but he may
have gotten his job as *Mary Celeste* first mate because of his
relationship to James H. Winchester, the ship's majority
shareholder. *Photograph Courtesy Peabody Essex Museum*

Briggs seemed as satisfied with his crew as he was with his business
partner. While he knew Winchester only slightly, Briggs was well acquainted with the *Mary Celeste*'s first mate. Albert G. Richardson had
sailed with Briggs before and handled himself impressively on a ship.
When he heard that Richardson would serve as his mate aboard the
Mary Celeste, Briggs had boasted to his wife that they would be in
"good hands."

Richardson, twenty-eight, was a dapper man of slight build with a thin mustache. A native of Stockton, Maine, Richardson had taken a break from sailing to serve three years during the Civil War. By the time Briggs took over the *Mary Celeste,* Richardson had sailed on Winchester ships for two years. It was a job he may have gotten as much for familial relations as seamanship. Richardson's wife, Fannie, was the niece of Winchester's wife.

Briggs did not know the rest of his crew. The second mate was Andrew Gilling, a twenty-five-year-old New Yorker. The steward and cook was Edward William Head, a newlywed of twenty-three who would leave his wife, Emma, to fend for herself in Brooklyn while he made the Atlantic run.

Four German men, ranging in age from twenty-three to thirty-five, rounded out the *Mary Celeste*'s crew complement. There is not much surviving biographical information on Arian Martens, Gottlieb Good-schaad, and the brothers Volkert and Boz Lorenzen, except that they were all either 5'8" or 5'9" and they all were going to be paid $30 per month for the voyage—the twenty-first-century equivalent of about $435. Martens looked shorter than he was and—perhaps because of his round face and beard—resembled a leprechaun. The Lorenzen brothers were working their way around the world with every intention of re-turning to their homeland. They were from Fohr, a German island in the North Sea not far from the country's border with Denmark. Volk-ert Lorenzen sent most of his pay home to his wife and daughter, who were living in poverty on the island, while Boz was engaged to a local girl. The sailors were quiet, and showed signs of being veteran seamen: they packed lightly for the long voyage—the Lorenzen brothers even shared a single sea chest. Based on how quickly they loaded the cargo, Briggs thought they seemed to be good workers. Just before the ship sailed, Sarah Briggs wrote home to her mother-in-law that "Benj. thinks we have got a pretty peaceable set this time all around if they continue as they have begun. Can't tell yet how smart they are."

On Sunday, October 27, Sarah and Sophy arrived in New York, traveling in fine style aboard a Fall River Line steamer. After spending the week in Queens while the *Mary Celeste* loaded much of its cargo,

Benjamin met his wife and daughter at the company's North River terminal. They had left Marion the previous morning packed for a long trip, and Sarah Briggs certainly didn't skimp. In addition to trunks of clothing and two hats for herself, she had shipped a melodeon, a sewing machine and a case of coloring books, as well as toys and dolls to keep Sophy busy on the long, dull passage. She claimed to know nothing about sailing, but Sarah Briggs was at the very least a savvy passenger.

It was a happy family reunion, Benjamin Briggs overjoyed at seeing little Sophy and "Sallie," his pet name for Sarah. Briggs led them to the *Mary Celeste*'s new berth at the foot of Montgomery Street, Pier 50, where they settled into their quarters. The captain spent the rest of the day with his daughter. He played with Sophy's dolls—Sarah Jane and Daisy—making them bang on the melodeon's keyboard after Sarah finished playing a cheerful tune. He looked at the family album with Sophy, who called out for her brother Arthur and pointed to pictures of "Gamma Bis."

Little Sophia was nosy, and explored the ship despite suffering a cold that her parents nursed with a steady diet of hash, bread and butter. The toddler discovered the ship's cat meowing in the cargo hold—where it was kept to kill mice—and called it "Poo-uh Poo." Later that evening, Sophy curled up in a bunk and, rocked by swells made by the passing ships, was soon asleep. As Sarah composed a letter to Arthur, Benjamin wrote to his mother that the voyage would do Sophy "lots of good."

While Sophy was mesmerized by her new surroundings, her mother thought it was just another creaky ship. And if there was anything worse than living on a ship at sea, Sarah thought, it had to be staying onboard one while it is in port. The noise made by the men loading the ship and the racket coming from other piers were getting on her nerves.

"The fact is there is such an amount of thumping and bumping, or shakings and tossings to and fro of the cargo, and of screeching and growlings by escaping steam that I believe I've gone slightly daft," she wrote in one letter to her family from aboard the *Mary Celeste*.

Sarah probably wrote those lines with an amused smirk on her

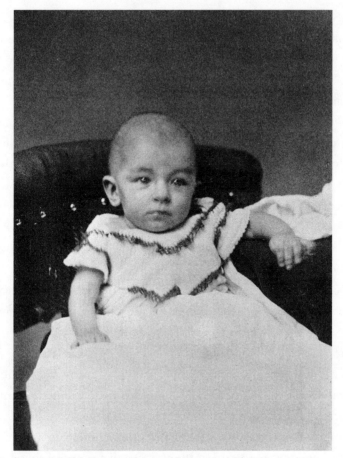

Sophia Matilda Briggs celebrated her second birthday on
October 31, 1872, just days before the *Mary Celeste* sailed from
New York. She was a curious, active child, and had her father's
eyes. *Photograph Courtesy Peabody Essex Museum*

face. She certainly was exaggerating her frustration. In more than a
decade of marriage to Benjamin Spooner Briggs, Sarah had gotten
used to shipboard life. She was a no-nonsense woman who had
proven that, like her husband, she could handle just about anything. At
thirty, the mother of two had grown into a confident woman who
bore little resemblance to the schoolgirl she had been.

Sarah Cobb was the daughter of Leander Cobb, Mother Briggs's
brother. Cobb was the minister at Marion's Congregational church, a
white clapboard building on the town's main street. Compared to the

reserved Briggs family, the Cobbs seemed somewhat wild. James Briggs remembered his uncle's fiery style in the pulpit, which he considered "wild west ways" because Cobb had been a missionary preacher in Indiana. "He pounded the pulpit as he expounded the text and sometimes awakened me from a sound sleep by stamping on the floor."

In spite of her lively family, Sarah had been a shy young girl except when she was singing. She was a regular in the church choir, and her friends and relatives remembered her having a lovely voice. Although she set a prim and proper example in public, the preacher's daughter was developing a quick wit and a playful sense of humor. Soon she too would be able to surprise the Briggs boys with her quips. And as she grew older, Sarah Cobb also realized that she had become smitten with her cousin, Benjamin.

Even in her teens, Sarah considered the somewhat older sailor a perfect match. The fact that Benjamin was often gone on sailing jobs by the time he was seventeen only made him seem that much more mature and appealing. Soon they became sweethearts, and Sarah didn't mind waiting for him to come home, at least not too much. By the time they married, surely she knew what she was getting into.

Because of her husband's profession, Sarah Briggs was forced to run her household's affairs, something that many American women had become accustomed to during the war, but that wives of ship captains had done for years. Sarah handled the job gracefully and seemed to enjoy it. More often than not, Sarah wrote the letters to Benjamin's parents when they were at sea. Sarah looked after her mother-in-law while her husband was gone. It was "Sallie" who kept the busy Captain Briggs's spirits up with letters while he was gone. Better than anyone, she understood how much her husband wanted to call it quits, and she made sure he knew he was not forgotten at home.

"I never heard Arthur say so much about you when you were gone," Sarah had written to Benjamin just a few months earlier. "He thinks it seems real lonesome without father and hopes he will get home soon. Baby had quite a howl for you under the bed clothes when she woke this morning."

Most likely, Sarah complained about the noise on the ship only because she was in the big city and not getting to see much of it. For nearly five days, she had been stuck with Sophy on board the *Mary Celeste*. Winchester later recalled that during his daily visits he alternately found Sarah browsing through Benjamin's books, playing her melodeon and tending to Sophy. She was bored.

Not only was Briggs busy preparing for the trip, and thus had less time to spend with his family, but they also were confined by circumstances beyond their control. A horse disease was running rampant on the East Side that fall and few carriages were running in the area. Benjamin tried for most of the week to find a way to keep them entertained, but it must have seemed like torture to the social Sarah Briggs. She would be cooped up on the ship for a solid month, and wanted to take in the sights and stretch her legs while in town. She knew this was her last chance to do anything for a while, and there was a lot to see in the city.

Even to world travelers like the Briggses, New York in 1872 was a sight to behold. At the end of the pier, gaslit streets led to ornate, imposing banks and towering insurance buildings that suggested a sophisticated city unlike any other they knew. Although its prosperity and growth were driven by business and commerce, New York was also the only settlement in the New World that captured a European air of culture. Museums, theaters and some of the finest hotels in the world were within walking distance of the docks, including the brand-new Metropolitan Museum of Art, which had opened on Fifth Avenue just that February. There was shopping in the city like nowhere else in the country, marked by the grand opening that very month of the Lord & Taylor Dry Goods Store.

Signs of the booming Industrial Age were everywhere. Refineries dotted the skylines of Brooklyn and Queens, new railroad tracks weaving amongst them, and steam ships were beginning to outnumber sailing vessels in the harbor. But nowhere was man flexing his engineering muscles more than a mile downriver of the *Mary Celeste,* where rising out of two caissons were the towers of what would become the longest bridge in the world, a span stretching over the East River from Manhattan to Brooklyn. From the deck of his ship, Briggs could see workers climbing on the tower across the river, which was already more than a hundred feet high.

It seemed that much of the country's excitement was centered in New York. Just a year after exposing the corrupt political network of William Marcy "Boss" Tweed, the newspapers of the day titillated with suggestions of fresh scandal, chronicling the end of Horace Greeley, the controversial founding editor of the *New York Tribune* and that year's compromise Democratic candidate challenging President Ulysses S. Grant. While the Briggses were in the city, the *New York Times* published daily front-page stories lauding the demise of Greeley's Democratic machine (Greeley would die only a few weeks later). Briggs, himself a Democrat, probably did not appreciate the not-so-subtle insinuations about his party's integrity.

Sarah finally got her trip into the city on Thursday, October 31. It was Sophy's second birthday—and the day some Americans were beginning to celebrate the European holiday of Halloween—but the impetus for the trip was a surprise visit. Sarah's younger brother Willie, in town with his wife, Emmie, dropped by the *Mary Celeste* as the family was celebrating Sophy's birthday. It was the first time Sarah had met her sister-in-law, an introduction made somewhat amusing when Emmie Cobb embarrassed herself by losing her bonnet on the cabin's low ceiling. Benjamin and Sarah were so happy to see anyone in the family that they hired a private carriage to take them across the island to Central Park, a trip that cost about ten dollars. It was pleasant in the park with the temperature hovering around fifty degrees—practically a spring day for the New Englanders. Sophy, Briggs reported to his mother, "behaved splendid and seemed to enjoy the ride as much as any of us."

While he was in New York, Briggs checked the local shipping news columns every day and kept an eye on the harbor for the *Julia A. Hallock*. Oliver was due in port any day, after having his ship prepared for the trip to Spain. The two brothers planned to meet up in Messina that winter, but Benjamin wanted to see his favorite brother earlier if they happened to be in the city at the same time. But the days passed with no sign of Oliver Briggs.

That Saturday night, November 2, the crew finished loading the *Mary Celeste*. In all, there were 1,701 barrels marked "alcohol" and they were not packed in too tightly. They took up little more than half the ship's cavernous new hold. Still, it was a pricey charter. The freight alone was worth $36,000—more than the ship's value by a long shot. Atlantic Mutual, a shipping insurance agency already thirty years old, held the policy on the cargo's freight. That protected Meissner, Ackersman, and Co. in case the ship was lost or the casks busted in a rough crossing, a very real threat.

In twenty years of hauling all manner of cargo around the world, Briggs had never carried alcohol before. It would have been natural for him to be nervous about it. Because of its flammability, alcohol was at the time considered, along with coal and hay, one of the three most dangerous cargos for a ship to haul. In the stories that would come, much was made of the alcohol onboard the *Mary Celeste* and what, if any, role it had in the crew's disappearance. Most people assumed the alcohol was some sort of distilled spirit and spun wild tales of a drunken, mutinous crew. But there was little chance this crew would be tying one on during the voyage. The generic alcohol the *Mary Celeste* carried was most likely some sort of industrial ethanol or methanol, something that not even sailors could drink.

Briggs did not even allow his crews to carry their own liquor on board. It was a rule inherited from his father, who swore off alcohol as a boy after an old blacksmith slipped him a drink of moonshine. In his day, Nathan Briggs never let his sailors carry beer, whiskey or wine on his ships, and soon many captains followed his lead. It became a fairly standard part of shipping contracts, even though it was not a popular policy among sailors, who were famous for enjoying their grog. It was expected, though. Particularly on a Briggs ship, there was no getting drunk and rowdy.

That Monday, Briggs visited Winchester's office and signed the bills of lading before making his way to the New York Custom House, where he hurriedly completed the necessary paperwork for the *Mary Celeste*'s trip. He signed Articles of Agreement "Benj. S. Briggs"—the

Captain Benjamin Spooner Briggs in later years, not long before he took command of the *Mary Celeste*. His icy, wolflike eyes belied his gentle nature. *Photograph Courtesy New Bedford Whaling Museum*

same way he endorsed everything—and filed a list of his crewmen. While he was there, Briggs may have run into a familiar face at the Custom House in those days, a man who twenty years earlier had published a novel about a great whale. But *Moby-Dick* wasn't selling all that well, so poor Herman Melville had to do his writing on the side, after he got off work at the Custom House.

Before returning to the *Mary Celeste* to oversee last-minute preparations, Briggs mailed a letter to his mother that he'd finished the night before. At the top of one page, he underlined the words "Shall Leave Tuesday Morning" for emphasis. They were the last recorded words from the captain.

In the note, Briggs said the last two weeks had been hectic, "tedious, perplexing, very tiresome" but he had adjusted. He told of his brother-in-law's visit, and said that having Sarah and Sophy with him helped calm him considerably.

I hope we shall have a pleasant voyage. We both have missed Arthur and I believe I should have sent for him if I could have thought of a good place to stow him away. Sophia calls for him occasionally and wants to see him in the Album which by the way is a favorite book of hers. She knows your picture in both Albums and points and says Gamma Bis. She seems real smart, has got over her bad cold she had. . . .

I was in hopes Oli might get in before I left but I'm afraid not now. We finished loading last night and shall leave on Tuesday morning if we don't get off tomorrow night, the Lord willing. . . . hoping to be with you again early in the spring, with much love I am, Yrs. Affly. Benj.

He asked his mother to write them with all the news from Marion in about twenty days. Send it to Genoa, he said, in care of the American Consul.

Although Briggs did not find his brother among the captains coming and going on the waterfront, he bumped into several other people he knew on his last visit to the great city. One of those was a bear of a man from Nova Scotia named David Reed Morehouse. Morehouse commanded another brigantine, the *Dei Gratia,* which would be sailing for Gibraltar in two weeks. Morehouse had been in town nearly a month, first unloading his ship's cargo in Brooklyn, then moving to the Venango Yards in Hoboken to load his ship with more than 1,700 barrels of petroleum. For years, people would claim the two ships were tied up alongside each other on the East River, but there is no evidence of that. Nonetheless, the men knew each other from ports all over Europe, and apparently were friendly. It is not terribly coincidental that they would run into each other, even in a city as large as New York. The waterfront was, in some ways, a small world.

Almost fifty years later, Morehouse's wife claimed the two captains

had a meeting that was never revealed during the scandal that followed. On their last night in port, Mrs. Morehouse said, Benjamin and
Sarah Briggs met her husband for dinner. They dined at the Astor
House, a palatial hotel on Broadway, perhaps the finest in the country
at the time.

Whether the Briggses dined alone with Morehouse or there were
other sailors present that night, no one knows. What the two men
talked about Morehouse never said, and he told very few people
about the dinner in later years. He mentioned to his wife only that he
was quite fond of Briggs and that they had realized they would be in
Italy at the same time. Before the evening ended, the men made plans
to meet up "on the other side."

In the November 5, 1872, edition of the *New York Times,* three brigantines are listed as having cleared: the *Osprey,* the *Pedro* and the *Mary
Celeste.* Aside from the ship's name, the only information the newspaper revealed about the *Mary Celeste* was the captain and the port for
which it was bound: "Genoa."

That morning, people around the country went to the polls to re-
elect President Grant as the crew of the *Mary Celeste* cast off its mooring lines and pushed away from Pier 50. There was a nasty nor'easter
blowing off the Atlantic, and rain clouds darkened the morning sky.
Still, Briggs was intent on leaving. He ordered Richardson to have the
crew unfurl the sails and make for the channel, but the storm was so
bad that they really couldn't *see* the channel. The ship barely made it
across the harbor before Briggs was forced to change plans. The *Mary
Celeste* dropped anchor off Staten Island, where it would stay for two
days before the crew saw calmer weather.

Later, Mother Briggs would be surprised to receive one final note
from her daughter-in-law. With the foul weather keeping Sarah holed
up in the cabin for two days, she took the opportunity to update
Grandma Briggs on their progress, or lack thereof. Dated November
7, 1872, "Off Staten Island," Sarah Briggs's letter recounted the ship's
final days in port and alluded to the dinner she'd enjoyed so much at

the Astor House just a few nights earlier. She passed along her regrets for missing a party that would soon be held in Marion and assured her once again that Sophy missed her "Gamma Bis."

Dear Mother Briggs,

Probably you will be a little surprised to receive a letter with this date, but instead of proceeding to sea when we came out Tuesday morning, we anchored about a mile or so from the city, as it was strong head wind and B. said it looked so thick and nasty ahead we shouldn't gain much if we were beating & banging about. Accordingly we took a fresh departure this morning with wind light but favorable, so we hope to get outside without being obliged to anchor. Have kept a sharp lookout for Oliver, but so far have seen nothing of him. It was rather trying to lay in sight of the city so long & think that most likely we had letters waiting for us there, and be unable to get them. However, we hope no great change has occurred since we did hear and shall look for a goodly supply when we reach G.

Sophy thinks the figure 3 & the letter G on her blocks is the same thing so I saw her whispering to herself yesterday with the 3 block in her hand— Gam-gam-gamma. Benj. thinks we have got a pretty peaceable set this time all around if they continue as they have begun. Can't tell yet how smart they are. B. reports a good breeze now, says we are going along nicely.

I should like to be present at Mr. Kingsbury's ordination next week. Hope the people will be united in him, and wish we might hear of Mrs. K's improved health on arrival. Tell Arthur I make great dependence on the letter I shall get from him, and will try to remember anything that happens on the voyage which he would be pleased to hear.

We had some baked apples (sour) the other night about the size of a new-born infant's head. They tasted extremely well.

Please give our love to Mother & the girls, Aunt Hannah, Arthur and other friends, reserving a share for yourself.

As I have nothing more to say I will follow A. Ward's advice, and say it at once.

Farewell,
Yours aff'ly Sarah

Sarah's final letter home was mailed by a New York harbor pilot named Burnett, who went aboard the *Mary Celeste* on November 7 to guide the ship through a shortcut just east of the main channel. Because of its relatively slight draft, the *Mary Celeste* could cut the corner after passing through the Verrazano Narrows and save several miles getting out to sea. But there was a danger of running aground on sandbars if the man at the helm didn't know the exact route. Once the ship cleared the shallows, Burnett bid the captain and crew farewell, collected his forty-dollar fee, and promised to send off their mail before climbing over the rails into his waiting boat. He was the last person to ever see any of the ten people on board the ship.

As the pilot made his way back into the harbor, the German sailors climbed into the rigging to unfurl the rest of the foresails. After two days of harsh winds and foul weather, it was a bright morning with exasperatingly light wind. They needed all the canvas they could fly to make up for the time lost while anchored in the harbor—Briggs was a man who liked to be on time. For the better part of an hour, the crew would have climbed around the rigging untying the sails on the foremast before stringing the jibs and repositioning the ship's huge mainsail.

Slowly, the canvas caught the wind and the ship's mast felt a light tug that caused it to lumber forward. But for a moment, it seemed to just hang there. As its square sails rippled in the newfound breeze, the *Mary Celeste* began its eastward trek. From the harbor, the ship's dark silhouette grew smaller and smaller, until finally it disappeared over the horizon.

A week or so later, the *Julia A. Hallock* sailed into New York City with Captain Oliver Briggs at the helm, eager to begin his final transatlantic voyage. He had visited Rose Cottage before sailing to New York and told his mother he was going to try to catch up with Benjamin there. Sophia Briggs worried about her boys—she didn't have many left—but Oliver assured her they would be fine. Ben had a good ship, Oliver said, and he was looking forward to spending some time on it while listening to Sarah play the melodeon. Checking with the

New York harbor pilots when he arrived, Oliver Briggs discovered he was too late. The *Mary Celeste* had sailed. Perhaps, as he made his way into port, Briggs even passed Morehouse's ship, the *Dei Gratia,* about to depart.

Arthur Briggs would hear from his mother one final time. Days after the *Mary Celeste* left New York, a letter arrived at Rose Cottage addressed to the boy in his mother's familiar script. It was a chatty note she had written a few days before they sailed, before the final note to Mother Briggs.

In the letter, Sarah asked Arthur to behave, to study his lessons and get plenty of wood inside for grandmother, because "you are the man of the house now you know."

> *I suppose you have been to meeting and Sunday school today with Grandma and Uncle James. I hope you heard some good things that you will not soon forget . . .*
>
> *I think if you remember that verse in your 'First Reader' beginning 'I will not fear,' you will not be afraid to go after milk if it is dark.*

Sarah Briggs left New York worried about her seven-year-old son being afraid of the dark. But it was a fear that would pass more quickly than she realized. Arthur Briggs would soon learn—and never forget—that there were things he should be more afraid of, things much more terrifying than anything in the dark.

FOUR

The Silence of the Sea

It began as a mercifully slow day on the Atlantic.

The brigantine *Dei Gratia* trudged through heavy swells, its sails fluttering languidly, its bow bucking in protest as the occasional whitecap smacked its hull. Although this was the first clear day her crew had seen in quite a while, it was also a dreary one. Winter was well on its way to the northern latitudes.

When the weather is bad on the Atlantic, the sea and sky can blur into a bland shade of gray, creating a featureless world that is maddening in its monotony. It had been that way for weeks, a steady drizzle interspersed with daily storms—violent gales and roiling waters fighting the change of seasons. This season had been particularly bad, worse than most years. On this day, a Wednesday, there was finally enough contrast to see the horizon, but it was drab. The crew did not complain. They were thankful for a break from the rain.

Now the ship was being bathed in a fresh wind from out of the north, a crisp breeze on the port beam that made everything feel clean. For the men of the *Dei Gratia,* it was a welcome change. The foul weather had kept the ship buttoned up for the entire voyage and, frankly, the cabins were getting a bit ripe. The main hatch, they would later recall, had not been open for more than an hour. Being cooped up down below, besides negatively affecting the ship's aroma, had made the crossing seem all the more slow and tedious.

The men of the *Dei Gratia* had begun counting the days till they reached land. They would arrive in Gibraltar in little more than a week, perhaps even sooner if the wind cooperated. It would be a short stop—a few days at most—but at least it was a break in the routine, time enough to stretch their legs, socialize with other sailors, and hoist a few pints of ale. Those were the thoughts that drifted by on afternoon watch, the things the *Dei Gratia*'s crew dreamed of to get through the endless march of swells.

For a while, none of them noticed the speck of a ship creeping toward them from out of the northeast.

It was just after 1 P.M. sea time, a fact that Captain David Reed Morehouse dutifully noted in the ship's log. From his perspective that meant it was now December 5, as sailors in the nineteenth century changed the date at noon while at sea (the courts would later use the civilian date, December 4). Morehouse updated the log slate alone in his cabin. More often than not, his wife accompanied him, but she had backed out of this voyage at the last minute—sick, she said. Now he was left with an empty bunk, not his favorite way to travel.

They had been at sea nineteen days and in that time had sailed from New York nearly all the way to Europe. By Morehouse's reckoning—and he marked this in the logbook, too—the *Dei Gratia*'s position was 38°20' north latitude, 17°15' longitude. It was not the most desirable address in the world: They were traveling through a deep, dead area of the North Atlantic, halfway between the Azores island chain and the coast of Portugal—roughly 400 miles from each. But Morehouse didn't gauge his progress by either of those landfalls, he was concerned only with the distance to Gibraltar. He estimated the ship was 630 miles from the British outpost, where he would find a cable from the ship's owners telling him where to deliver the 1,735 barrels of petroleum he was carrying. Morehouse figured they would be going to Italy, a relatively short but slow cruise across the Mediterranean. But he didn't have to concern himself with that for another week, so he didn't. Morehouse recorded the *Dei Gratia's* heading as Southeast by ½ East, same as it had been yesterday, and closed the logbook. Weary of the quiet cabin, he went up on deck to get an estimate of the ship's speed and the wind direction.

The *Dei Gratia* was a solid ship, a brigantine much like the modified *Mary Celeste*. The two vessels were of similar size, design, and sail plan—both adopting the half brig mix of square sheets on the foremast, fore-and-aft sails on the main. Although the *Dei Gratia* was a decade newer and slightly larger, to an amateur the two ships would have been hard to tell apart. Most likely they competed for the same business. Even their origins were similar. The *Dei Gratia* hailed from Bear River on Nova Scotia's west coast, across the Bay of Fundy from Maine. Morehouse, from the same county, sailed her on shares, and his co-owners were also his neighbors. It was a traditional arrangement, a traditional ship. The *Dei Gratia,* a name that translated as "By the Grace of God," still flew the British flag from its mainstay.

It was cold on the deck of the *Dei Gratia* but not unbearably so, especially for a Nova Scotia sailor. To Morehouse, a burly man with short, tousled hair and a beard that stretched nearly to his chest, the light breeze must have felt as comfortable as an old sweater. In nearly twenty years at sea he had learned to enjoy whatever mild weather there was, because there wasn't much of it.

Morehouse found the men on his watch about an hour into their shift. John Wright, the second mate, stood bow watch on the forecastle and John Johnson, the quiet one, steered. Augustus Anderson lingered near Johnson at the stern, ready to relieve him at the helm if needed. They had been a good crew so far, Morehouse thought, and had held the *Dei Gratia* together nicely through the bad weather. In some ways, the captain preferred the storms to the weather they were in now. The ship's speed had slowed considerably since yesterday and

The *Mary Celeste,* abandoned. The Ghost Ship as she appeared to the crew of the
Dei Gratia on December 4, 1872, from a wood engraving by Rudolph Ruzicka.
Photograph Courtesy Peabody Essex Museum

the breeze was easing up still more. By evening, years of experience
told Morehouse, the *Dei Gratia* would barely be moving.

Morehouse was the first to spot the anonymous vessel, sometime after
1:30 P.M. Standing at the port rail, Morehouse sighted a ship on the
horizon; he guessed it was about six miles away. At first he thought little of it—even in that desolate patch of the North Atlantic so many
merchant vessels traversed the shipping lanes that it was not uncommon for ships to pass within hailing distance. But something about
this dark little ship soon gave Morehouse pause, inspired him to reach
for his long glass to take a better look.

At first, he couldn't decide exactly what it was that bothered him
about the vessel, but Morehouse felt there was something amiss. As he
continued to stare at the vessel through his telescope, he realized what
it was: The ship was hardly flying any sails. In such a light breeze, she
should have been showing acres of canvas. There was no good reason

to loiter in this dead patch of ocean, he knew. The ship could be in trouble.

"Mr. Johnson," he called out to the helmsman, according to his later testimony, "bear up toward that vessel. Two points."

A tall ship responds to her rudder slowly, and the *Dei Gratia* was no exception. Almost imperceptibly, the brig swung its bow around into the wind, slightly toward the East-Northeast—two points translated into about a 22½-degree turn. A sailor learns a lot of patience steering a tall ship. Without landmarks for reference, modest turns are made on faith in the compass and the stars. At least with another vessel in the distance the helmsman could tell the ship was reacting to his steering.

After twenty minutes, the gap between the two ships had been closed to just over four miles. As they drew closer Morehouse saw that he had been right: The ship was showing almost no cloth. It looked as if it was flying only one jib and a foresail that was reefed (which meant that part of the sail was tied up; it wasn't completely unfurled). In the light wind, it would not have been uncommon to see the ship flying nearly two dozen sails in an attempt to draw as much speed as possible out of the flaccid breeze. With a following wind, the ship should have had its largest foremast sails unfurled, at the very least.

Wherever this ship was headed, Morehouse thought, it appeared to be in no hurry to get there.

The ship was also fighting its course, bucking like a rodeo bull. It was yawing—its bow pitching to port and starboard alternately, as if its course were determined only by the swells nudging it. These movements disturbed Morehouse, and when he peered through his long glass again he saw something that alarmed him even more. He thought he could see a distress flag flying from one of the yardarms.

At that moment, Oliver Deveau was suffering through his watch below deck, supervising his men as they went through the drudgery of cleaning the *Dei Gratia*. Morehouse's first mate could hardly have been any less interested. A former captain himself, Deveau was overqualified to be mate on a small freighter. He had as much experience as the captain—in fact he was a half year older than Morehouse—but he lacked a Master's Certificate, the document a sailor needed in those days to take command of a ship. Many men would have resented this station, and it could have caused trouble on some ships, but if Deveau felt that way he didn't let it show. He was an accomplished sailor, and the captain and crew knew it. Morehouse treated him respectfully, much as an equal, and for that Deveau was appreciative. He just wanted to do his job and quickly get back to his young family in Nova Scotia, where his son would be talking any day now. When Morehouse called out for his first mate, Deveau welcomed the distraction—anything to get out of the cabin for a minute. He could not have realized he was walking into a scene that would change his life.

Deveau found Morehouse leaning on the port rail, staring off into the distance. The captain might have been daydreaming, except for the squint of his eyes. Something was out there, Deveau realized. When he reached the rail, Morehouse wordlessly handed him the glass. There was only one thing to see, so he knew what he was supposed to look at: a ship, pitching fitfully over the swells, barely making any progress. Deveau guessed it was four or five miles away.

It was a sight that would stay with Oliver Deveau for the rest of his life; the image of a small ship riding up the waves and then falling off. The silent vessel was ambling along without purpose, silently running before the wind. The scene would be re-created hundreds of times over the next century, sketched, painted, described by historians and journalists throughout the world. Deveau was looking at what would become the classic profile of a ghost ship.

Deveau took in the scene for a moment before the captain spoke.

Morehouse feared the ship's crew was in trouble. He wanted to speak with the vessel's captain to see if they needed any help. In deference to his mate, he asked Deveau for his opinion. After studying the odd little ship a moment longer, the first mate had to agree and, as such, knew what to do next. Deveau called his men on deck and told them to haul up; they were coming around. The crew scrambled, familiar with the routine. The sailors moved to their duty stations and braced the arms on the foremast, which basically meant pulling lines that rotated the yardarms, altering the angle at which the square sails caught the wind. The *Dei Gratia* was changing course more drastically than Morehouse had ordered just minutes earlier. They were going to intercept the mystery ship.

For the better part of an hour, they stood there like that— Morehouse and Deveau watching the distance close between them and the strange vessel. It was a dark-hulled ship—a brigantine, just like the *Dei Gratia*—but that was all they could confidently infer. It had no flags flying, no distinguishing markings. It could have been American or European; the only thing they could guess with any certainty was that it was a merchant ship. There were hundreds of similar vessels on the ocean in 1872.

The strange thing was that, even as they sailed closer, neither Morehouse nor Deveau could make out anyone on the other ship's deck.

Just before 3 P.M. the *Dei Gratia* passed within 400 yards of the ship. Morehouse and Deveau alternately used the spyglass to inspect the brig, perplexed by its lifelessness. There should have been a watch on deck, at least a couple of sailors milling about on the bow, another at the wheel—but there was no one in sight. Morehouse used the glass to look for the signal he thought he'd seen an hour earlier. He spotted it quickly, but immediately realized his mistake. It was not a distress flag he'd seen—it was the tattered remains of a sail.

Something was wrong.

It took only a few minutes for the *Dei Gratia*'s crew to launch a lifeboat, using block and tackle to lower the skiff into the churning sea. The shredded sail and the absence of any crew on deck had convinced Morehouse they should board the ship. He sent Deveau to investigate and told him to take two men. There might be sick or injured people on board, and it might take extra hands to handle the situation, he said. Both men knew there could be trouble as well, but neither mentioned it. Deveau chose John Wright, the second mate, and John Johnson, the sailor who had been at the wheel. Together, the three men climbed over the rail and down into the lifeboat.

The small boat gave the men an entirely different perspective of

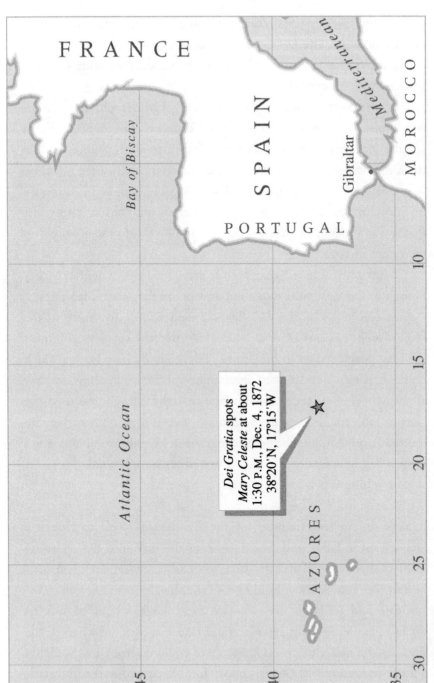

FRANCE

SPAIN

PORTUGAL

Gibraltar

MOROCCO

Mediterranean

Bay of Biscay

Atlantic Ocean

Dei Gratia spots
Mary Celeste at about
1:30 P.M., Dec. 4, 1872
38°20'N, 17°15'W

AZORES

10

15

20

25

30

35

40

45

Map by Gill Guerry

the ocean and the weather. On board the *Dei Gratia,* the swells produced a gentle rocking that was almost comforting, slow and easy. The lifeboat, however, jarred their teeth as its bow fell off the tops of swells and slapped the trough behind them. It was, Wright later recalled, "tolerably heavy seas" that the men fought to row over to the ship, but still it took only minutes to cover the distance.

As they approached the black hull, Deveau and his men searched for signs of damage. There were no holes; in fact the copper sheathing appeared fairly new and in good shape. It looked as if it had seen some rough weather; it was dragging a few lines—rigging, they guessed. But the rudder was intact and the ship seemed to be riding correctly in the water. Circling the ship to find a place to tie up, Deveau steered around to the stern, where the sailors discovered its name: *Mary Celeste.* It was a New York ship.

The brig sailed so slowly that she seemed almost completely still, and it took little effort to pull up alongside her. As the men rowed abeam of her, Deveau grabbed one of the lines hanging over the side. The ropes provided a way to hold on to the ship, but not wanting to risk losing their boat, Deveau left Johnson to tend it while he and Wright explored. They climbed up the side of the ship's hull, telling Johnson they would be right back.

The deck of the *Mary Celeste* was unnaturally calm. The wind had died down, leaving the ship silent save for the occasional rustle of the jib or the creak of a random, protesting deck plank. Tattered pieces of a sail dangled from one of the yardarms and the wheel turned itself as the current slapped the rudder. The portside rail was lying on the deck and another torn piece of sail was draped over the galley's stovepipe. The deckhouses were dark—inside one, a cabin door swung back and forth, keeping time with the swells. When it struck the doorframe, it produced a bang that cracked the silence enough to startle the men. Deveau called out once, and then again, but knew he would get no answer. There was no one on board.

It took Deveau and Wright more than a half hour to explore the *Mary Celeste,* and they later recited what they found almost matter-offactly. Their stories supported one another, the inconsistencies in them suggesting conflicting memories or differing perspectives, not contradictions of fact. If they had been rehearsed, as some people suggested, there likely would have been no variation in their accounts. There was no doubt they had stumbled upon an unnerving scene. If Deveau and Wright were spooked by it, though, they said nothing of it in the court hearing that was to follow.

Deveau testified that the first thing he did was sound the pumps to see how much water was in the *Mary Celeste*'s hold. But most likely he did that only after peeking in the deckhouses—it would have almost defied human nature not to check for bodies. When Deveau looked in the cabins he would have noticed that everything on the ship was saturated—there was several inches of water standing in the galley. Had he not thought of it himself, the water in the galley would have suggested to Deveau that he needed to see if the ship was taking on water.

It seemed someone else had had the same idea.

The two pumps for the *Mary Celeste*'s bilge were located just behind the mainmast. They resembled well pumps with long, detachable handles. To take a sounding, the pumps had to be removed from a pipe that reached from the deck to the bottom of the bilge. But Deveau did not have to bother—the pumps were already off. It appeared that somebody else had thought to take a measure: the ship's sounding rod—a metal bolt tied to the end of a rope—was lying next to one of the pump boxes. Deveau dropped the bolt into the hole and pulled it back out with the line. He measured 3½ feet of water in the bilge— enough that it should be pumped out, but not an alarming amount. The *Mary Celeste* was in no danger of sinking.

Deveau had not believed the ship was taking on serious water, he was just being cautious. In fact, he couldn't imagine there was anything seriously wrong with the ship. The *Mary Celeste* looked almost new—the hull and deck wood was still fresh. It would have been hard to convince Deveau the ship was nearly a dozen years old. He noted the new spars and decking (although Wright conversely thought the rigging looked old and ratty, an opinion that may have been based on the damage to it).

Deveau did not believe there was a dangerous leak. The water in the hold meant nothing; "waterproof," he knew, was a myth. Every ship leaks, and they all have to be pumped out regularly. There was a more obvious explanation. All of the ship's hatches were open—the fore hatch, the main hatch and the lazaret, as well as the entrances to both deckhouses. Even the skylight in the captain's cabin was propped up. With every doorway and several windows open, it would not take much more than a couple of waves breaking over the bow, a following sea or a steady rain to soak the entire vessel.

Even if the *Mary Celeste* hadn't suffered a hard blow, it appeared she had been knocked around a bit. Aside from the ripped sail and mangled rigging, the binnacle—the box used to store the ship's compasses and other equipment—had busted on the deck, where Wright found it lying in pieces. It looked as if the box had been ripped from the roof of the aft deckhouse, where cleats held it in place for the helmsman. One of the cleats was lying on the deck and the compass had fallen out of the binnacle, its glass broken, its innards smashed. Deveau picked it up and turned it over in his hand. Very odd, he thought.

Just as Deveau started to walk away, out of the corner of his eye he saw something move. It may have startled him briefly, until he realized it was the ship's wheel. He had noticed it when he came aboard. The wheel was connected directly to the rudder—just as it moved the rudder, the rudder could move it. The water pressure on the rudder turned the wheel as if a ghost helmsman was steering the ship. Deveau wondered why the crew had not tied off the wheel, as any sailor would have done when leaving the deck of a ship that wasn't sinking. The wheel should have been lashed tightly alee so that instead of being completely at the mercy of the wind, the ship would sail in something of a circle. It at least explained why the *Mary Celeste* had been bobbing around so strangely. The waves were steering her.

Leaving Wright to poke around on the forecastle, Deveau squeezed his huge frame through the companionway leading down into the main cabin. Perhaps the ship's log could tell him what had happened if it was still on board. As he reached the main cabin,

Deveau found himself facing the entrance to the captain's quarters. The door was slightly ajar. He stepped inside.

The cabin smelled musty and damp, but—save for the captain's bed, which was unmade—it was remarkably neat. The shelves were lined with charts and books, there was a sewing machine on the table, and in one corner, an elegant musical instrument made of fine wood. It was like a piano but smaller: a harmonium or melodeon, he did not know which was the correct name. From spying the soiled dress draped over the chair, Deveau figured there had been a woman on board. The captain's wife. There was a child, too—toys were piled in one corner and there were a few pieces of children's clothing lying out.

The main bunk was big enough to hold all three people, he noted, although there was another bed in the cabin. He made a cursory scan of the room, but couldn't find a log of any sort. Maybe they took it with them. Deveau turned to walk out of the cabin. Glancing back, he saw something that gave him a slight chill. In the damp covers of the captain's bunk he could make out the distinct impression of a child's form. It looked almost like a death mask, popular on infant tombstones of the day.

Deveau next checked the first mate's quarters, which he found behind the only other door in the main cabin. There was a chart hanging over the mate's bed with a line drawn on it representing, he guessed, the *Mary Celeste*'s course across the Atlantic. It meandered along nearly straight and due east from the tip of New York, stopping just west of the Azores, a spot several hundred miles west of the ship's current location. The date of the final plotting was November 24—ten days earlier. That meant nothing: the mate could have grown bored with charting the course; they didn't really need it as long as they kept latitude/longitude records. He could have caught it up later.

Deveau found another chart beneath the bed, but it had no markings on it. On the mate's desk, however, he found a book. It wasn't a log; it appeared to include receipts for cargo, ship's expenses—nothing recent and nothing that told anything of the crew's fate. As he sat the receipt book down, Deveau saw the log. It had been behind the other book. He flipped through the pages until the writing stopped. It was all pretty standard stuff—businesslike notations of course, speed and wind direction. The final entries were made on November 24, same as the chart. He scanned the writing, but it told him nothing.

Deveau found the log slate lying on the table in the main cabin. The crew used the erasable slate to keep their hourly observations, recording them in the log once a day. The slate had notations for November 25, the day after the log ended. That made sense, but it didn't provide any answers. In fact, it was devoid of any clue to what had happened. The slate suggested that November 25 had been a routine day.

The *Mary Celeste* had been making good time. With a fresh wind, the ship had been cruising at a solid eight knots, speeding to nine knots just after dark the previous evening (which was the night of November 24, based on civilian time).

The last entry on the log slate was made the morning of November 25. The *Mary Celeste* had maintained its eight knots throughout the night, indicating there had been good wind. After the long sail from New York, the crew had finally spotted land. They first sighted the island of Santa Maria—or as American sailors called it, St. Mary's—at five that morning. Three hours later, the ship passed the southernmost of the Azores. The final entry on the slate read, "At 8 Eastern point bore S. S. W. 6 miles distant."

And there, six miles east of the last island in the Azores, the log stopped. The line for a 9 A.M. entry, and all beyond it, was blank.

Deveau was perplexed. There was no mention of harsh weather, of illness or any problem with the ship. The log simply ended. There was only one other thing on the slate, scribbled in the corner. In the last line on the left-hand side, someone had scratched the words, "Francis my own dear wife Francis N. R."

And there the writing abruptly stopped.

While Deveau explored the cabins of the aft deckhouse, Wright had looked around the ship's forecastle. In the forward deckhouse, he found a mess. The stove had been knocked over and there was water standing several inches deep, held in by a nine-inch doorsill meant to keep water out. Cooking utensils littered the floor, pots and pans floated about.

Deveau ignored the galley, wading through to reach the crew quarters. He passed the second mate's cabin, which had but a single bunk in it, and then came to the largest room in the deckhouse, where the rest of the men slept. There were four bunks and three sea chests. It stopped Deveau, but only momentarily. Sailors sometimes shared chests (he would have immediately made the connection, had he known two of the four sailors bunking in the room were brothers). At the time, Deveau thought one of the chests could have been taken.

Deveau found it strange the men had left behind their belongings, a luxury most poor sailors did not have. When he saw the first pipe, it barely registered with him. But then he spied another one, and another one on the table—four in all. Deveau was a smart man, and twenty years of sailing told him that sailors went absolutely nowhere without their pipes. This disturbed him almost as much as seeing the outline of the child on the captain's bunk. But there was more, and he was beginning to take note of things he'd overlooked before. Hanging from pegs mounted on the cabin wall, Deveau found the men's foul-weather gear—four sets. He'd noticed the same thing in the captain and mate's cabins, but it hadn't struck him as that unusual. In the crew's quarters, however, it seemed almost mind-boggling. This time of year sailors almost always wore their foul-weather gear at sea. With the rough weather plaguing the Atlantic in the past month, these men would have hardly been out of their gear (and there was no question of any lowly deckhands having an extra set). If they had left the ship during a storm, which Deveau was beginning to suspect, they would have been wearing their foul-weather gear when they left. Yet here were four bunks and four sets of foul-weather oilskins. It didn't make sense.

Obviously they had abandoned ship.

There was no other answer, of course. But that raised other nagging questions: When and where had they left the ship, and why?

Those puzzles were almost secondary, at the moment anyway, to the question of *how*. Deveau could not tell whether the crew had launched a lifeboat—or even find a sure sign that they had carried one. Part of the portside rail had been taken down, but there was no rigging to indicate anyone had lowered a boat from the spot.

Wright believed they had carried the boat on the stern, pointing out two davits mounted there, but Deveau knew better. There was a spar lashed to the davits, which is how crews protected the hoisting cranes when there was no boat attached. If there had been a boat there, Deveau knew they would not have lowered it and then taken the time to lash a spar in its place, but there were no other davits or any other way for the crew to lower a boat. The lines they found hanging over the side were part of the rigging, but surely the crew could not have used that to lower a boat. How did they leave, Deveau wondered.

For years afterward, some people would claim the *Mary Celeste* had not carried any lifeboats on that trip. Although there didn't appear to be another place to hang a skiff, and there was no abundance of space on deck, there were clues that suggested one boat had been aboard. Deveau noticed fenders lying around the main hatch that might have been used to cushion a boat strapped down over the opening. But then, what would they have done if they wanted to open the hatch, Deveau wondered. It would take several minutes to move the boat each time they opened it.

Perhaps they had not needed to get into the hold, the *Dei Gratia* sailors thought. Down the hatch, Deveau and Wright saw rows of barrels marked "alcohol" but no other supplies or equipment. There was some water between decks—no surprise, given the condition of the cabins—but that was all that seemed to be wrong. Everything else appeared to be in good condition.

Deveau and Wright were not overly concerned with the mystery of the empty ship, but found it perplexing nonetheless. For every clue that pointed in one direction, there was another that suggested the opposite. Together, none of it made any sense. Deveau and Wright had been onboard the *Mary Celeste* for half an hour, enough time to search the entire ship, but still had no idea what had happened. Although everything was in its place, Deveau had the feeling that they left "in a great hurry." The question was why. The ship was in satisfactory condition. The rigging was a mess, but they assumed that had happened since the crew deserted. If the log was accurate, the *Mary Celeste* had been sailing around the North Atlantic untended for more than a week. When the crew last recorded its position, the ship had been sailing east, toward the Mediterranean. Now it was sailing southwest, at least 350 miles from its last recorded position. The ship had sailed east since the last log entry and, at some point, turned completely around.

There were signs the ship had encountered nasty weather before the crew departed. More than half the portholes had been boarded up or covered in canvas, probably the crew's attempt to protect the glass during high winds. Certainly the *Mary Celeste* had sailed through the same rotten weather that had plagued every other ship on the Atlantic that month. But if the crew abandoned ship during a storm, why had all the hatches been off and the skylight open? If there had been a storm, why had the crew not been wearing foul-weather gear?

Deveau told Wright that he suspected the sounding rod was the answer to the mystery. The crew found a fair amount of water in the bilge and, fearing that the ship was sinking, took to the lifeboat. It didn't make complete sense, but then, nothing did. Deveau didn't consider it long; he already had other things on his mind. After Wright disappeared over the side, Deveau took one last look around, climbed over the gunwale and into the waiting lifeboat.

It was after 4 P.M. when Deveau, Wright and Johnson made it back to the *Dei Gratia*. Their shipmates were eager to hear what they'd found and as soon as they climbed aboard, Deveau gave Morehouse a report. Most of the crew loitered within earshot of the two men, who stood together at the *Dei Gratia*'s stern.

Deveau had weighed the situation the entire way back. While the scene might have frightened a less experienced sailor, Deveau saw only opportunity. A ship with a hold full of cargo was worth a lot of money, and the salvage on it would be handsome. He laid out what he'd found optimistically, putting emphasis on the good condition of the hull and the sails. Deveau knew Morehouse well enough to realize he would be reluctant to go along with the plan he'd devised.

The ship was "apparently in good condition," Morehouse recalled Deveau saying, but for some unknown reason had been abandoned. There was 3½ feet of water in the hold, but it could be pumped with little effort. There were some small problems with the rigging, a few sails were torn, but nothing that couldn't be repaired. The ship was, Deveau told the captain, nearly new—and there was a hold full of unmolested cargo.

"I think we should take it in," Deveau said.

Salvage is the law of the sea. Any untended, damaged, wrecked or abandoned vessel can be claimed by anyone who comes upon it or can get it to port. The way it works, in reality, is that a maritime court determines an award price for any derelict brought into its jurisdiction. The owners of the ship pay that price to the salvers or they don't get it back. When Deveau inspected the *Mary Celeste,* he didn't see a ghost ship—he saw dollar signs. He knew that if they could sail her to Gibraltar, which wasn't much more than a week away, the ship's owners could probably use their insurance to pay a salvage award. It might be as much as $40,000 or $50,000 for the cargo and ship combined, he figured. It would make a huge difference in his life, and give his wife and young son a little security.

As Deveau had no doubt expected, Morehouse was wary of the idea but took it seriously. The salvage of a ship of that size with nearly 200 tons in cargo would bring enough money to make men do dangerous things—it was almost like finding buried treasure. Morehouse told his mate to think about the consequences, of all the bad things that could happen over 600 miles of open water.

"Consider the risk we are running," Morehouse said, according to court testimony. "The risk to our own ship or our lives and property."

Consider, Morehouse said, that he would bear all the blame and loss—not Deveau. He reminded him how stubborn the weather had been on the trip.

Deveau didn't need the facts laid out for him. The *Dei Gratia* carried a crew of eight—two watches of four men who worked four hours on deck, then had four hours off. This bare-bones crew complement was a penny-pinching measure by the ship's owners, and the sailors paid a hefty price for it. A minimal crew left no room for error, no allowance for sick or tired men. In the weather the *Dei Gratia* had sailed through in the past few weeks, there had been several times when both watches were needed on deck. Taking away men to put a skeleton crew on the *Mary Celeste* left the *Dei Gratia* vulnerable. "What if more bad weather comes up?" Morehouse asked.

"I think we can make it," Deveau told him, if they have "favorable conditions."

Morehouse was not a tyrant and, like Deveau, knew the salvage could have a big impact on their lives. The captain called the crew aft, where he laid out the facts, Deveau's scheme, and his reservations. Morehouse played out the dangerous scenario that would come up if they were hit with more bad weather. He told them that if they followed the first mate's plan they would share the risk and, for the better part of two weeks, they would work almost constantly. If they were successful, however, they would also share in what almost certainly would be a handsome salvage award.

There was likely very little debate. It had to be an extremely tempting idea to the sailors. Like the crew of the *Mary Celeste*, most of the men on the *Dei Gratia* were sailing for a pittance—thirty or forty dollars a month. The salvage award Deveau envisioned might earn them several hundred dollars each—more than they made in a year (the *Dei Gratia*'s owners would still get the biggest share, and it would be split from there). Still, even a small slice of the ultimate reward would be a huge windfall for the poor men. Their decision was unanimous. The men of the *Dei Gratia* would salvage the *Mary Celeste*.

Although Morehouse was willing to go along with his first mate's plan, he hedged his bets. He only allowed Deveau to take two men with him to run the *Mary Celeste;* Morehouse would keep four in addition to himself to handle the *Dei Gratia*. Aside from the *Dei Gratia* being his first priority, it was a heavy ship that was hard to maneuver. If there was going to be an advantage, he wanted it. He allowed Deveau to pick which two men he wanted, however, and Morehouse later told the court that his mate chose the best two. Deveau took Charles Lund, from his watch, and Augustus Anderson, a crewman from the captain's watch. Neither had been along on the first search party.

Morehouse gave the men the smaller of *Dei Gratia*'s two lifeboats, a barometer, a compass and his own pocket watch. They took a small amount of provisions, unsure of the food onboard the *Mary Celeste*. Deveau took many of his personal navigation instruments with him. By the time the three men set out in the small lifeboat the sky was darkening, the wind had died completely, and the seas were flattening to a dead calm. In the Atlantic dusk, Deveau made his second trip to the ghost ship, now just a silhouette a quarter mile away.

More than fifty years after the crew of the *Dei Gratia* found the *Mary Celeste,* after Morehouse and Deveau were dead, a new claim about that day surfaced. Desiah Foster Morehouse, long since widowed and living in Massachusetts, told a Boston reporter of her husband's acquaintance with Benjamin Briggs. It was she who said the two men dined at the Astor House shortly before they sailed. She said, "In fact, they were friends of many years." If that is true, then when Deveau returned to the *Dei Gratia* and reported the derelict's identity, Morehouse knew it was Briggs who was missing. Mrs. Morehouse suggested that while Deveau, Lund and Anderson readied the *Mary Celeste,* her husband took the *Dei Gratia* on a desperate search for the lifeboat he knew was out there somewhere with Briggs, his family and crew aboard.

Unless he feared losing sight of the derelict, or the last date on the log slate convinced him that whatever happened had occurred hundreds of miles away, it would have been normal for a conscientious sailor such as Morehouse to have searched. Perhaps he did. Morehouse knew the crew would not last for long in a lifeboat on the open Atlantic—storms and rogue waves could capsize and sink a skiff in a matter of minutes. The water temperature was in the low sixties, meaning anyone in the water would succumb to hypothermia in less than a day, if they didn't drown first. The crew's best hope, Morehouse knew, was a passing ship. Although it was a dead area of the Atlantic, the stretch between the Azores and Portugal was on the normal trade route. Maybe someone picked them up, Morehouse thought, as unlikely as that was.

In his later testimony, Morehouse was vague about the *Dei Gratia's* actions that night. He only said that they "tried to set sail" but ultimately stayed with the *Mary Celeste.* If he was keeping quiet about his search efforts, he had his reasons.

It was a long night.

When Deveau and his party reached the *Mary Celeste,* it was dark and they were greeted only by the familiar creaks of a wooden sailing ship rocking in gentle swells. Because the wind had died down, they would have an easier time working on the rigging. The darkness didn't make much difference. Sailors were accustomed to working by starlight and in nearly blind conditions.

Deveau had Lund and Anderson measure the water in the bilge again. If the ship were taking on significant water, the level would have changed since he'd checked it a few hours earlier. Both men claimed to have used the sounding rod and said the ship still carried 3½ feet of saltwater in her belly—no change, which was reassuring. Lund spent the next three hours pumping the bilge dry as Deveau and Anderson inventoried the sails and made sure they had rigging enough to maneuver the ship. Anderson stayed on deck most of the evening, and didn't go anywhere near either of the dark deckhouses for some time after boarding the *Mary Celeste.* He later said it was because he was too busy.

Late that evening, the ship was pumped dry. The wind was too light to make much progress east, so they worked as best they could through the night to make further repairs, shadowed by the dark outline of the *Dei Gratia* nearby. At about 10 P.M., Morehouse had the *Dei Gratia* drift close to the *Mary Celeste's* stern to check on his mate's progress. The captain shouted to Deveau and the huge man shuffled to the rail. Morehouse asked if he'd gotten the ship pumped dry and then, according to later court testimony, made a less technical query.

"Do you feel safe on her?"

"I think we're all right," Deveau called out, "but don't leave me tonight."

By midnight, Deveau and his makeshift crew had a few sails hoisted—it would take them days to fully repair the rigging—and the ship sluggishly started east in the intermittent breeze.

The next morning, Deveau, Lund and Anderson were already exhausted and still had 600 miles to make port. At the wheel, Deveau was counting his money. Occasionally, he stopped to look out across the vast desert of the North Atlantic and wonder what had happened to the ship's crew, and why they had abandoned this ship. He never thought to worry about his own safety on the ship, or what he'd gotten himself into.

Deveau had little time to devote to such thoughts. It would be a long, hard run down the coast of Portugal and he hoped to avoid the weather he convinced Morehouse they would miss. Encouraged by a fresh breeze and thoughts of a lucrative salvage, Oliver Deveau steered the *Mary Celeste* for Gibraltar.

PART II

FIVE

News From Overseas

On Saturday, December 21, the *New Bedford Evening Standard* carried an ominous notice in its "Marine Intelligence" column. Buried beneath a list of the harbor's arriving and departing ships was a terse but disturbing dispatch that cast a pall over Christmas at Rose Cottage:

> *Brig* Mary Celeste, *from New York Nov. 17 for Genoa, is reported by cable as having been picked up derelict and towed into Gibraltar 16th inst. She was commanded by Capt. Benjamin Briggs, of Marion, who had his wife and child with him, and much anxiety is felt for their safety.*

While the news sounded dire, the family tried to take solace from the fact that at least some of the report was just plain wrong. James Briggs and his mother knew from Sarah's final letter that the newspaper was mistaken about the date the *Mary Celeste* had left New York. They did not realize the item contained two other errors as well: the date the ship arrived in Gibraltar and that it was towed into port. Those inaccuracies, the first of hundreds, only made the situation seem even worse than it was. A ship that had to be towed probably was unsafe to sail, and suggested the vessel had been through violent weather. If that were the case, the crew very easily could have been swept overboard—a horrifying prospect reminiscent of the fate of Maria Briggs and her husband.

Such sloppy reportage was common in newspapers of the era, but even if the Briggs family had known of the discrepancies it would have been of small comfort. The bottom line was the same— Benjamin, Sarah and baby Sophy had been missing for several weeks.

Over the years, the Briggs family had learned all too well how to receive news of maritime disasters: They expected the worst. Throughout their traditional New England Christmas, they spent much of the time praying. In some ways, it felt as if the family was huddled in tragedy. While members of the Cobb family were in and out of the house, most often there was only Mother Briggs, Arthur and James, who—following the death of his wife Rebecca—had moved back to Rose Cottage. With her passing already weighing on them, the family tried not to let this news dampen holiday spirits any further. They spoke little of the trouble with the *Mary Celeste*—and not a word of it in front of Arthur. The boy would not be told of his parents' disappearance. Not yet. On that point, Mother Briggs was insistent.

By the time the *New Bedford Evening Standard* reported the news, the story had been circulating through the seaports of New England for almost a week. It began with a series of cables from Gibraltar, one of which was sent by Captain David Reed Morehouse to a New York shipbroker who owned a stake in the *Dei Gratia*. Morehouse's cryptic note said only, "Found fourth and brought here '*Mary Celeste*' abandoned seaworthy admiralty impost notify all parties telegraph offer of salvage."

Word reached the rest of the city through a State Department telegraph and, picking up on an error included in it, the New York papers mistakenly identified the ship as an Austrian brig. The next day, on December 14, dateline Gibraltar, the papers updated the story with a single sentence: "The brig *Mary Celeste* is in possession of the Admiralty Court."

Arthur Briggs, shown here in a photo taken more than a year before the accident, would not be told of his family's disappearance
for months after the *Mary Celeste* was found abandoned at sea in
December 1872. *Photograph Courtesy Peabody Essex Museum*

Although these mentions raised more questions than they answered,
the story initially drew little attention. It was just another disaster at sea,
something so common it hardly stood out in the shipping news. The
same week the first notice of the *Mary Celeste*'s discovery appeared in the
New Bedford Evening Standard there were at least a half dozen other
tragedies listed in the "Marine Intelligence" column. The steamship
Adriatic broke up at sea; the ship *Gustave* was lost with all hands; an unknown schooner went down off Cape Ann; and the ship *Radnagore* from
Quebec became unmanageable and was abandoned at sea.

The difference between these ships and the *Mary Celeste* was that only her crew was missing, which made it less tragic to the most avid readers of the maritime reports—that is, the men who owned the ships. After all, the vessel had been saved. A missing crew was not even all that uncommon at the time. In one seven-year stretch of the late nineteenth century, the American Hydrographic Office listed 1,628 derelicts found on the Atlantic—an average of more than nineteen a month. There were probably more, but many abandoned ships were swamped and sank long before anyone ran across them. The fact that the *Mary Celeste* survived whatever peril forced its crew to leave it should have been only a minor curiosity. In fact, there was no guarantee yet that there was even loss of life. Since most ships followed the same basic route between Europe and America, there was a chance that a passing vessel had rescued the ship's crew.

On the New Bedford waterfront, the *Mary Celeste* incident attracted some interest because Briggs was held in such high regard in the maritime community. News of his disappearance sparked speculation among the Buzzards Bay sailors—*Have you heard anything of Briggs?*—that was informed by the scandalous talk from overseas. It would not let up anytime soon, and before it subsided would only grow more intense, fueled by news of the salvage hearing in Gibraltar's Vice Admiralty Court, which was already into its third day of testimony. Within weeks, the hint of crime and scandal would move the dispatches from the "Marine Intelligence" column to the front pages of newspapers across the country.

The *Mary Celeste* was becoming a big story, for it appeared something sinister had occurred.

Sailing the *Mary Celeste* into Gibraltar with a skeleton crew had been a tougher job than Oliver Deveau expected. For one thing, the ship's rigging was more tangled than he initially thought and it took him nearly two full days to get everything back in order. The problem was not a lack of materials, or even damage to the ship. The *Mary Celeste* had extra sails to replace the ones that had been ruined, and Deveau and Charles Lund found new lines for the rigging. But the men had to restring that rigging, replace the sails and keep pace with the *Dei Gratia* as they crossed 600 miles of open ocean. If they had encountered rougher weather than they did, Deveau might have lost his gamble. As it was, sailing a 100-foot ship with only two other men was very nearly suicide. The weary men struggled just to keep the *Mary Celeste* on course. Only one of them could rest at any given time, and then just for a scant few minutes. The three sailors barely got any sleep for more than a week.

With light breezes most of the way across, the *Mary Celeste*—despite being shorthanded—had more often than not stayed within sight of the *Dei Gratia*. Three or four times, the ships sailed close enough that Deveau and Morehouse could shout to one another. That is how it went for a week, until they reached the Strait of Gibraltar, the narrow neck of water that connects the Atlantic to the Mediterranean and separates Europe from Africa. There, just as the crew of the *Dei Gratia* sighted Cape Spartel and the Moroccan coast on December 11, a storm blew in that separated the two ships. Throughout the night, the men on board the *Mary Celeste* fought to keep an even keel, and keep themselves from being washed over the ship's stubby gunwales.

The heavier *Dei Gratia* fought the weather better than the *Mary Celeste* and was able to make the turn north to reach Gibraltar's harbor quicker. Meanwhile, Deveau found himself dangerously close to the southern shore of the strait. To avoid running aground, he was forced to turn east and the ship sailed—or was pushed by unfavorable winds—nearly forty miles up the coast of Spain. By the time the *Mary Celeste* fought its way back west far enough to sight the towering profile of the Rock of Gibraltar, it was the morning of December 13, a Friday no less.

The *Dei Gratia* had arrived at 4 P.M. the previous afternoon, and Morehouse immediately alerted local authorities that his crew was bringing in a derelict. Aware that Deveau was struggling with the ship, the captain prudently waited until the *Mary Celeste* safely reached port before wiring a request for salvage back to New York.

When the *Mary Celeste* reached the marina, Morehouse greeted Deveau on the docks. The captain had not spoken with his mate for a few days and was shocked by his appearance. Morehouse found Deveau gaunt, skinny and slightly disoriented. He had suffered mightily just to make port, Morehouse later said, and recalled that Deveau looked "fatigued and sleepy."

Of course, Morehouse had been right—it was a reckless venture. If the storm had been any worse both ships would have been at risk. But that was a point Morehouse refrained from making for the moment. He simply congratulated Deveau on successfully delivering the ship to port. But he noted that his once optimistic mate no longer seemed so eager.

"I don't know that I would attempt it again," Deveau said.

Thomas J. Vecchio, marshal of the British Vice Admiralty Court, took custody of the *Mary Celeste* shortly after it arrived in Gibraltar. Great Britain had controlled the port, just a few square miles of land overlooking the Mediterranean, since 1704. The English found it an extremely advantageous location. The huge limestone Rock of Gibraltar jutting 1,400 feet out of the sea marked a fortress that, by the nineteenth century, had gained the rightful reputation as one of the world's most impregnable. It was a handy outpost for what at the time was the world's greatest navy. The port was also a hub of commerce, a harbor with dozens of ships from around the world coming and going every week, many stopping after a hard trek across the Atlantic, before sailing on to other European cities.

The *Dei Gratia* crew had been bound for Gibraltar to pick up telegraphed orders on where to deliver their cargo, a common practice in those days. American sailors knew Gibraltar well, and since English was the official language, they felt comfortable there. The volume of traffic underscored its importance and also kept the Admiralty Court quite busy. Nonetheless, the court scheduled the *Mary Celeste* salvage hearing for the next week's docket.

Oliver Deveau believed the matter would be settled quickly, perhaps more quickly than he'd prefer. Even after a full night's sleep, Deveau felt whipped, and did not want to consider going back to sea for a while. The *Dei Gratia* sailors felt their physical exhaustion bolstered the request for a high salvage; they had worked hard to save the *Mary Celeste,* and expected the court to see it that way as well. A week in

port awaiting the salvage hearing was welcome news to them. Deveau, Lund and Anderson knew they would be lucky to get rested up
before they were scheduled to testify.

For that entire week, Deveau remained optimistic about the hearing, convinced that his testimony was just a formality. The day after arriving in Gibraltar he wrote to his wife back home in Digby County,
Nova Scotia, expressing his sorrow that he hadn't received a letter
with news of his son, James, and bragging about the crew's "luck" in
finding the derelict *Mary Celeste.*

> *I took two men out of the brig and brought her in here . . . and I had a
> hard time of it. I would not like to undertake it again. I had very fine
> weather for the first two or three days, and then we had it hot and heavy.
> I made the land all right and it was blowing a gale at the time, and I got
> drove through the gut [the Strait of Gibraltar] and 40 miles to leeward.*
>
> *I shall be well paid, for the* Mary Celeste *belongs to New York and
> was loaded with alcohol bound for Genoa, Italy, and her cargo is worth
> eighty thousand dollars besides the vessel. We do not know how it will be
> settled yet. I expect the captain will have to stop, and I will proceed on the
> voyage with the* Dei Gratia. *They seem to say that we will draw half sal-
> vage. I think you will see this reported in the papers.*

Although Deveau had no doubt heard the outcome of many salvage hearings, he was a little naive about the value of the cargo and
the ship—his estimate on both was more than double the actual insured price. He also held some misconceptions about the court pro-
ceedings. Deveau expected the salvage hearing to be resolved quickly,
and assumed Morehouse would be the main witness for the salvers. To
him, it all seemed almost predictable. He didn't realize that the Admiralty Court considered this anything but a routine matter, or that it
would be him—and not his captain—whom the British Admiralty
judge was most interested in questioning.

Morehouse realized from the start that nothing good could come of
a salvage hearing. Whether it was because he was wary of the Admi-

ralty Court marshal, or the local attorney general had already been
sniffing around, Morehouse tried desperately to avoid any legal en-
tanglements. He asked local diplomats to help them reach a salvage
agreement before the case went to trial. In a telegram to the U.S. State
Department sent just hours after the *Mary Celeste* docked, Horatio
Jones Sprague, the American consul at Gibraltar, announced that he
was trying to help Morehouse do just that.

> *The Master of the* Dei Gratia *claims salvage and would prefer settling
> this matter out of court, if possible to avoid court formalities and other ex-
> penses.*
>
> *I have telegraphed to the New York Board of Underwriters, and also to
> Genoa on the subject of this disaster, and though prepared to do all in my
> power for the protection of the interests of those concerned, I can do noth-
> ing more for present, as the Vice Admiralty Court will not recognize any
> party claiming the property in its hands unless accompanied by a power of
> attorney from the rightful owners . . .*

Sprague asked the State Department to try and sort out the details
in New York while he considered ways to circumvent the salvage
hearing locally. He knew from experience to expect trouble from the
British bureaucrats. Sprague was so certain the case would get tangled
in red tape that he did not find it imprudent to cable his counterpart
in Genoa to report that the *Mary Celeste* would almost certainly arrive
far later than it had been expected.

Sprague had been the American consul in Gibraltar for more than
two decades, succeeding his father in the post. He knew the town like
a native, which he was, and that made him quite good at his job. The
State Department in the mid-nineteenth century had nearly 400
consuls stationed around the world, men whose sole purpose was to
promote American commerce and assist sailors in foreign ports,
particularly if they were in distress. Given Gibraltar's importance to
international shipping, Horatio Jones Sprague was a key consul, familiar to several generations of sailors. The tall, friendly and distinguished Sprague often facilitated their mail to and from the United

States, and tended to other tedious paperwork duties. To many sailors, he was a benevolent father figure.

While it was his job to help the New York owners of the *Mary Celeste,* Sprague felt a special compulsion to assist in this case because he knew Benjamin Briggs. In a profession with more than its share of rough and questionable characters, Sprague thought Briggs stood out as an honorable man, a true gentleman. They shared an acquaintance of nearly twenty years, speaking each time the captain sailed into town, which was often. Benjamin Briggs spent so much time in Gibraltar that he had joined the local Masonic lodge, and it was very likely Sprague had even met Sarah Briggs.

This connection may have helped to spare the Briggs family some of the harshest innuendo that would follow. As the accusations and insinuations flew, Sprague never entertained any notion of foul play, simply because he knew Briggs. He was certain the captain would not be a party to anything illegal or unethical. He made that point every chance he got.

Still Sprague worried about the talk.

Suspicions of foul play were already being whispered around town, and it was hard to avoid them in a place as small as Gibraltar. That meant the court officers had heard them, too, and might feed off it. He knew the British bureaucracy occasionally took things a little too far, particularly the local attorney general and the queen's advocate and proctor on maritime law, a fussy seventy-one-year-old man named Frederick Solly Flood.

The salvage hearing began the following Wednesday, December 18, in the court of Sir James Cochrane, the judge and commissary of the Vice Admiralty Court of Gibraltar. The room was filled almost exclusively with witnesses and attorneys, including Henry Peter Pisani, who had been retained by Morehouse to serve as advocate for the *Dei Gratia's* crew. Pisani appeared with the sailors who had been aboard the *Mary Celeste,* but not the captain. Either on the advice of Pisani or for reasons he kept to himself, Morehouse declined to testify—his excuse being that he did not know much, that he had not gone aboard the *Mary Celeste* until it was docked in Gibraltar. The judge seemed unmoved by the decision. At least initially, it appeared the court did not intend to spend much time on the case. Oliver Deveau, John Wright, John Johnson, Charles Lund and Augustus Anderson were all scheduled to testify in a single day.

That turned out to be a very ambitious agenda. At first, the questions were routine, but unsatisfactory answers sparked others. Very quickly an adversarial tone surfaced, the mood grew tense, and soon the simple salvage hearing took on overtones of something much more serious. Ultimately, the first round of testimony would expand by several days—into the weekend, in fact—mainly because of Flood.

Most of what is known about the *Mary Celeste* incident comes from the notes taken during the salvage hearing. Without the court's transcript, the story would survive only in a handful of State Department documents and starkly conflicting newspaper accounts. But the court's notes leave out a fair number of facts. While the transcript of the Vice Admiralty hearing records the testimony given by Deveau and the other *Dei Gratia* crew members, it does not—except in rare instances—include the comments and questions of the court or the queen's proctor. It is possible only to surmise the general nature of the inquiries based on the answers. Still, even with only the vaguest notion of what the *Dei Gratia* sailors were asked, it appears clear that Flood suspected some sort of conspiracy nearly from the beginning.

Oliver Deveau took the stand first and outlined the *Dei Gratia's* voyage from America and the subsequent discovery of the *Mary Celeste*. They had left New York on November 15 bound for Gibraltar, he recalled. On December 5, sea time, the captain called him on deck to see a "strange sail on the windward bow apparently in distress requiring assistance." Deveau mistakenly gave the time of the sighting as 3 P.M.

Deveau continued almost uninterrupted as he told the court about finding the empty ship, sounding its pumps and exploring its cabins. The crew had seemingly just vanished, but he couldn't say exactly why. "There had been a great deal of water" throughout the ship, he said, enough that it had ruined the vessel's clock. He told of finding the *Mary Celeste*'s logbook and slate, how the rigging was mangled

Oliver Deveau, first mate of the *Dei Gratia,* imagined he was due
a handsome salvage award for bringing the *Mary Celeste* to
Gibraltar. He did not realize that, from the start, the local attorney general was suspicious of his story. *Photograph Courtesy Peabody
Essex Museum*

and how, save for a few ragged pieces of canvas still flying, most of her
sails had been furled.

"There seemed to be everything left behind in the cabin as if left
in a great hurry but everything in its place," Deveau testified.

The judge seemed most concerned about the crew, questioning
Deveau about the *Mary Celeste*'s lifeboats and whether the anchor was
still on board. The anchor was secure, he said, but there were no
lifeboats—and no sign that there had been more than one onboard.

Cochrane knew the men could not survive long in a small boat on the Atlantic and seemed to be seeking clues the ship had been close to land. Failing that, he turned his attention to determining why the crew had deserted. Eventually, Cochrane relegated himself to asking all the *Dei Gratia* sailors about the water in the ship's bilge, repeatedly inquiring what they'd found each time they sounded the pumps.

Flood was not so interested in the mundane facts.

The attorney general asked the sailors when they had first seen the *Mary Celeste,* and if they had spotted any other ships during their trip. He asked where the *Dei Gratia* had been on November 24 and 25, the last dates recorded in the *Mary Celeste's* log. Based on his answers, it seems that Deveau could hardly comprehend what Flood was insinuating.

"We spoke to one other brigantine on our voyage bound to Boston, but we did not pass nor see any other vessel of similar class on our outward voyage," Deveau's testimony reads. "Therefore the first time we could have seen this vessel was the day we found her as we did deserted. I cannot say without referring to my log where our ship was on the 24th or 25th. I do know we were North of the other vessel. I know that we were between the Latitudes 40 and 42. I only know that we were North of the vessel from seeing her track traced on the chart."

Flood wondered if the *Dei Gratia* could have been at St. Mary's island around the same time as the *Mary Celeste.* He asked Deveau how well he knew the island. *Could he sail into its port?* A leading question if there ever was one, but Deveau answered nonchalantly.

"We did not sight St. Mary's during any part of our voyage. I do not know the Latitude or Longitude of St. Mary's [but] then I never was at St. Mary's, never saw it," Deveau said. "I think I could enter St. Mary's by help of charts and sailing directions as well as any other part to which I have not been without reference to a chart or sailing directions. I do not know what sort of harbor St. Mary's [has]."

Flood demanded Deveau describe the ship's interior in excruciating detail, stopping him occasionally to ask questions that made him seem almost rabid with suspicion. Years later, the Briggs family would dub Flood the "excitable Irishman," and his performance in the Vice Admiralty Court supports the label. After Deveau mentioned the table in the main cabin, Flood wanted to know if there were any knives lying out. When Deveau said he found another compass— besides the one that had broken—a few days after taking over the ship, he had to explain that it was normal for a vessel to carry more than one. No, Deveau said once during cross-examination, he had not found any "beer or spirits whatever in the ship."

Based on his questions, Judge Cochrane seemed to believe the Mary Celeste's crew had been lost, or abandoned ship during a storm. In the early stages of the hearing at least, his inquiries were calm and simple; compared to Flood, he must have seemed a comfortably sage authority figure. Cochrane had been the chief justice in Gibraltar for thirty-one years, and had held Flood's job for eleven years before that. In that time, he no doubt had heard similar cases, and his comments appear to draw on vast experience. Besides his numerous questions about the ship's pumps, Cochrane asked Deveau if it appeared the ship had been on her beam ends at any time. That could not have happened, Deveau said, or her hatches would have been washed overboard.

All the Mary Celeste's hatch covers were found lying very near the opening that they normally covered, the Dei Gratia's mate testified. It may have been the first time that fact had occurred to Deveau, who from the start had suggested harsh weather scared away the crew. But in his testimony, Deveau was forced to admit the weather could not have been too bad or many of the things on the Mary Celeste's deck would have been long gone by the time they found her, including the hatches.

To some people, it seemed that Deveau was contradicting himself.

As the day wore on, it became obvious the court had not heard what it expected or wanted. Late in the day, an enervated Deveau expanded on his theory, perhaps hopeful that it would quell the line of questioning.

"My idea is that the crew got alarmed and by the sounding rod being found lying alongside the pumps that they had sounded the pumps and found perhaps a quantity of water in the pumps at the moment and thinking she would go down, abandoned her."

Deveau's testimony had taken the entire day, and the court was not yet finished with him. With the *Dei Gratia* first mate still on the witness stand, the Vice Admiralty Court adjourned until Friday.

A day off gave the *Dei Gratia's* crew more time to rest, and when they returned to court Deveau seemed more clearheaded. He began by correcting the timeline from his original testimony. It had been 3 P.M. when he boarded the *Mary Celeste,* he said—not when the captain first sighted her.

To Flood, it seemed that Deveau was trying to change his story, and it sent him into a frenzy. The attorney general peppered Deveau with the same questions he had answered just two days earlier. Flood quizzed him again on the Azores, asking what route the *Dei Gratia* had sailed around them. He seemed unsatisfied by Deveau's contention that the two ships had taken opposite courses around the island chain, as if that were somehow unusual or suspect.

He asked how the *Mary Celeste* had gotten from six miles off St. Mary's to a spot several hundred miles away. *Could it have sailed there on its own?*

"I cannot give an opinion as to whether the derelict could have run the distance where we found her in the interval with the sails she had set," Deveau testified. "She was going steadily from 1½ to 2 knots when we saw her with the wind on her beam. She might have had more sails set at first, she would not run steadily before the wind with her rudder unlashed."

After nearly a day and a half of testifying, Deveau was excused so the court could hear from the other sailors. The attorney general next called John Wright, the *Dei Gratia's* second mate who had first investigated the *Mary Celeste* with Deveau. Wright gave a brief statement to Pisani before Flood cross-examined him. In his testimony, Wright re-created his thirty minutes aboard the derelict and answered the court's obligatory questions about sounding the pumps and water damage to the *Mary Celeste.* He was not asked any leading questions and was quickly dismissed. But when Charles Lund testified next, Flood attempted to trip him up with inconsistencies about how closely the *Dei Gratia* and *Mary Celeste* had sailed on the trip to Gibraltar. Deveau had said the *Mary Celeste* lost sight of the *Dei Gratia* only a day before arriving, but Lund said it had been two or three days before amending his answer by saying, "I am sure it was two days, it was bad weather."

Repeatedly, Flood asked about the timeline, implying that the men had unfinished business to tend to before the *Mary Celeste* could be brought into port. He was practically insinuating there was evidence to destroy.

The *Dei Gratia* sailors were not accustomed to such interrogation, and either ignored or were oblivious to most of Flood's thinly veiled accusations. If they were guilty of a crime, it wasn't bad acting. Like a bunch of backwater rubes, they rambled at length about measuring the water in the *Mary Celeste*'s bilge, the broken binnacle and how damp everything was on board. But they weren't answering—they couldn't answer—the one thing that Flood wanted to know: What happened to the crew of the *Mary Celeste*?

Growing more suspicious by the hour, Cochrane and Flood soon made it clear the hearing would stretch into the weekend.

On Saturday, December 21—the day the news reached New Bedford—Augustus Anderson took the stand. Anderson was not only one of the better sailors on the *Dei Gratia,* he also made one of the best witnesses. Anderson seemed to have an almost photographic memory and quickly answered every question the court threw at him. He succinctly recounted the events of the night that Deveau, Lund and he had readied the derelict for sailing.

"I went up second from [the] boat immediately after mate [Deveau]," Anderson said. "Her masts and spars were all right, the topgallant and royal yards bent, the standing rigging was all to pieces, the ratlines were all to pieces . . . In the cabin there were three windows on starboard side and two windows on the port side and one window in the fore part facing the bow. All the windows were covered with plank—they are all covered yet—except the one in the mate's room which was also covered but he opened it, the cabin window facing the bow was covered also, I am sure, the companion door was open."

Anderson said he had examined the compass and the binnacle but could not repair them. To the judge's query, Anderson said that the anchors were made fast to the cathead, where they should have been when the ship was underway.

Perhaps Anderson's thoroughness set off Flood, or maybe the proctor thought the sailor was being insincere. Flood opened the *Mary Celeste's* logbook, which Deveau had kept up after boarding the ship, and read off every notation, stopping to ask Anderson if it was correct. To every question, Anderson answered with a simple, "Yes."

Flood's protracted silence loudly suggested a measure of disbelief.

The last of the *Dei Gratia's* crewmen to testify was John Johnson, who had been at the wheel when the derelict was spotted and later held the lifeboat at the *Mary Celeste's* side while Deveau and Wright investigated the ship. Johnson made a few simple statements for the court at Pisani's coaching, but his inability to speak fluent English frustrated Flood, who declined to cross-examine him. As such, the Russian sailor never had a chance to offer his account of the incident.

Instead of questioning Johnson, Flood complained to the judge that Pisani and his clients were hiding evidence from the throne. He demanded the log of the *Dei Gratia,* ostensibly to search for contradictions in the testimony—proof that the men were lying about their whereabouts on the day the *Mary Celeste's* crew disappeared. Cochrane seemed as irritated with Flood as the *Dei Gratia's* crew must have been, and dressed down the queen's proctor in the middle of the hearing— one of the few instances in which the court reporter recorded the exact words of the Vice Admiralty Court's officers.

"You have the opportunity of seeing the log of the *Dei Gratia* now if you please and therefore if you do not choose to avail yourself of it, it is your own fault," Cochrane said.

"I have asked for it twenty times a day and [have] not been able to procure it," Flood said.

"The log is here in court and has been always accessible to the queen's proctor," Pisani replied.

That snippy exchange ended three days of testimony, but brought the hearing no closer to a conclusion. Cochrane's instructions made that much clear. He ruled that the ship would not be released to deliver its cargo and the court would not set a salvage price until a few more questions were answered, including some by the ship's owners. Cochrane may have been irritated with Flood, and less conspiracy-minded than the attorney, but their opinions on matters of law differed little. If James Henry Winchester wanted the *Mary Celeste* back, he would have to come to Gibraltar to get it.

For a persnickety bureaucrat such as Flood, not getting the answers he demanded aggravated him greatly, and that put the crew of the *Dei Gratia* in a precarious position. Flood was a dangerous man, as Horatio J. Sprague or anyone else in Gibraltar in 1872 could have attested. A private attorney in London for most of his career, Flood had been forced to take a job with the Gibraltar court seven years earlier because, at the age of sixty-four, he could get no other work. That was his most constant source of irritation. Flood had expected by that time to be retired to a farm in Ireland, but gambling debts had cost him everything—or so the stories around town went. Some said Frederick Solly Flood was such a con man that he had swindled his own son out of an inheritance from his maternal grandfather. To most people, though, he just seemed a bit daffy or excitable, as the Briggs family would later say.

The *Mary Celeste* case certainly excited Flood, whatever the reason. He was convinced something nefarious was going on and, whether he was intrigued by the mystery or just wanted to meddle, Flood was determined to get to the bottom of it. Although the salvage hearing would not resume for weeks, Flood could not let the matter wait. The next Monday, December 23, Flood hired a surveyor at the court's expense to give the *Mary Celeste* a thorough inspection. Flood ordered John Austin to report on the condition of everything on the ship and keep his eyes open for anything that seemed out of place. Clearly, Flood did not trust the men of the *Dei Gratia* to tell him everything.

Flood also hired a professional diver named Ricardo Portunato to go beneath the *Mary Celeste* and inspect her hull. That suggests the attorney general had not completely ruled out an accident, as damage to the ship's underside would constitute proof of a wreck or some other mishap, and most likely rule out foul play or conspiracy. Perhaps Flood was only being cautious, or maybe he really did just want answers. If there was no serious damage to the hull, then something else forced those people off the boat. And he intended to find out what— or who—it was.

Whether Flood was fueling speculation himself or news of the salvage hearing had traveled the shipping lanes, questions about the *Mary Celeste* were suddenly coming from both sides of the Atlantic. Using local news accounts of the salvage hearing, the London papers reported the strange tale at length, and some papers in New York City declared outright that a crime of some sort had been committed.

Just before Christmas of 1872, the New York *Shipping and Commercial List* reported that "The strange feature about the *Mary Celeste* is the fact that she was in seaworthy condition. There was no evidence that she had been run into, or that she had encountered unusually heavy weather. The inference is that there has been foul play somewhere, and that alcohol is at the bottom of it."

As was so often the case in nineteenth-century newspapers, the source of that intelligence was not attributed, but it echoed theories Flood was developing. Around that same time, Sprague wrote a cautious note to the U.S. State Department to warn his bosses that the "queen's proctor suspects foul play." While it is unlikely that Flood was corresponding with reporters, he was speaking with sailors who passed through Gibraltar, and they were spreading his theory for him. By the end of the year, the conventional wisdom in the merchant marine was that whatever happened on board the *Mary Celeste*, it was more than a simple accident.

The insinuation infuriated the ship's owners, and they did not hesitate to say so. Either at the insistence of J. H. Winchester & Co. or Meissner, Ackersman, and Co. (which owned the freight aboard the ship), the *Shipping and Commercial List* recanted its allegations a few days later, allowing that it was only entertaining "apprehensions of foul play":

> It seems that the closing sentence of the paragraph was misconstrued into a reflection upon the honesty or good faith of the shippers, although it really bore no such interpretation. The shippers of the cargo of the Mary Celeste are known to us as being among the most honorable of firms, and not the slightest suspicion is entertained of fraud on their part, so far as we are aware. The impression we intended to convey was that the crew had possibly been making free with the Alcohol, and that foul play had resulted. This, of course, is mere conjecture, and until the affair has been fully investigated, the real cause of abandonment cannot be known—perhaps it never will be.

The clarification did little good; the seeds of doubt had been planted. Just as the tales of sea monsters and the *Flying Dutchman* grew taller with each succeeding version, the mystery of the *Mary Celeste* became more foreboding with each retelling. If the ship's owners wanted to snuff out the talk, which was certainly bad for business, they were going to have to act quickly.

On the last day of 1872, Horatio J. Sprague sent a letter to Flood announcing the pending arrival in Gibraltar of James H. Winchester, majority shareholder of the *Mary Celeste*. Although Sprague needed the official record, he probably preferred sending a note to briefing the attorney general in person. He also hoped, optimistically, that the news would allay some of the attorney general's suspicions.

"For your information and that of the court, I beg to state that a telegram has just been received to the effect that the owner of the *Mary Celeste* is already on his way to this port from New York for the purposes of claiming his vessel and settling salvage and court expenses appertaining to the *Mary Celeste*.

"So far, nothing is known of the missing crew."

While giving every appearance of cooperation, Sprague was not above making his own attempts to thwart the court. Things were getting out of hand quickly, so Sprague asked one of the most respected sailors he knew—the U.S. Navy Captain R. W. Shufeldt—to also examine the *Mary Celeste*. Clearly Sprague did not trust Flood's cronies to offer unbiased testimony any more than the attorney general trusted the *Dei Gratia*'s crew. While Shufeldt's findings likely would hold no sway with the court, there was a chance they could affect public opinion. Sprague just hoped Shufeldt could make it to Gibraltar before the hearing resumed in January.

For David Reed Morehouse, the days stretched miserably into weeks. With the hearing stalled, he knew the accusations eventually could reflect badly on him and his crew. So far, most theories hinted at some sort of wrongdoing by Briggs's own crew, but Morehouse knew the tide might eventually turn. The attorney general and even the judge appeared to be suspicious, and at some point they might start pointing fingers in another direction. That could explain one of the lingering mysteries of the case.

While he was in Gibraltar, Morehouse never mentioned that he and Benjamin Briggs were acquaintances, much less friends—as his widow would claim. Even if they weren't particularly close, it would not have been terribly coincidental for two twenty-year veteran New England sailors to at least know each other in passing. There is also little doubt Flood would have exploited even the most tenuous link between the men.

That is why Morehouse said nothing—like any good sailor, he could tell which way the wind was blowing. If it got out that Morehouse and Briggs were friends, speculation of a conspiracy might never end. It could severely damage his career. These maniacal bureaucrats might even throw him in jail. Perhaps that is why Morehouse was vague about his actions on December 4, and why he initially refused to testify. He wanted to keep his mouth shut.

Morehouse had a family, a job, commitments and—salvage hearing or not—he could not be steered off course. On the same day Flood led his inspection of the *Mary Celeste,* Morehouse sent the *Dei Gratia*—with Oliver Deveau in command—to Genoa, Italy, to deliver the 1,735 barrels of petroleum that had been held up for nearly three weeks. He had to know the court might not like his men leaving, but Morehouse had customers and shareholders to consider.

For his part, Deveau was more than happy to go. After his grilling by Flood, Deveau had realized the quick riches he'd imagined weren't going to just be handed over to him and he was growing to regret his scheme. Morehouse may have even outlined for him the trouble they might find themselves in if the judge decided they had a hand in the disappearance of the derelict's crew.

With those unhappy scenarios playing out in his mind, Deveau set sail with the rest of the crew aboard the *Dei Gratia* on Monday, December 23, right under the nose of Flood's inspection team. Deveau planned to relax and take his time in Genoa. He didn't care if he ever saw the Rock of Gibraltar again.

Oliver Briggs celebrated the New Year unaware that his older brother was missing. He had sailed from New York before word reached the States that the *Mary Celeste* had been found derelict. The *Julia A. Hallock* crossed the Atlantic in milder weather than the *Mary Celeste* had to contend with, and made the north coast of Spain in late December. Oliver Briggs was in good spirits—his final voyage as a ship captain was going well. He dreamed about the lot he had cleared for his new home near Rose Cottage, and perhaps even thought with some pride of the stone wall he'd already built.

The *Julia A. Hallock* delivered its cargo in Gijón in perfect condition—Oliver was no slouch as a captain, either. Not having any cargo to carry to the next port of call, Barcelona, the ship took on fifty tons of coal for ballast. From there, just after the New Year, Oliver Briggs set sail on what he fully expected to be his last trip in command of a ship. It would not be an easy route; he would very nearly have to circumnavigate Spain, sailing out of the Bay and into the Atlantic, through the Strait of Gibraltar and into the Mediterranean to reach Barcelona. There, he planned to take on more cargo and then rendezvous with Benjamin in Messina. But he never made it that far.

The bad weather that Oliver Briggs had avoided on the Atlantic caught up with him in the Bay of Biscay. On January 8, 1873, a fierce storm hit, knocking the *Julia A. Hallock* around like a child's toy in a bathtub. The ship took on water and, as the crew tried to pump out the bilge, coal dust clogged up the works. Before they realized it, the ship was past the point of no return and in its death roll. The *Julia A. Hallock* sank in minutes. Like the alcohol his brother had been hauling, coal also was considered one of the more dangerous cargos to carry.

Oliver Briggs had not survived the seafaring life so long to give up without a fight. When he hit the frigid water, Oliver looked for whatever flotsam or jetsam he could reach to serve as a life preserver. He soon found one of the *Julia A. Hallock*'s deckhouses, which had broken loose and was floating free in the Bay. There he met the ship's only other survivor, his second mate, a man named Perry. Together, they rode out the storm on the last pieces of a ship that Oliver had never liked much anyway.

Four days later, another merchant ship spotted the floating deckhouse. Lying atop it, the ship's crew found Perry, shivering and near death from exposure and dehydration. When he was pulled aboard the ship, he told the men of the disaster and informed them of their unfortunate timing. The *Julia A. Hallock*'s captain, Oliver Briggs, had given up and slipped beneath the waves just two hours earlier.

Months later, after Perry had recovered and returned to his home in Massachusetts, he sent word through a family friend that he would like to pay a visit to Mother Briggs at Rose Cottage. Perry wanted to tell the Briggs family matriarch of her son's last hours—the things he did, the valiant effort he put forth to save the crew. All the things a grieving mother doesn't want to hear.

In her long life, Sophia Briggs had heard enough sad stories and was still clinging to the diminishing prospects that her Benjamin and his family were still alive. Her heart was already broken beyond repair, and she didn't think she could bear to hear of any more tragedy. She didn't consider the request for long.

"Tell him not to come," she said.

SIX

"A Moment of Panic"

By early January, Frederick Solly Flood had the evidence he needed to confirm his worst suspicions of violence and conspiracy. The Admiralty Court surveyor had discovered a sword hidden onboard the *Mary Celeste*—and its blade appeared to be smeared with blood.

In the month since the ship had been brought into Gibraltar, the queen's proctor had grown more steadfast in his belief that something nefarious happened on the *Mary Celeste*. The report of John Austin—and the sword—gave Flood the ammunition he needed on two fronts: it offered real proof suggesting the crew met a violent end, and quelled any notion that he merely suffered from an overactive imagination. The surveyor's findings only strengthened Flood's resolve to press for a criminal investigation.

The Austin report provides the best contemporary description of the *Mary Celeste*'s condition in early 1873. The surveyor recorded details that either escaped or were overlooked by the *Dei Gratia* sailors. In fact, the report was almost too much. The detailed affidavit, which rambles on for nearly thirty pages, is the model of officious bureaucratic thoroughness, outlining every move Austin made in his five

hours examining the ship. It is filled with exact measurements and an-
alytical commentary that suggests an unquestionable, even arrogant,
expertise.

It was exactly what the attorney general had asked for.

Aside from the sword, Austin wrote at length about strange markings on the hull, which to him was a sign of the vilest sort of cover-
up. The "cuts" were so obvious and noticeable, the report implied, that
it was amazing no one had mentioned them before. The surveyor left
no doubt that he believed the damage was in some way related to the
crew's disappearance.

"On approaching the Vessel," Austin wrote, "I found on the bow
between two and three feet above the water line on the port side a
long narrow strip of the edge of one of her outer planks under the cathead cut away to the depth of about three-eighths of an inch or about
one inch and a quarter wide for a length of about 6 or 7 feet. This injury had been sustained very recently and could not have been effected
by the weather and was apparently done by a sharp cutting instrument
continuously applied thro' the whole length of the injury."

The starboard side of the hull was marked in the same manner, and
Austin speculated both grooves had been made in the same fashion at
the same time. This uniformity ruled out any possibility the damage
was accidental. But as meticulous as Austin's report was, it offered no
theory about what had cut the *Mary Celeste*'s hull.

Perhaps not coincidentally, Austin refuted the theory of the *Dei
Gratia*'s crew that foul weather chased away the crew, noting that the
rigging did not appear to have been damaged in the way the sailors
had described. In fact, Austin questioned whether the ship had seen
any harsh weather at all. He found almost no trace of water damage,
and did not believe the hold had been wet at all. The report went out
of its way to dismiss the simplest explanation for the crew's disappearance.

It seemed that Flood himself had a hand in editing, if not writing,
Austin's entire report. It all too neatly debunked Deveau's testimony
while giving weight to the attorney general's own ideas. But there is
no evidence Flood pressured or directed Austin on what to include or

ignore in the report. Perhaps the best evidence that Flood didn't meddle too much is that the mention of blood doesn't come until near the end—something the queen's proctor most likely would have highlighted. Austin makes much more out of the cuts to the hull. Uncharacteristic of the rest of his report, Austin is almost matter-of-fact concerning the ornate cutlass found in Briggs's cabin.

"I also observed in this cabin a Sword in its scabbard which the Marshal informed me he had noticed when he came on board for the purpose of arresting the vessel. It had not [been] affected by water but on drawing out the blade it appeared to me as if it had been smeared with blood and afterwards wiped."

It was a long, slender blade with a gold scabbard and inlaid wood on the handle and the cross of Navarre on the hilt. It seemed more ceremonial than functional, an observation that neither Austin nor Flood made. All that mattered was that it was there, and it could have been used for foul play. The sword stoked the fires of conspiracy because, for Flood, it pointed in only one direction: murder.

Flood initially had suspected he was dealing with a case of insurance fraud. After the discovery of the sword, he decided mutiny was more likely, but believed there could be even more to it. That none of the *Dei Gratia* sailors had mentioned the sword—one that appeared to be smeared with blood!—in their expansive testimony only made Flood that much more skeptical of their story, and of them.

Whether it was intended to do so, the rest of the evidence in the surveyor's report did little to allay Flood's misgivings. Not only did Austin rule out foul weather as a reason for abandoning the ship, the diver's report said the underside of the *Mary Celeste* was in nearly new condition. It had not run aground, hit a reef, or become stuck on rocks so far as he could tell. In fact, Ricardo Portunato said, "the hull stern, keel sternpost and rudder of the said vessel were thoroughly in good order and condition."

Together, the two reports did not describe a ship that veteran seafaring men would abandon. The *Mary Celeste* was, in fact, in nearly pristine condition.

Either hungry for more incriminating evidence or showing a rare measure of caution, Flood decided he needed more proof. He was anxious to go over the *Mary Celeste* once again for what he termed "a still more minute examination for marks of violence." So, on January 7 Flood led a contingent of a half dozen captains aboard the ship for more sleuthing.

Flood was on a full-fledged witch-hunt.

The queen's proctor soon had his additional evidence.

Where Austin had been reluctant to characterize the minor damage to the ship as anything out of the ordinary, Flood had no such reservations. Not only did the attorney general and his posse find more strange cuts on the ship, but also what he believed was blood splattered across the *Mary Celeste's* deck.

Flood later reported to the London Board of Trade that the sailors he took aboard the *Mary Celeste* agreed the marks on the derelict's hull "had been effected intentionally by a sharp instrument." Even more disturbing, Flood claimed the starboard rail had blood on it and the "mark of a blow apparently of a sharp axe." There were a few other specks of red on the deck that Flood assumed was blood. In the hold, he vaguely noted, it appeared one of the barrels of alcohol had been "tampered with," but offered no further details.

Flood was taking the investigation well beyond the realm of a salvage hearing. On what apparently was his sole authority, he ordered tests on the new evidence. The queen's proctor hired a doctor to take samples of the ruddy substance on the sword, the railing, and the deck. If tests proved there was in fact blood on the ship, Flood felt it would be the final piece of evidence he needed to build a criminal case for the murder of the *Mary Celeste's* officers. Based on these new findings, Flood believed the crew of the *Mary Celeste* had killed the captain and then deserted the ship. He suspected the crew cut the hull to leave the false impression the ship had run aground, a plausible reason for them to abandon her.

On January 22, the attorney general wrote to the Marine Department's Board of Trade in London seeking an official inquiry.

Without accusing the crew of the *Dei Gratia* of any wrongdoing, Flood nevertheless dismissed their theory out of hand. He related only the facts he found important—the last charted position of the *Mary Celeste* by her own crew, where she was found sailing, the lack of weather damage. There were considerable valuables left on board, Flood added, but did not say what that might indicate. The queen's proctor outlined for the board the first of several theories he would offer over the next decade.

> *My object is to move the Bd. of Trade to take such action as they may think fit to discover if possible the fate of the Master, his wife and Child, and the crew of the derelict. My own theory or guess is that the Crew got at the alcohol and in the fury of drunkenness murdered the Master whose name was Briggs and wife and Child and the Chief Mate—that they then damaged the bows of the Vessel with the view of giving it the appearance of having struck on rocks or suffered from a collision so as to induce the Master of any Vessel [which] might pick them up if they saw her at some distance to think her not worth attempting to save and that they did sometime between the 25th Novbr. and the 5th Decbr. escape on board some vessel bound for some north or South American port or the West Indies.*

It was a fantastic tale, an intimate look into the dark imagination of Frederick Solly Flood. As unlikely as the story was, though, there was no conflicting evidence or witnesses to refute it, so people began to listen. The attorney general made a good first impression, anyway, and professed noble intentions for his inquiry—he claimed to be Captain Briggs's only advocate. Before sending his letter, Flood amended it the next day, arguing that the *Mary Celeste* had not been abandoned until several days after November 25 because it could not have sailed so far on its own. The attorney general was becoming famous for these addenda to his letters—he always had something else to say.

Flood was determined to have the final word.

James H. Winchester felt like he had walked into a trap. The owner of the *Mary Celeste* arrived in Gibraltar on January 15 completely out of sorts. He had sailed from New York on Christmas day on the steamer *Abyssinia,* bound for Liverpool, and from there booking passage to Gibraltar. He'd left his business and a sick wife on the other side of the Atlantic, undertaking a round trip that would cost him a minimum of two months away from both, to conduct business he should have been able to settle by telegraph or through the State Department.

Although annoyed he had to make the trip, Winchester nevertheless had reacted quickly to the Admiralty Court's edict. He realized the voyage was the only way to salvage his ship, and perhaps his company's reputation. That was of the greatest importance to him. Winchester & Co. was one of the most reputable ship merchants in New York, but the postwar economy was in a slump and there were plenty of other hungry freighters waiting to take his business. He didn't want anything to steer business away from his company.

Winchester was also worried about upsetting an important client such as Meissner & Ackersman. The alcohol in the court's custody was already a month overdue and this was taking up more valuable time. In fact, Winchester had been so caught up in these business matters that he'd barely had time to consider that Benjamin Briggs was missing. But he could not avoid that realization any longer when the Admiralty Court reconvened on January 29 and he was asked to identify Briggs's signature on the bills of lading.

In his testimony before the Vice Admiralty Court, which was lost for nearly a century, Winchester is professional but curt in his cross-examination by Frederick Solly Flood. Years later, Winchester's relatives claimed the two men clashed so terribly that the whole family had memorized the exchange. Flood was relentless that day. He asked Winchester his name, his citizenship and finally a derogatory question about his lineage. "Of what descent are you?"

At that point, his family said, Winchester spat out a vitriolic answer: "British, sir, but if I knew where the British blood was I would open my veins and let it out."

The salvage hearing transcript does not include the statement, but it is clear that Flood subjected Winchester to a harsh round of accusatory questions, quizzing the shipping merchant about minutiae he could scarcely have known. The queen's proctor asked if there had been a sextant and quadrant onboard the Mary Celeste when it left port, if he was familiar with the Azores, and—most brazenly—if the ship had been smuggling anything that did not show up on the manifest.

At one point, Flood showed Winchester a photograph of Oliver Briggs, asking him to identify the man as Benjamin Briggs. Although the brothers bore a striking resemblance, Oliver was more slender and had a thinner face. Anyone who knew the two could easily tell them apart. Winchester knew enough to tell Flood he had the wrong man. Winchester also said he barely knew Sarah Briggs, but recalled visiting the couple on another ship ten years earlier—perhaps the Forest King—and remembered, "The lady played on a melodeon or musical instrument . . . I saw a melodeon put on board the Mary Celeste, but I cannot say whether it was the same that she played on previously."

Quoting from the Austin report, Flood grilled Winchester about the sword and the cuts in the Mary Celeste's bow. There, the attorney general got his only satisfactory answer from the ship merchant. Winchester worriedly conceded that the marks on the topgallant rail and along the hull were new.

They "are not in the same condition that they were in New York," Winchester said, claiming to have never seen the sword before. "I do not know whether either of them [Briggs or the first mate] carried a revolver or gun, which would be a much more likely weapon for them to have."

Although Winchester found this line of questioning unusual, it was not until his second day on the witness stand—January 31—that he became convinced something devious was afoot. While he agreed that it appeared something strange had occurred on the ship, Winchester said he couldn't imagine it was anything sinister. But he conceded there was nowhere near enough damage to the Mary Celeste to make Briggs abandon her in favor of a lifeboat. After that, his denials of any conspiracy fell on deaf ears.

I am still in total ignorance of what has become of the Master B.S. Briggs his wife and the crew of the Mary Celeste. *I have received no intelligence of them whatever. Since my last examination in this court on Wednesday last I have been on board the Brig* Mary Celeste *now lying in this bay and have examined her thoroughly and am perfectly certain she is the* Mary Celeste *of New York. From what I have seen of the state and condition of the vessel I cannot believe that she was abandoned by her Master, officers and crew in consequence of stress of weather only. I had plenty of time to examine her thoroughly and feel very certain that she was not abandoned through perils of sea . . . I knew Benjamin S. Briggs and also the mate Richardson and [they] both bore high characters as able seamen and I add here to what I have previously stated respecting their characters and that I am very certain both men would remain by their ship to the last and that neither would have deserted the ship unless forced to do so for fear of their lives.*

Flood was unmoved by Winchester's testimony and informed the merchant that he had not brought along the proper papers to take custody of the *Mary Celeste*. To clear matters up, Winchester would have to put up bail for all latent claims—including any that Benjamin Briggs might later make—and pay the court for "salvage expenses."

Flood's threatening tone and demand for large sums of cash must have reminded Winchester of the U.S. customs official who had solicited a bribe from him a year earlier. This time Winchester was in no position to gamble with this ship. He had too much invested in the *Mary Celeste*'s refit, not to mention the cargo, to tell the court to keep her. George F. Cornwell, who was Winchester's attorney in Gibraltar, said his client was willing to provide reasonable bail but argued that Flood's demands were out of line. Cornwell asked Cochrane to intervene, but the judge was not in a charitable mood that day. Cochrane had just learned Oliver Deveau left Gibraltar on the *Dei Gratia* without asking—or informing—the court. How the ship had slipped out of such a small town without someone noticing is unknown. It didn't matter—Cochrane was furious, and warned that it would have a bearing on the case.

There are certain matters which have been brought to my notice respecting this vessel my opinion about which I have already very decidedly expressed and which make it desirable and even very necessary that further investigation should take place before the release of the vessel can be sanctioned or before she can quit this port. The conduct of the salvers in going away as they have done has in my [opinion] been most reprehensible and may probably influence the decision as to their claim for remuneration for their services.

Cochrane was beginning to have his own misgivings about the *Dei Gratia's* crew. He found it odd that Morehouse had stayed in Gibraltar and sent his first mate away with his ship. Deveau should have remained in Gibraltar, Cochrane said, not Morehouse—who seemed to have few, if any, of the answers the court wanted.

The judge's decree had a chilling effect on Horatio J. Sprague, David Reed Morehouse and especially James Winchester, who did not have the money the court demanded and wasn't sure it would do any good anyway. The Americans had hoped that Flood's ranting did not reflect the opinion of the court, that the charges would be dismissed out of hand and a salvage verdict rendered soon. But Cochrane was perturbed, and his diatribe signaled that he in some ways at least sympathized with the attorney general's viewpoint.

The press had picked up on the suspicions of the Vice Admiralty Court and reported them as fact. In that morning's *Gibraltar Chronicle,* a story on the hearing recounted most of Flood's allegations—that the ship had no weather damage and one barrel of the alcohol had been "started"—and the surveyor's conclusion that "there exists no apparent reason why the vessel should have been abandoned."

"In addition to the above facts, a sword was discovered which, on its being drawn out of its scabbard, exhibited signs of having been smeared with blood and afterwards wiped," the *Chronicle* reported.

No doubt Flood provided the information to the paper, as "F. Solly-Flood, Esq." is mentioned as having ordered the special survey. The *Chronicle's* story soon spread to larger newspapers on both sides of the Atlantic, prompting stories that implicated the crew of both the

Mary Celeste and the *Dei Gratia* in some sort of conspiracy. In the press, if not the courtroom, the salvage hearing was quickly becoming a criminal trial. Like Flood, the newspapers couldn't decide what crime had been committed, but agreed one almost certainly had.

Winchester was dejected about these new developments. He had hoped to see the cargo on its way before he left port, and in anticipation had even hired a new captain for the *Mary Celeste,* George W. Blatchford. Winchester told Blatchford to raise a crew in Gibraltar and sail the ship to Genoa. But it appeared Blatchford was in for a long wait.

Sitting idly by was not in Winchester's nature. As anxious as he was to settle this salvage mess, Winchester was more desperate to return to New York. Shortly after being dismissed by the court he traveled to Cadiz, just over the Spanish border. There, Winchester met a familiar ship captain—Henry O. Appleby—who lent him the money he needed to pay the ship's bail. Winchester sent the money to Gibraltar, care of Horatio J. Sprague, along with a note that he was in Lisbon about to take the Anchor Line steamer *Caledonia* for New York. Winchester had become convinced that he was on the wrong side of the Atlantic. Whether or not he made the remark about his British blood in court, there is little doubt he harbored the sentiment.

When he arrived in New York nearly a month later, Winchester sent Sprague a long note apologizing for his hasty departure. He offered obvious reasons—that he was anxious to get home to his wife and his business, that he could do no good while there—but also hinted that there was more to it. Winchester wrote that he was worried the Admiralty Court officers thought he had something to do with Briggs's disappearance.

"A gentleman came to me while at Gibraltar and told me that after the judge and the attorney general had used up every other pretense to cause delay and expense they were going to arrest me for hiring the crew to make way with the officers. The idea was ridiculous but from what you and everybody else in Gibraltar have told me about [Flood] I did not know but they might do it, as they seem to do just as they like."

His sojourn to Spain had been intended as only a brief visit, Winchester told Sprague, and he'd planned to come back for the remainder of the salvage hearing. But the American consul at Cadiz told him to run.

In early February Sprague received the report he'd been awaiting from Captain R. W. Shufeldt. More than a month earlier, he had asked the Navy commander to come to Gibraltar and inspect the *Mary Celeste*. It was not a random request. Shufeldt, a career Navy man and veteran of the American Civil War, was often called on for such purposes. In 1867, he had investigated the controversial wreck of the American schooner *General Slocum* and the disappearance of its crew in Korea's Ping Yang River. Intelligence sources said the crew had been murdered during what may have been a secret U.S./British mission to establish trade with the nation. Shufeldt, who was serving in the Navy's Asiatic Squadron at the time, sailed in, examined the wreck, and questioned Korean officials. His report to Washington concluded that there had been some foul play aboard the *General Slocum*.

To Sprague, however, Shufeldt could present no such finding. After arriving in Gibraltar on February 5, Shufeldt spent the next day examining the ship, and sailed the following day. Before leaving, he delivered to Sprague a letter that said simply that the *Mary Celeste* had been deserted prematurely.

"I am of the opinion that she was abandoned by the master and crew in a moment of panic and for no sufficient reason," Shufeldt wrote.

Shufeldt said the *Mary Celeste* showed minor signs of weather damage but nothing harsh enough to make experienced seamen leave her. There was not even a hint of serious damage to the vessel. Also, Shufeldt said there were no signs of mutiny on the ship, no trace of violence anywhere. The "cuts" in the hull that Flood and his surveyor had elevated to evidence of a sinister plot were "nothing more than splinters made in the bending of the planks which were afterward forced off by the action of the sea—neither hurting the ship nor by any possible chance, the result of an intention to do so."

Shufeldt said that such splintering was common in new hull planking (it's unclear if he knew of the *Mary Celeste*'s recent refit). He did not address the uniformity of the marks, which raises questions about how uniform the marks actually were. He was basically, and very diplomatically, saying that Austin and Flood were idiots.

Overall the ship was staunch and seaworthy, Shufeldt wrote, and he hoped they soon would hear from a distant port that another vessel had rescued the *Mary Celeste*'s survivors. But Shufeldt was only being sympathetic. It had been nearly two months since the crew of the *Dei Gratia* discovered the ship. Prospects for a happy ending, he realized, were growing dim.

"But if we should never hear from them again I shall nevertheless think they were lost in the boat in which the master and men abandoned the *Mary Celeste*—I shall remember with interest this sad and silent mystery of the sea."

Sprague was not optimistic that a report from a United States Navy officer would hold much sway with the British Vice Admiralty Court, but he shared the findings with Cochrane and Flood anyway. As relieved as he was by the report, Sprague found it disheartening. If he had any lingering hope that Benjamin Briggs, his family and crew might be found alive, Shufeldt's letter did nothing to encourage him. Instead, the report prepared everyone for the increasing likelihood that Benjamin Briggs and the crew of the *Mary Celeste* were dead.

By the time Sprague received Shufeldt's opinion, Flood had held the results of the bloodstain analysis for more than a week. The report would not be shared or even entered into the court record. Years later it was found unopened, untouched since the day it was delivered. That's because Cochrane would not admit it in court and Flood had no reason to open it—he already knew what it said. And he didn't like it.

In his report, Dr. J. Patron said that he had examined "some red brown spots about a milimetre thick and half an inch in diameter" on the foredeck. In all, he found four such spots and, using a chisel, separated them from the deck of the *Mary Celeste*. He also took a sample from a cut in the ship's topgallant rail, but reported that he could not find even minute traces of anything resembling blood in the ship's cabins.

Patron initially thought the reddish brown stains on the sword were indeed traces of blood. The granules of substance on the blade exhibited traits consistent with blood on first look, but further tests contradicted that impression. It appeared the blade was speckled with traces of "a yellow and imperfectly crystallized substance," citrate of iron. Even more discouraging to Flood, Patron said none of the other samples he'd collected contained the first drop of blood, either.

Flood was also disappointed by the latest report of Thomas J. Vecchio, marshal of the court. Vecchio had completed a new search of the *Mary Celeste*'s hold, perhaps to further investigate the "tampering" with the alcohol that Flood had alleged. Vecchio and his men removed fifty casks and found them to be in "excellent order." The marshal said the barrels had not been handled in any way, and that they were still full. The report greatly relieved Winchester and his clients, if no one else.

Although the court sent a wire to Italy ordering Deveau to return to Gibraltar, Flood felt his case was slipping away. As much evidence as he had collected to suggest something sinister, Flood could not make all the pieces of the puzzle fit into a single, solid theory. He could not proceed with his plans without a stronger case, no matter how desperately he wanted to. There were too many contradictory facts. That may be why he was unable to stick to one conclusion in later years, why he seemed to be grasping at straws. Perhaps that is why in late February Flood finally agreed to Sprague's request to release the *Mary Celeste* to her rightful owners.

In a cable to the U.S. State Department on February 25, Horatio Sprague wrote that the "formalities required" for restitution had been dropped and the *Mary Celeste* had on that day been turned over to the owners. The Vice Admiralty Court also agreed to surrender the crew's personal belongings, save for a few items that were the private property of Benjamin Spooner Briggs. Evidently, Flood still had use for some of those things—a signal that not everything had been settled completely. His criminal case might have been evaporating, but the queen's proctor still had a mind to make someone pay for this crime. Just because the court was through with some of the evidence did not mean that Flood and Cochrane were finished with the crew of the *Dei Gratia*.

They meant to punish someone.

By the time the court reconvened to settle the claim of the *Dei Gratia* salvers, it was March of 1873. The *Mary Celeste* and its cargo had been arrested in Gibraltar for nearly three months, and although the ship had been cleared to leave port, Captain Blatchford was still trying to raise a crew. The ship had become a familiar sight to sailors stopping in port, but few of them wanted to sign on—they already considered the *Mary Celeste* unlucky. Idle talk about her crew's untimely demise was spreading quickly. Bad weather was never considered a possibility. Most of the stories centered on mutiny and murder and, soon, piracy. If Flood didn't have a case, the press had not yet caught on.

In mid-February the *Spectator* wrote that, "The *Gibraltar Chronicle* relates a story which might have given a hint to Edgar Poe or Coleridge." The *Spectator* claimed there was no chance the *Mary Celeste* had sailed through "any seriously heavy weather" because nothing on board the ship had been upset—even a spool of thread had been found still sitting upright on a table (an erroneous fact that would find its way into countless versions of the story).

The newspapers reported whatever anyone said about the *Mary Celeste*, no matter how contradictory the stories might be. At the New York offices of Atlantic Mutual, which held a $3,400 policy on the alcohol in the *Mary Celeste*'s cargo hold, employees pasted newspaper clippings of their customers' vessels in ornate ledgers. The ledgers, which survive to this day, show two stories wildly at odds that appeared in the final week of February 1873. A February 25, 1873, *New York Herald* story began:

No tidings have yet been received from the crew of the brig Mary Celeste. *"They may, however, have gone on board a vessel bound on a dis-*

tant voyage, in which case sufficient time has not yet elapsed to hear of their arrival. Since the brig was taken into Gibraltar she has undergone a thorough examination, and it is stated that suspicions of foul play are entertained, in consequence of finding some spots of blood on the blade of a sword in the cabin and on the rails with a sharp cut in the wood, indicating the use of force or violence. Capt. Briggs, who belongs to Marion, Mass. had his wife and child on board, and as many things were found in confusion on the vessel (including ladies' apparel) this circumstance has added to the suspicion of some outrage on the part of the crew. They were mostly foreigners, and in case of mutiny by breaking into the cargo the men might have become inflamed by liquor to the commission of murder.

In one rambling paragraph, the article referred to evidence collected by Shufeldt and Flood, an indication that a mishmash of information was circulating or—perhaps more telling—purposely being distributed. It was almost as if Flood and Sprague were playing a sort of nineteenth-century public relations damage control.

As bad as most of these stories were, they could not compete with the sheer sensationalism of the article that ran in another New York paper just three days later, on February 28. In a long, meandering style, the story reported that, "the New England vessel, the brig *Mary Celeste,* of Marion, Mass. was seized by pirates."

The article warned that piracy was still alive in the Atlantic and sensationally speculated that "the Yankee captain and his delicate wife" may have been forced to walk the plank. This revelation came after two long paragraphs of exposition on the demise of piracy in the Atlantic, how it had not been a threat in the modern century (although it was still prevalent off Malaysia and in the Chinese seas, the journalist noted). There was no attribution for the "announcement" and the article ultimately rambled on with other theories, the bottom line seeming to be only that something bad certainly had happened.

"That she was deserted is alone sufficient evidence that her commander had been foully dealt with, for, had he voluntarily abandoned her in order to defraud the underwriters, he would certainly have taken the precaution to sink or destroy her. Other evidence, however, was not wanting that a great crime had been committed."

The article erred in reporting that the ship's cabins were completely ransacked and that the valuables were stolen by "brutal cutthroats." The alcohol was mentioned suspiciously, and the crew called "inevitable" mutineers. A fierce struggle for control of the ship is even attributed to the men—details that no one knew, but some people were obviously willing to make up. It would have been labeled yellow journalism had the term existed in the 1870s.

In three months the *Mary Celeste* had gone from one-line notices in shipping news columns to a front-page sensation, a mystery with just enough hint of criminal activity—and just enough provocative facts—to ignite a ravenous curiosity. Given the amount of ink the newspapers devoted to the *Mary Celeste,* the story obviously was selling.

On March 3—the same day the *Boston Advertiser* ran a small notice about the "damning spots" on the cutlass—the Vice Admiralty Court met to hear the final testimony in the *Dei Gratia's* sailors salvage hearing. Shortly after convening, Thomas J. Vecchio was waving that very "blood-stained cutlass" around in the Gibraltar courtroom in a final attempt to stir controversy.

In court, following his unexcused absence, was Oliver Deveau. Deveau had caught passage back to Gibraltar aboard another ship, leaving the *Dei Gratia* in Genoa, along with the rest of the crew. He told the court Charles Lund was in a Genoa hospital being treated for injuries sustained while sailing on the *Mary Celeste.* No one suggested it publicly, but it is likely that Morehouse ordered Deveau to leave the *Dei Gratia* in Italy, safely out of the Vice Admiralty Court's jurisdiction. The court officers had shown they were capable of anything, and Morehouse did not want his ship seized under whatever pretense Flood might invent.

All that remained in the hearing was for Henry Pisani, the attorney for the crew, to offer proof in support of their salvage claim. But Flood, who still hoped to find a crack in the case, tried to call Deveau

David Reed Morehouse, captain of the *Dei Gratia,* may have been reluctant to testify in the *Mary Celeste* salvage hearing because he did not want to reveal his friendship with Benjamin Briggs. *Photograph Courtesy Peabody Essex Museum*

to the stand first to grill him on the new "findings." He was ruled out of order.

In his argument, Pisani outlined the danger the men of the *Dei Gratia* had faced to salvage the ship, how splitting the crew had endangered both vessels. He said that with its hatches left open, the *Mary Celeste* was in "imminent danger of being lost or waterlogged." His clients had risked their lives to save the ship and were entitled to a just reward. Pisani had to know he was treading water, that after Cochrane's last outburst the court might not give them any salvage award at all. In what may have been a desperate bid to bolster their case, Pisani surprised the court by calling Captain David Reed Morehouse to the stand.

Morehouse's testimony, which remained undiscovered for nearly a century, sheds new light on the *Mary Celeste* incident and offers greater detail about certain aspects of the case than Deveau's did. Morehouse was by far the best spoken of the *Dei Gratia's* crew. He came across as a sensible, educated man as he calmly laid out his story: How he'd spotted the ship, called Deveau on deck to confer with him, and then sent the mate and two others to investigate a ship "which I thought was in distress and required assistance."

Morehouse contradicted his crew's account of the direction in which the *Mary Celeste* was sailing when they found it (this may have had more to do with his better command of maritime terminology than erroneous information from his crew) and revealed that one of the first things that had attracted him to the *Mary Celeste* that day was what he thought was a distress flag.

Morehouse told the court he had opposed the salvage because of the danger to his own ship, but allowed his crew to vote. When they unanimously chose to bring in the *Mary Celeste,* Morehouse said he agreed and gave Deveau "the two best men." Sailing shorthanded had cost him at least four days, Morehouse said, because with fewer hands to operate the ship he had to make conservative decisions. He was politic enough not to mention the time he had wasted sitting in Gibraltar.

"Whenever the weather looked doubtful I was forced to prepare for taking in sail longer than I should have done had I had my full complement of men and took longer to make sail and therefore a loss of time," Morehouse said. "The work with a shorthanded crew is also much harder than with a full crew."

Flood used his cross-examination to rehash questions about the *Dei Gratia's* location on the day the *Mary Celeste* was allegedly abandoned, and conditions on the day when they had supposedly found her. He apparently hoped that Morehouse would contradict Deveau, but the captain did not provide him any ammunition. His story matched his crew's.

Morehouse attempted to appease Flood by conceding some of the attorney general's more benign observations, agreeing with the proctor's idea of which tack the *Mary Celeste* had been on when it was spotted. He also appeared to give serious consideration to Flood's contention that the ship could not have sailed so far with so few sails flying. Morehouse agreed that it was odd.

"I have seen vessels behave so strangely that it is impossible to say how or what they will do," Morehouse said. "She was yawing coming into the wind and then falling off again. I watched her for two hours doing that. . . . My opinion is that the vessel had worn round before I picked her up. By the yards being left square, I should say that when she was abandoned she was running before the wind."

The rest of the cross-examination was more contentious. Shown a portion of one sail, Morehouse conceded that it appeared to have been cut with a knife, but he wasn't sure. He argued his position gently to Flood.

"I have seen sails torn by the wind in every sort of way, across and against the grain," Morehouse said. "The flag or what I thought was a flag from the port yardarm we found when we got up to it was part of the upper topsail hanging down torn."

Morehouse allowed that he, too, had seen one curious feature of the Ghost Ship that his crew had failed to mention in their testimony, "I also saw the marks on the bows of the *Mary Celeste*," Morehouse said.

He was clearly troubled by the marks and feared what they might imply, but Morehouse said he could not even venture a guess as to what had made those strange cuts in the *Mary Celeste*'s hull. Flood was, as usual, left unsatisfied.

The next day, March 4, Deveau was recalled to the witness stand. He had been cross-examined about his earlier testimony the afternoon before, but on this morning Flood wanted another shot at the *Dei Gratia*'s first mate to explore inconsistencies in the evidence and his testimony. Deveau appeared ready for Flood this time. He argued over several points in the surveyor's report, noting that he had replaced the *Mary Celeste*'s peak halyards with used rope and that's why the rigging did not appear to have been changed. Deveau said there was little sign of water damage because they had dried much of the ship by airing it out, and the crew's personal belongings by laying them out on the deck to sun. This time, Deveau had done his homework.

Deveau said he hadn't noticed the cuts in the rail, but didn't think he or his men had made them—they didn't have an axe, and hadn't found one onboard the ship. Deveau admitted he had seen the captain's sword, but didn't mention it because he did not think it of much consequence.

"There was nothing remarkable on it," Deveau said. "I do not think there is anything remarkable about it now, it seems rusty."

That remark did it—the proctor was off on a rant.

Flood was infuriated by the suggestion that he was mistaken and— no doubt upset that he could not uncover the plot he suspected— launched into a wholly unsupported and nearly nonsensical scenario that baffled Deveau and most likely everyone else in the courtroom. Flood said that the sword had been cleaned with lemon, "which has covered it with a citrate of iron which has destroyed the marks of the supposed blood which therefore is not blood at all as at first supposed but another substance put there to destroy and disguise the original marks of blood which were once there."

Flood said there had been blood on the deck, but that it had evidently been washed away by seawater. Flood could not have made these statements without reading—or knowing the contents of—Dr. Patron's report on the blood analysis, which he should not have legally been able to do, since it was sealed. Cochrane would not allow it into the hearing, but Flood managed to work some of its conclusions into his remarks (and, later, the newspapers). By the time he was finished, the sword was about the only thing left untainted.

With a mountain of contradictory evidence and nothing solid to build a case on, Flood was becoming desperate, if not hysterical. But throughout the proctor's ranting, Deveau—who most likely had been coached by Pisani—remained calm. He said that it had never occurred to him, nor had he seen anything to make him believe, that there had been any violence on the *Mary Celeste*. If Flood relied heavily on Austin's report, Deveau almost parroted Shufeldt's.

"I used often when at the wheel to think how and why the vessel had been abandoned by her crew and came to the conclusion that she had been left in a panic, that being also strengthened by the sounding rod found near the pump and her sails being rather injured," Deveau said. "She was so sound and stout that I cannot think that if I had been on board I should have abandoned her. I should have considered her safer than an open boat unless she was on the rocks."

Things weren't going as the attorney general had hoped. Even the *Gibraltar Chronicle* seemed to be turning away from Flood and his theories. That morning the newspaper reported Captain Shufeldt's findings, which almost certainly had been supplied by Horatio Sprague. The paper's editors seemed to have decided that the loss of the *Mary Celeste*'s crew was more curious than criminal.

"For the present the mystery remains unsolved, but it is satisfactory to note that the opinion of a practical man, such as Captain Shufeldt, and an analysis made by Dr. Patron, of this City, of the alleged bloodstains coincide in refuting the theory of violence," the *Chronicle* reported. "The possible fate of those who were on board the *Mary Celeste* is sad enough without the addition of mutiny and bloodshed."

Flood could not have been pleased by the story, even if he did not pick up on the subtle jab the paper made at him, calling Shufeldt and Patron "practical." The attorney general was not deterred for a minute. With the hearing drawing to a close, Flood made one last stab at ferreting out the conspiracy. He accused Deveau of changing his story and launched into more queries about whether he had really tried to dry the personal belongings of the ship's crew. After someone— apparently Cochrane—said something about his line of questioning, the attorney general defended his cross-examination as "necessary in the ends of justice in order to endeavor to solve the mystery of the abandonment of the ship by her master and crew."

"I alone represent the interests of the master," Flood declared.

The next day, the mood in the courtroom was sullen. Flood read the affidavits of John Austin and Ricardo Portunato and the rules of salvage were recited. In his closing remarks, Henry Pisani—making a final plea to Cochrane—said that the merits of the case were great and deserved serious consideration.

"The vessel was entirely abandoned, found drifting in the middle of the ocean in the winter, the stormy season of the year, with her hatches and skylights open," Pisani said, asking that the court consider, "the chances of her going down and being absolutely lost, the chances of her being run into by some other vessel, perhaps to the loss of both.

"There was great courage and risk to both vessels in dividing the crew of the *Dei Gratia* as was done and great skill in bringing the two vessels safely into the port of Gibraltar as has been done."

Pisani reminded the judge that salvage is rarely more than half, but seldom less than one-third the value of the ship and its cargo. Cochrane made no comment. He simply dismissed the case, saying he would deliver his verdict for a salvage award on Tuesday, March 11.

The day before the salvage verdict was expected, the *Mary Celeste* sailed out of Gibraltar. Captain George W. Blatchford had been waiting more than a month to finish the voyage the ship had begun in November. He could have left earlier, but it had taken three weeks to raise a full crew. Almost no one wanted to sail on the *Mary Celeste,* a problem that would follow the ship for the rest of its days.

At the offices of the American consul, Horatio Sprague was left to clean up the mess. He had begun to take inventory of the crew's sea chests—mostly clothes, books and knickknacks—that he would have to send to the families of the lost sailors. It was a sad task, sorting through the few remaining artifacts of ten people. There were cherished letters, a silver watch and, the thing that must have tugged at Sprague's heart more than anything else, a hood for a small child, a tiny piece of cloth meant to keep Sophy's head warm while she was on the cold, lonely ocean. It would no longer do her any good.

Oliver Deveau left Gibraltar at about the same time as the *Mary Celeste*. As soon as the court excused him, he sailed for Genoa to retrieve the *Dei Gratia* and her crew. Deveau would take the ship to Messina to pick up a load of fruit before sailing back to America, while Morehouse remained in Gibraltar to collect the salvage award.

That is, if there was going to be one.

It was March 14—four months since the derelict had arrived in port—before that figure was handed down. In his brief statement, Judge Cochrane reluctantly awarded the crew of the *Dei Gratia* £1,700 for salvage of the *Mary Celeste*. That amounted to about $8,300 U.S., and was based—the court said—on the ship's value being about $5,700 and the cargo worth little more than $36,000. While the estimated value of the cargo closely reflected its insured value, the court's assessment of the ship was preposterous. Even as the wrecked and jury-rigged *Amazon,* the ship had sold for more than that amount five years earlier. Winchester had put twice that much money into its refit and claimed to have a new appraisal that said it was worth $16,000.

By any means of accounting, it was a pitiful reward for all the work and trouble the men had been through. The court awarded an 18 percent salvage award—based on a low estimate—when twice that amount would have been common. The message in Cochrane's award seemed to be that the men barely deserved anything. Clearly, the judge suspected the *Dei Gratia*'s crew had done something wrong and this was the only way he could punish them.

To add to Morehouse's disappointment, Cochrane decided that out of their award the salvers would pay the cost of the reports and analyses done at the court's insistence. The judge castigated the crew of the *Dei Gratia,* particularly Morehouse and Deveau, for their handling of the situation. They would pay for the investigation because, he said, they had caused it to be necessary.

The next day the *Gibraltar Chronicle & Commercial Intelligencer* reported the confusing reasoning behind the low judgment.

> *The Judge further thought it right to express the disapprobation of the Court as to the conduct of the master of the* Dei Gratia *in allowing the first mate, Oliver Deveau to [go] away with the ship which had rendered necessary the analysis of the supposed spots or stains of blood found on the deck of the* Mary Celeste *and on the sword.*

Not only had Cochrane shorted the *Dei Gratia* crew on their salvage, his remarks sparked talk that implicated them in the evolving conspiracy theories surrounding the *Mary Celeste.* Given statements that Flood made a decade after the fact, this may not have been coincidental. After Cochrane died in 1883, Flood claimed he and the judge had expected to conduct a criminal trial sometime shortly after the salvage hearing. The reason Cochrane had refused to admit the bloodstain report at the hearing, Flood said, was that he did not want to taint evidence or potentially interfere with the criminal trial they hoped would follow.

Whether or not the judge intended it, his words cast a bad light on the crew of the *Dei Gratia.* Newspapers throughout Europe and America picked up on the insinuation and soon began to publish the sentiments Cochrane had only suggested. During the three months the *Mary Celeste* sat in custody of the Admiralty Court, all the theories of foul play had centered on her own crew. Soon, Morehouse and Deveau would be considered accomplices, and the accusations would follow them the rest of their lives. Even though there would be no formal trial, the *Dei Gratia's* crew would be under suspicion in the court of public opinion forever.

As disappointed as he was in the salvage—and as worried as he must have been for his career—Morehouse was more relieved just to be free. He took the paltry salvage award and caught the next ship to London, where he would find passage home. On the long voyage to Nova Scotia, David Reed Morehouse had a lot of time to reconsider his actions and it almost always came out the same: he wished that he'd made other choices on that cold winter day when he first spied the *Mary Celeste*.

SEVEN

In the Wake of Misfortune

On September 1, 1873, the *Mary Celeste* slipped past Boston Light and into the city's expansive harbor, nearly ten months after she had sailed from New York.

The voyage was mercifully uneventful, a slow cruise without even the slightest threat of a tropical storm in the northern latitudes. The new crew most likely welcomed the pace. No doubt the men had heard the stories and, although they signed on anyway, there were still concerns about the ship. That she might have structural damage, that she didn't sail right. That she was, well, cursed. But for the entire trip, the only thing that called to mind the ship's recent unpleasantness was the occasionally flaccid state of the sails, the sight that had originally drawn the *Dei Gratia*'s attention.

By all accounts it was an insignificant homecoming. The ship docked anonymously at Boston's waterfront without the festive welcome that accompanied the return of many oceangoing vessels. There were no happy family members to greet this replacement crew, a ragged lot assembled from various European ports along the route. The ship had been forced to return light—that is, without a cargo to defray the cost of the run. It was just one final insult added to the disastrous trip. With nothing to unload, the sailors were simply released, left to find work on any vessel that might carry them home.

By nightfall the *Mary Celeste* was deserted at its moorings, a ghost ship once again. But she would not go unnoticed for very long.

Captain George Blatchford was grateful to be back in Massachusetts for the first time since Christmas. He had little to show for his time away from home, for the trip had not been successful by any measure. After escaping Gibraltar in March, the *Mary Celeste* delivered its cargo of alcohol to Genoa less than two weeks later. When it was finally unloaded, the freight was found to be in good shape. Only nine of 1,701 barrels were empty—a most respectable delivery rate, especially given the time in transit.

There was no explanation for why those nine barrels were empty, whether the casks had leaked or busted open. It seemed unlikely the alcohol in just a few barrels evaporated, but the bureaucrats who normally would have studied such trivia gave it little notice. O. M. Spencer, the American consul at Genoa, wrote to Horatio J. Sprague simply that the cargo was in "excellent condition."

After its hold was unloaded, the *Mary Celeste* was hove down for a proper hull examination. Winchester and Blatchford did not want to risk a transatlantic crossing without some assurance the ship was completely seaworthy and, having no explanation for the crew's disappearance, they had to consider everything, including structural damage, a possibility. And perhaps with good reason, Winchester did not trust the Vice Admiralty Court's stamp of approval; he wanted to see for himself. But the inspection ultimately supported the court's report. The *Mary Celeste*'s hull was fine.

While the ship was docked, Blatchford had searched for a charter back to America. Winchester had lost the contract to haul fruit from Messina, and he desperately wanted to avoid losing more money on this devastating excursion. Insurance paid the greatest share of the salvage settlement, but the trip was still costing Winchester & Co. handsomely. To sail back without a charter would eat up hundreds of dollars in operating costs. But Blatchford could find no one who was hiring—at least not hiring his ship. He lingered in Italy until the end of June before finally giving up and setting sail for America.

Winchester did not have the appetite to calculate how much the *Mary Celeste* had cost him. Not only was there the four months out of service and the lost revenue from missing a charter, there was also the damage to his reputation. The ongoing speculation about the missing crew was bad publicity, especially since some of the fanciful stories even implicated him. Winchester felt the ship had become his own personal albatross, and he was ready to cast it off. While the ship was moored in Boston, J. H. Winchester & Co. put the *Mary Celeste* up for sale.

Winchester would not shed his demon so easily, however. For weeks, there were few nibbles and no bites. It soon became apparent that no one in Boston wanted the ship, so he sent a crew to sail the *Mary Celeste* back to New York. He hoped for better luck in that city.

"When she arrived a great many people came to look at her, but as soon as they found out her history they would not touch her," Winchester later recalled.

More than anything else, it was a curiosity.

If the ship did not attract any potential buyers, the *Mary Celeste*'s fame—or infamy—eventually drew plenty of attention, luring a steady stream of gawkers to the waterfront. Had Winchester been a more creative or enterprising man—say, more like P. T. Barnum—perhaps he would have thought to charge admission to see it. He might have made up for the lost charters, as there was no shortage of prurient interest. Nearly a year after the *Mary Celeste*'s crew vanished, the fate of the sailors was still a popular topic in New England harbor towns. It was dockside parlor talk, and the speculation ran the gamut from the probable to the impossible. The buzz had scarcely let up since March, when conjecture had been at a fever pitch.

Some of the more eloquent sailors had their opinions published. Captain Ansel Weeks, Jr.—who lived in Mattapoisett, only a mile or so from the Briggs family home in Marion—proclaimed in the *Journal of Commerce* that there was no mutiny, piracy or fraud, only tragedy.

Weeks said Briggs and his crew deserted because the ship was in danger of crashing into the rocky coastline of St. Mary's Island.

In his argument, the captain displayed a commanding knowledge of the seas around the Azores and relied on the log entries of the *Mary Celeste* that were publicized during the salvage hearing. Weeks said the circumstances added up to only one possible solution: the *Mary Celeste* had floundered in light winds only six miles from shore, where she drifted dangerously close to the breakers on the rocky, windward side of St. Mary's, a result of "a heavy northerly swell rolling toward and on the island, as is generally the case during that season of the year." Anchoring was out of the question, Weeks said, because the water around the island is too deep. If it appeared the ship would be swamped or rolled in the breakers the only sensible alternative was to abandon ship.

"At that late season, with the boat overcrowded by the captain and family, officers and crew, and on the weather or inaccessible side of the island, and taking for granted that the vessel was doomed, they would naturally pull away and endeavor to make a landing on some accessible part," Weeks speculated. "They may have been deceived by appearances (a surf never showing its worst from offshore) and may have been swamped, or even may have been swamped in trying to reach the port on the south side of the island, and of course all on board would have perished."

After that, the ship needed only to catch the right gust of wind to sail out of danger and, eventually, away. While some people quickly endorsed Captain Weeks's reasoning, including James Briggs, others argued there was a hole in the story: no sign of the lifeboat or the crew ever washed up on St. Mary's. But Weeks knew all too well that in the ocean nothing is a certainty.

Samuel W. Dabney, a U.S. consul in the Azores, said the crew might very well have disappeared around the island chain, but on purpose. Dabney told his bosses at the State Department that dozens of sailors jumped ship in the Azores because of the temperate climate and abundance of food. He said the islands were a paradise, to many men

preferable to working on a whaling ship, for instance. Dabney said officials should not rule out the possibility the *Mary Celeste*'s crew had
gone ashore at St. Mary's. State Department officials paid no attention
to the consul, partly because he sounded like a tourism official.

As time wore on it became clear the crew would not turn up in some
South American port on their rescue vessel. Without any remnants of
a lifeboat—without remains—it was anyone's guess where they had
gone. When news of the case stopped coming from Gibraltar, the
story of the *Mary Celeste* and her missing crew should have died. But
many people kept guessing. The story took on a life of its own; the
number of theories grew almost weekly. Within months, people debating the mystery fell into four main camps, alternately blaming
mutiny, pirates, insurance fraud or foul weather for the loss of the
Ghost Ship's crew.

According to some newspaper accounts of the day, Winchester
himself considered mutiny a possibility. In the March 11, 1873, edition
of the *Bath Daily Times* of Maine, a typically unattributed dispatch announced that Winchester had uncovered proof the crew had mutinied
against Briggs:

> *J. Winchester & Co. ship brokers of New York, whose brigantine, the*
> Mary Celeste, *was abandoned at sea near Gibraltar under suspicious cir-*
> *cumstances some time ago, have now received additional information leav-*
> *ing little doubt that the crew mutilated and overpowered the officers, killing*
> *them or taking them prisoners.*

With an admirable show of creativity and attention to sinister detail, the article read much like one of the most horrific stories from
Edgar Allan Poe:

> *The officers were probably surprised, and quietly gagged and bound. A*
> *sword was found that seemed to have been stained with blood, and the*
> *foretop gallant sail was cut as with some sharp instrument, and perhaps in*

a struggle with the man on lookout, as they must have been near land.
Nothing has been heard of Captain Briggs, his family or crew, and until
some of them are found their fate will be a mystery.

It's doubtful Winchester was the source of the article. Mutiny was
not an idea he cared to promote, and one he eventually denounced.
Reports of mutiny on one of his ships hardly could have been good
for business, and that was his first and foremost concern. The story
more likely trickled down from Frederick Solly Flood, the Gibraltar
attorney general. He first suggested the possibility of mutiny in his
letter to the London Board of Trade months earlier. Later, Flood
bizarrely suggested that Winchester may have paid the crew to
mutiny—to what end, it was never clear. Flood rarely concerned himself with such trifling matters as motive.

In the nineteenth century, mutiny on sailing ships was rare, but not
unheard of. In the years since the *Bounty* incident, mutiny had become somewhat romanticized. Part of that notion, the British author
Leonard F. Guttridge wrote, was the "inborn readiness to flout authority." Often mutiny was attributed to abused sailors rising up
against captains who treated them much like prisoners, something
that the descendants of American colonists could appreciate. But such
shipboard conditions, Guttridge noted, were much rarer than most
people believed.

Documented accounts of insurrection and insubordination onboard sailing vessels date back hundreds of years, at least to Ferdinand
Magellan's voyages of discovery. In the nineteenth century alone there
were several famous incidents: the whale ship *Globe,* the slave ship
Amistad. But at the time the *Mary Celeste* was found adrift, the most
memorable mutiny in America was still the *Somers* incident of 1842.

The USS *Somers* was a brigantine, similar in size to the *Mary Celeste,* that the Navy had selected to serve as a training ship for cadets.
A crew of teenagers would sail alongside the ship's regular crew, running dispatches back and forth across the Atlantic. For the regular
crew it was busy work, but the voyages would give cadets valuable

square-rigger experience before they were turned loose on the U.S.
Navy's burgeoning fleet.

On its maiden training voyage, the hundred-foot *Somers* was ob-
scenely overcrowded: seventy-four cadets shared space with the regular crew of forty-seven. With such inhuman living conditions, it
should not have been surprising that there would be trouble. The
brig's official mission was to deliver orders and mail to the *Vandalia,* a
frigate patrolling for renegade slave ships off the west coast of Africa.
But the *Somers* did not provide a stellar example to its young trainees.
After a few weeks of trying in vain to intercept the *Vandalia,* Captain
Alexander Slidell Mackenzie gave up, changed course and sailed for
America.

During the return trip, Mackenzie learned that some members of
his crew were plotting a mutiny against him. Before they could act he
had the three sailors arrested. Then the real problems began. Mackenzie, an author and politically connected career Navy man, found himself in a dilemma. Holding the men in chains could spark another
mutiny attempt, but if he let the plotters go they might be even more
inclined to proceed with their plan. After debating this quandary with
his officers for days, Mackenzie came up with a novel solution: He
hanged the three men from one of the ship's yardarms—either to
keep the alleged mutineers from rallying the crew, or to scare anyone
with similar ideas. Or both.

When the *Somers* and its story reached New York, the nation was
shocked. One of the hanged mutineers was the son of the secretary of
war, giving the incident even deeper political ramifications. The
Somers incident quickly became the favorite story of New York papers, which ran sensational articles (much as they would three decades
later about the *Mary Celeste*) that took all sides in the issue. Even the
author and naval historian James Fenimore Cooper weighed in, criti-
cizing Mackenzie for his actions. Despite the vitriolic controversy, a
board of inquiry eventually acquitted the captain.

The *Mary Celeste* mutiny as it was portrayed in the *Bath Daily Times*
and other newspapers more closely resembled fiction than any actual

event of the era. In particular, the gruesome details very closely mirrored Poe's *Narrative of Arthur Gordon Pym*. In Poe's only full-length novel, drunken mutineers take over the whale ship *Grampus* and "a scene of the most horrible butchery ensued. The bound seamen were dragged to the gangway. Here the cook stood with an axe, striking each victim on the head as he was forced over the side of the vessel by the other mutineers. In this manner, twenty-two perished . . ."

It is unlikely that the crew of the *Mary Celeste* killed Briggs and Richardson and then escaped in a lifeboat. The immigrant sailors under Briggs's command had little motive for such a risky, violent act. Mutineers who were caught were often killed, as the crew of the *Somers* witnessed firsthand. Maritime lore is filled with similar tales. As a blatant warning to others with mutinous ideas, Magellan had one attempted insurrectionist stabbed to death and another beheaded. Other captains through the centuries had adopted Magellan's model—including, of course, Mackenzie. As a result, mutiny was not something that sailors entered into lightly. More often than not it was sparked by one of several common circumstances on board a ship, and none of those conditions applied to the *Mary Celeste*.

Occasionally mutiny was tied to political uprising, a revolt against a tyrannical captain or untenable living conditions, such as the *Amistad* slave ship mutiny in the 1830s. But Briggs was by all accounts a fair, if not gentle, man. No one who ever sailed with him complained of his demeanor. Even if he had been a harsh commander, it is unlikely he would have abused such a small crew, if not for humanitarian reasons, because he needed them to sail the ship. The sailors, in fact, weren't mistreated in any way. There was plenty of food on board, so there was no rationing. As Guttridge noted, "In their own practical interests, conscientious captains strove to keep their people well nourished." Weaklings did not make very good sailors.

Mutiny plots were sometimes borne of men with little to do when off duty but sit around and talk, stirring each other into a frenzy—a luxury the crew of the *Mary Celeste* didn't have, especially with the weather on that particular voyage. Flood believed the men murdered the captain in a drunken rage after getting into the alcohol in the hold. It became a popular theory, but the entire premise is flawed. Briggs did not allow the crew to carry their own liquor aboard, there was none found on the ship and the men could not have drunk the alcohol in the hold. The 1,701 barrels of alcohol the *Mary Celeste* carried were most likely some sort of industrial alcohol. If the crew had foolishly tapped one of the kegs they would have been half dead before they could have worked themselves into a drunken rage. It was perhaps the most outlandish of all the theories, but the idea of a drunken, rampaging crew lingered for years.

By the middle of the nineteenth century, the most common motive behind mutiny was greed. The *Somers* mutineers had planned to take the ship and use it for piracy off the coast of Africa. If the *Mary Celeste's* crew had mutinied for such reasons, they weren't very proficient. Not only did they fail to steal any of the valuables onboard, they left behind their own belongings and clothing—not to mention the ship. The *Mary Celeste* and her cargo were worth a handsome sum, the Admiralty Court's ruling notwithstanding. If the crew had forcibly taken the ship, they would have meant to profit from it.

Captain R. W. Shufeldt, who examined the *Mary Celeste* for the State Department, said there were no signs of violence on the ship, and he had an eye trained to find just those sorts of clues. Although the powers of perception among the *Dei Gratia's* crew seemed no more than average, it's hard to argue with Shufeldt's findings. The alleged mutineers were a simple group of immigrants, not criminal masterminds who would have taken the time to cover up the crime. If there had been a mutiny, there simply would have been more evidence.

The same logic that rules out mutiny on the *Mary Celeste* also undermines the idea that pirates kidnapped or killed the crew. The theory of piracy dates back to February 1873 newspaper articles and may have been prompted in part by the alleged blood on the deck and the sword. Even though the court's bloodstain analysis was kept sealed, its contents made it into some reports. Within two months after Flood breathlessly announced he'd found blood, the claim had been openly debunked. But as conspiracy theorists have always done, contradictory facts were ignored.

Stories of murderous swashbucklers overtaking the *Mary Celeste*'s crew flourished because pirates, who had received very little attention at the height of their plundering days, were becoming idealized outlaws in the nineteenth century. The legend of Maiden's Cave, with its fancy and chivalrous pirates, was one of the best-known tales in the Nova Scotia countryside where the *Mary Celeste* was built. In America, the stories were even more widespread. Pirates were the maritime equivalent of the train robbers and hold-up men storming the American West. Hardly ten years after the *Mary Celeste* incident, in fact, Robert Louis Stevenson made his name with the wildly popular, pirate-infested adventure *Treasure Island*.

Piracy was a plausible solution because it so neatly explained how the crew could seemingly just vanish. It was not a completely baseless idea, either. The stretch of water between the Azores and the European coast was notorious for pirates in the early nineteenth century. Not so many years before the *Mary Celeste* sailed, the United States and Great Britain were paying "tribute" to Islamic Barbary Coast pirates to keep them off their merchant ships. Pirates often plundered ships and took their crews hostage, later selling them into slavery. The waters where the *Mary Celeste* was found had been a pretty common place to be attacked. The Azores, in fact, had been a base for some pirates.

James Briggs, Benjamin's younger brother, may have thought there some validity to the notion of a pirate attack based on his brief experiences at sea. The only Briggs man not to sail professionally took one voyage with his brother Oliver in 1861. On that trip aboard the brigantine *Samoset,* the Briggs brothers sailed through the waters where the *Mary Celeste*'s crew would disappear a decade later. James wrote admiringly of the "green hills and white cottages" of Corvo, one of the Azores, but said as the *Samoset* neared the Straits of Gibraltar one night, Oliver chose to keep his ship farther out to sea.

"He said that he had rather beat about all night if he did not make a foot than to anchor near that pirate-infested shore," James wrote years later.

While many sailors claimed piracy was a real threat well into the twentieth century, there were few confirmed reports of piracy in the

North Atlantic as late as the 1870s. By 1872 even Barbary Coast piracy had died out. Into the 1890s, there would be occasional reports of Riff pirates boarding ships in the seas off Gibraltar, but those accounts were few and far between. The pirates that remained were less bold than their more famous predecessors and set their sights lower. In some ways, though, that bolstered notions that the *Mary Celeste* incident fit the profile. In the late nineteenth century what few pirates remained preyed on slow, small freighters—such as hundred-foot brigantines.

But pirates don't tidy up.

If pirates had gotten aboard the ship—as one hoaxer in the early twentieth century claimed—Briggs and his men surely would have put up a fight before allowing themselves to be taken prisoner or killed. The ship would have suffered at least some damage in the melee, and pirates would have been even less likely than mutineers to destroy evidence. Shufeldt said what little damage there was to the ship could be explained in any number of other ways. The marks on the ship's rail, for instance, were more likely made by the crew cleaning fish or splicing rigging than some dramatic swordfight.

Then there's the ship. Pirates would have plundered the *Mary Celeste* for anything they could have sold or traded at the next port—it's how they made their living—but all the crew's valuables were still onboard. There wasn't even a sign that anything had been mussed in a search, much less plundered, despite some news reports of the day. Ultimately, the ship and its $36,000 worth of alcohol would have been more valuable than the people. Pirates likely would have taken the *Mary Celeste* before its crew.

As the Gibraltar salvage hearing drew to a close, some newspapers suggested the *Mary Celeste* incident might be nothing more than a clever insurance scam. The charge stemmed from the problems that Winchester had with the ship's registry two years earlier. An unnamed source told the *New York Sun* that the ship had been "improperly cleared and sailed under false colors." The *Sun* reported that theories of mutiny, abandonment or pirate attacks were not given much credence at the Custom House because a "Deputy Surveyor Abeel"—almost undoubtedly the source of the story—had discovered a deception in the ship's registry earlier and "took measures to seize the brig."

The article outlined the circumstances of the *Mary Celeste*'s 1870 change of name and registry (from the government's point of view) and said there was a huge difference in the ship's insured value and its actual worth. The *Sun*'s source said that when the *Mary Celeste* was seized in Boston, she was appraised at $2,600. But on the voyage in which Briggs and his crew disappeared, the ship had been insured for $16,000.

"This discrepancy furnishes a clue upon which the insurance companies will probably act," the *Sun* reported.

The figures were enough to raise the eyebrows of bureaucrats, underwriters and newspaper editors—and enough to send James H. Winchester into an unbridled rage. The ship merchant called the article "an atrocious falsehood" and challenged the paper or anyone else to prove wrongdoing on the part of his company. In a letter published in the *Sun,* he offered "the true history of the vessel, as far as we know, together with Mr. Abeel's connection."

Writing of himself in the third person, Winchester said Abeel had come to him years earlier claiming the ship's registries were fraudulent, but that he realized Winchester & Co. had nothing to do with it.

> *He said he knew we were innocent parties and did not want to be hard on us and that we could settle the matter. This looked so much like blackmail that Mr. Winchester told him if the vessel belonged to the United States government, they would have to take her, as we had no money to settle with him or anybody else.*

Winchester said the discrepancy in the ship's value was due to a major refit of the vessel that Abeel was either unaware of, or was conveniently ignoring. The *Mary Celeste,* he wrote, was "torn down to her copper and rebuilt and made a double-decked vessel at an expense of $11,500." He said the insurance on the ship was $14,000 on a ship now valued at $16,000. "And now we would ask if an attempt has been made to defraud the underwriters? What has become of the Captain, his wife and child, officers and crew?"

Winchester included a list of the insurance companies that held policies on the ship and cargo, inviting anyone who was interested to check out the figures for themselves.

For all of Winchester's outrage, it was not the first time he had heard an accusatory tone in questions about the ship's insurance. In this instance, insurance scam was the suspicion that deserved the closest scrutiny. Flood, and perhaps even the Vice Admiralty Court judge, had considered fraud a very real possibility and they had every reason to be suspicious: A ship turned up in port in fine shape, with its cargo intact, yet the insurance companies were forced to pay salvage. Winchester could have easily hired the men of the *Dei Gratia* to make the claim for a portion of the award. It would have been extremely profitable, and it would not have been the first time such a scheme was devised.

The idea was so feasible, in fact, that had the court known of a friendship between Briggs and the *Dei Gratia's* captain the entire episode might have been ruled an insurance scheme, or barratry—fraud against the owners—at the very least. Morehouse and possibly even Winchester would have gone to jail. That is most likely why Morehouse was reluctant to testify, and the reason he never revealed his acquaintance with Briggs. He was making a claim on the ship of a friend—a friend who had mysteriously disappeared. He knew what it looked like. It smacks of insurance fraud even today but, upon examination, that too is unlikely.

By the mid-nineteenth century some businessmen had already realized what a century later would become common knowledge: insurance scams, if successful, can be profitable. It seemed a victimless crime—an insurer paid out on the loss, diluting the cost among its policyholders. Certainly the *Mary Celeste* would later qualify as an unprofitable ship, but at the time it was—for all practical purposes—a new ship with some modest amount of promise. Winchester made the point in his letter to the *Sun* that there was nothing to collect on, as the ship was still there. As insurance still paid the salvage claim, it was a weak argument, and not even the best one he had. Had Winchester been interested in perpetuating some sort of fraud, would he have done it on the first cruise after a major refit? Would he have risked the investment of $11,000—in 1872 the equivalent of nearly $160,000? Even with a better payoff than the Vice Admiralty Court awarded, it would have been a lot of expense for an uncertain award. It didn't make business sense.

The sudden increase in the ship's insured value rightfully made the Custom House crowd suspicious, but once they had Winchester's explanation they evidently dropped their accusations. The government never launched an investigation, and the insurance companies never filed suit. Insurance companies would have investigated for months if they suspected a glimmer of truth to the fraud rumors.

Ultimately the theory collapses around questions of motive and execution. If Morehouse and Briggs had been planning a scam, they would not have devised such an attention-drawing mystery. Surely they would have preferred a neat explanation, a clear reason why the ship was abandoned and the crew lost. Even a note left in the logbook or on a table would have gone a long way to dispel some of the questions, to take the wind out of nosy bureaucrats and newspaper reporters.

There were some curiosities, however. Some people questioned why Morehouse had not taken his wife—who almost always traveled with him—on this particular voyage, the insinuation being that he didn't want her involved. But that is a question that could apply to Briggs as well. If Benjamin Briggs were going to abandon ship and disappear in the middle of the ocean, why risk the lives of his wife and baby daughter? It only complicated matters. And if he planned to disappear permanently with his family, why not take Arthur? And Briggs, like Winchester, would have lost money on a salvage claim. The bottom line is the best factor to debunk a scam theory.

In later years, David Reed Morehouse and Oliver Deveau were occasionally mentioned as accomplices to whatever scheme there was. Some even claimed the *Dei Gratia* crew murdered the *Mary Celeste* sailors for the salvage money. These stories were fueled by a few crafty hoaxers, including one who said on his deathbed that he was the *Dei Gratia* sailor who had thrown Benjamin Briggs and his wife overboard.

In the years following the Ghost Ship's discovery, Morehouse and Deveau escaped all but the smallest amount of scrutiny (outside of the Vice Admiralty Court, of course). The best defense for Morehouse and Deveau is the same one that eliminates the possibility of fraud: if the men of the *Dei Gratia* had any sort of criminal intent, surely they would not have left so many loose ends.

They would have come up with a better, less troublesome, story.

The *Dei Gratia* sailors blamed it on the weather.

Their argument garnered little publicity because it was so common and devoid of criminal activity, which made it unattractive to editors trying to sell newspapers. If a storm was the culprit, the *Mary Celeste* incident was nothing more than another mundane sea disaster. It wasn't sexy, but Oliver Deveau swore until the day he died that Briggs left the ship during a storm after discovering several feet of water in the bilge.

Deveau based this on the conditions on the *Mary Celeste* the day he first boarded her, and little else. While never publicly critical of the crew, Deveau's theory showed an almost offensive lack of respect for Briggs. There was some modest weather damage to the ship, but it was nothing serious—any sailor with Deveau's experience could see that. When the *Dei Gratia* sailors boarded her on December 4, 1872, the *Mary Celeste* had a little more than three feet of water in its bilge, not enough water to panic seafaring men. Deveau certainly had no reservations about sailing the ship across 600 miles of open water. Also, that water had accumulated over the days the ship had sailed with its hatches opened. As common as it was for men to abandon ship during a storm, in the case of the *Mary Celeste* it is the theory that least fits the facts.

In their court testimony, the *Dei Gratia* sailors said that on the *Mary Celeste* a couple of sails had been shredded, some of the rigging hung over the sides, and the binnacle was busted. While it seemed serious to the court, the damage was actually minor for a boat that had been untended for more than a week. In fact, the *Mary Celeste*—for

years criticized for its sluggishness and bad luck—showed almost remarkable signs of resiliency. It was, in many ways, a tough little ship.

Even if the *Mary Celeste* had been in that same ragged condition
the day the crew deserted, that alone could not have been enough to
scare them off. For a veteran sailor such as Benjamin Briggs to load his
wife, baby and crew into a small skiff on the open water, the *Mary Celeste* would have had to be in a death roll. A battered, leaky ship beats
a yawl or an eighteen-foot skiff at sea any day. When Briggs left the
ship, it was completely seaworthy. All the minor damage to the *Mary
Celeste* occurred during the time it was sailing untended through the
North Atlantic.

The ship's log reflected almost tranquil conditions on the day the
crew disappeared. Their foul-weather gear hung from pegs below
deck and the windows and hatches were left open. Unless the crew
was trying to sink the ship, there is one thing that is certain: whatever
happened, they crew of the *Mary Celeste* abandoned ship on what at
least began as an exceptionally calm day.

A week after the salvage hearing ended, Horatio J. Sprague mailed the
State Department an inventory of Captain Benjamin S. Briggs's shipboard desk. It was a dark wooden box with a large flat lid, filled mostly
with standard office supplies of the day—a pencil, ruler, paper, sealing
wax and U.S. stamps. Inside, there were receipts signed by J. H. Winchester and twenty-one letters from his family. These were Briggs's
most valued possessions, just about all the man had left behind.

Sprague was still faced with the mystery every day. He sorted, inventoried and packed the belongings of the various crewmen, and
found himself answering dozens of inquiries about the incident. One
letter came from N. W. Bingham, a Treasury officer from Boston, who
asked for his help with a fraud investigation. Bingham was interested
primarily in the alcohol the ship carried. "From information which I
have received I am led to believe that there may have been in the
transaction a fraud perpetrated upon the revenue of the United States
instead of the 'tragedy' which is proclaimed," Bingham said.

The Treasury agent believed the *Mary Celeste* was bootlegging al-

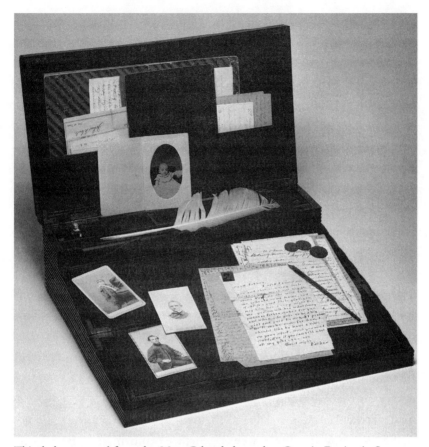

This desk recovered from the *Mary Celeste* belonged to Captain Benjamin Spooner Briggs and held his most prized possessions—letters from his family. *Photograph Courtesy Peabody Essex Museum*

cohol, but his investigation never flourished. Perhaps Mr. Abeel in the New York Custom House had stoked the Treasury agent's suspicions, but he had found no proof to back up the charges, and Sprague did nothing to help his case. The consul answered, diplomatically of course, that he didn't believe there had been any such attempt to evade taxes. Bingham probably thought, as many people did, that the *Mary Celeste* was hauling distilled spirits of some sort—whiskey or rum.

"The missing master, Briggs, I had known for many years and he always bore a good character as a Christian, and as an intelligent and active shipmaster," Sprague wrote dismissively.

Sprague was more intrigued by a long dispatch from T. A. Nick-elsen, a German official in Prussia who inquired about the ship, the Lorenzen brothers and whether the American had found "any signs of distress on board." Nickelsen assured Sprague that mutiny was not an option, as "I know three of the sailors personally and know them to be peaceable and first class sailors." Later, this unsolicited testimonial would strike Sprague as odd, but at the time, he was polite and ex-pansive in his reply.

"The general opinion is, that no violence took place on board, as no signs were found to that effect," Sprague wrote. "Should I learn anything about the missing crew or any other information relating to this mysterious affair, I shall not fail to address you on the subject."

That May, Sprague forwarded the log of the *Mary Celeste* to the con-sul in Genoa, where it was needed to process the ship through cus-toms. Sprague asked Consul O. M. Spencer to hold the book until Washington decided what to do with it. A receipt for its delivery shows up in State Department files, but the logbook soon vanished. Although the Admiralty Court had recorded notations that Deveau made in the *Mary Celeste*'s logbook, the transcribing secretary did not bother to copy the three weeks' worth of information Briggs and Richardson had posted in it. With the disappearance of the log, the conditions that the *Mary Celeste* encountered on the voyage—perhaps even some other clue to the fate of the crew—was lost forever. At the time, though, no one thought much of it.

The letters kept coming.

Sprague was more comfortable corresponding with fellow diplo-mats than writing the eventual notes of concern to family members, but he had to handle several of those as well. He received a sad note from Emma J. Head of Brooklyn, who referred to her new husband as "the late steward of the *Mary Celeste*." The widow Head wanted her husband's belongings shipped to J. H. Winchester's office so she could pick them up. She needed something to help her remember her young husband, she said, as they had been married for only a few months.

The note that must have affected Sprague the most arrived from

New Bedford that August. James C. Briggs, the younger and only surviving brother of Benjamin, requested that Sprague send along the captain's belongings as soon as possible. It was a sign the family had given up hope.

By the summer of 1873, James Briggs no doubt had told Arthur that his parents were lost. It was hard to avoid when the boy saw his mother and father's belongings divided up among cousins, aunts and uncles. James Franklin Briggs, James's son, long suspected Mother Briggs told little Arthur to never give up hope, that one day his family might come home.

Arthur Briggs continued on as his mother had instructed him to do in her last letter, learning his arithmetic and spelling as well as he could. He did his chores and kept to himself. He finally learned to skate, as she had asked about in that note. He held on to that small bit of happy news, waiting—hoping—that one day he could tell her.

James, who was initially appointed Arthur's guardian, in his letter to Sprague said he wanted Benjamin and Sarah's belongings for their son. They were tokens of a life—of a once large, happy clan—that by 1873 was all but gone. Not long after that devastating winter James sold Rose Cottage, ostensibly because he had taken work in New Bedford and Mother Briggs was too old to be left alone. But perhaps the grand home also harbored too many memories, too many recollections of a large seafaring family taken before its time. That sentiment came through in James's short note.

I am the last of a family of seven, six of whom have been lost to the sea. My brother left a little boy at home for whom I claim these mementos of his father and mother.

After that, the two men corresponded for months under the guise of business, but it seemed they were simply swapping memories and pleasantries. Sprague wrote that "Your brother was well known to me and therefore I was able to appreciate his merits."

James Briggs replied, saying that he was "glad on such an occasion to deal with a friend who knew my brother."

It wasn't much, but by that time members of the Briggs family had to take solace in anything they could.

Eventually the family drifted even farther apart. Mother Briggs lived until 1889 with James and his new bride, Mary J. Reynolds, who had been the fiancée of James's lost younger brother, Zenas. Little more than a year after his parents disappeared, Arthur went to live with his uncle, the Reverend William H. Cobb, some fifty miles away in Uxbridge, Massachusetts. Reverend Cobb eventually became Arthur's legal guardian and the boy became the oldest brother in a family of five children. As he grew to adulthood, Arthur clung to those final letters from his parents, wondering what terrible thing had cost him his family. The question would haunt him for the rest of his life.

Winchester had no better luck selling the *Mary Celeste* in New York. James Franklin Briggs later wrote that by the end of September 1873 the ship had a reputation "as wholesome as that of a haunted house." One unsubstantiated story had it that Winchester took a prospective customer by ferry to see the brig in Brooklyn. As they approached the ship, the man saw the name *Mary Celeste* on the ship's stern and cried "Oh Lordy!" before running to catch the ferry as it left the dock.

Winchester temporarily abandoned the notion of selling the *Mary Celeste* and hired a new captain. Coincidentally, John Q. Pratt hailed from Benjamin Briggs's home county of Plymouth, Massachusetts. After raising a new crew, Pratt took the *Mary Celeste* on a Caribbean run, arriving in Kingston, Jamaica, on October 31, which would have been Sophy's third birthday. It was an uneventful trip, and the ship's last as part of the J. H. Winchester & Co. fleet. In February 1874, Winchester finally sold her to the Brooklyn shipping partnership of Cartwright and Harrison. After the sale, Winchester calculated that he had lost more than $8,000 on the *Mary Celeste*—the early twenty-first-century equivalent of more than $115,000.

The ship soon lived up to its reputation.

David Cartwright put the *Mary Celeste* in service on his company's

West Indies route, where it routinely lost money. A load of lumber en route to Montevideo, Uruguay, tumbled overboard in a storm. Next she was chartered to carry horses to Mauritius, an island in the Indian Ocean east of Madagascar. But rounding Africa's Cape of Good Hope—in the waters haunted by the *Flying Dutchman*—the *Mary Celeste* ran into one of the area's infamous storms. By the time the ship arrived in Mauritius, few of the horses were still alive. Cartwright claimed that he had been sold a cursed vessel.

Edgar M. Tuthill, the *Mary Celeste*'s latest captain, searched for a return charter in ports around the Indian Ocean. Soon he found one in Calcutta, and it turned out to be his last voyage. During the trip back to America, Tuthill took ill. The ship was forced to stop in St. Helena, a South Atlantic island off the coast of Africa, as the crew looked for a doctor. Three weeks later Tuthill died on the island, leaving the first mate to bring the *Mary Celeste* home. The Ghost Ship had claimed her third captain.

At some point during those days of squalor, a photographer captured a single image of the *Mary Celeste.* In the sepia-toned portrait, the ship swings at anchor in an unidentified harbor, all its sails furled, a few sailors loitering on her deck. At first glance, it seems rather generic, just an old brig with the usual web of rigging strung between its masts. The most striking feature of the photo may be how dark the ship appears—forbidding, almost haunting. It could just be the quality of the picture.

Cartwright kept the *Mary Celeste* in service a few more years, sending it once again to Africa, a trip that cost him another $1,000. Disgusted, he finally sold her at a rock-bottom price in 1880, and calculated that he had lost $5,000. A few years later, after the ship's legend was cemented in maritime lore, Cartwright related its misfortunes under his flag for the *New York World* newspaper: "Do I remember the brig *Mary Celeste*? Well, I should think I did. We owned her for five years, and of all the unlucky vessels I ever heard of she was the most unlucky."

This undated photograph of the *Mary Celeste* shows the ship in an unidentified harbor in the days after Benjamin Briggs, his family and crew disappeared. *Photograph Courtesy Cumberland County Museum, Amherst N.S.*

Losing a little money, Cartwright said, was a small price to rid himself of the former ghost ship.

During those miserable last days of the *Mary Celeste,* the ship had a coincidental brush with its past. In August 1877, Captain George Spicer—the Spencers Island teenager who had carried the body of the ship's first captain home—found the former *Amazon* docked in New York.

Spicer was in the city to serve on a board investigating the loss of another vessel and came across the *Mary Celeste* one day while strolling the docks. He boarded the ship and walked her decks, remembering his early days before the mast. In fifteen years, she had changed dramatically. Not only had her features been altered considerably, she appeared run-down and neglected. Worse than her shoddy state of repair was her reputation—an infamy that Spicer knew all too well. He hardly could have avoided the stories.

Although as an old man he would defend the ship—or at least defend it as *Amazon*—he felt compelled to write little of this sad encounter in his personal diary. He noted simply that "Today I was on board the old brigantine *Mary Celeste* which used to be the *Amazon* that I sailed on for over two years."

Stanley T. Spicer, the captain's grandson and biographer, wrote that Spicer was fond of visiting his old ships and usually made some favorable, nostalgic comment about nearly every such vessel he encountered—calling it a "good sailor" or a "fine vessel."

But, Spicer noted, his grandfather evidently had few kind words for the *Mary Celeste* after that encounter.

Most sailors felt the same way. The Ghost Ship had proven one too many times that, even if it wasn't cursed, it was at the very least bad luck. They could not forget the ship's past.

Soon, no one else would be able to, either.

EIGHT

Conan Doyle's Statement

In some ways, it was almost elementary.

The story explained how a ship in perfect condition could turn up in the middle of the ocean sailing without a crew, why a group of seafaring men would leave all their belongings behind. Although it was an exotic solution, nearly unimaginable for the times, it gained credibility by playing to both the superstitions of sailors and the cultural fears of Europeans. It was nearly perfect.

There were, to be sure, more than a few puzzling discrepancies. So many of the facts were wrong that it could not be entirely accurate, yet so many details were dead-on the tale could not be easily dismissed as fancy. If the story could be proven true, there was no doubt it would have a profound effect on the mystery. For it meant that someone had survived the incident on the *Mary Celeste.*

When the "true confession" of a man who had been aboard the *Mary Celeste* appeared in January of 1884, officials in Gibraltar were skeptical. The name of the ship's captain and the date of the voyage were wrong. Even the name of the ship was slightly off. It was actually a sloppy yarn—amateurish, the bureaucrats thought, perhaps even

a vicious hoax. Whatever it was, the men in the British outpost were
not amused. More than a decade after the *Mary Celeste* had arrived in
Gibraltar's harbor, the town had not forgotten the Ghost Ship, had
not stopped pondering the mystery. But surely this was not the answer they had been seeking. In two separate government offices, two
very different men had the same reaction: American Consul Horatio
Sprague and Gibraltar Attorney General Frederick Solly Flood launched
investigations.

The story was published in London's prestigious *Cornhill Magazine*
and allegedly had been written by a New England physician. The
man, a Dr. J. Habakuk Jephson, claimed the ship's crew and passengers
were systematically killed on the trip across the Atlantic in a most sinister plot. His survival had been nothing more than a miracle, Jephson
claimed.

Shortly after reading "J. Habakuk Jephson's Statement," Frederick
Solly Flood telegraphed his unsolicited comments to London newspapers in an attempt to quell the speculation. The story was, he said,
"A fabrication from beginning to end." Even at eighty-two, Flood
was still an excitable Irishman. The stoic Horatio Sprague found himself in the unusual position of agreeing with his counterpart. The
American consul did not want to believe the story could be true,
either. He dealt in facts, and there were too many contradictions in
the tale, not just the name of the ship—called the *Marie Celeste* by
Jephson—but also the names of the entire crew. Jephson claimed that
a Captain J. W. Tibbs had been in command of the vessel. Tibbs was
an emotional man, Jephson said, with a "loud voice and hearty manner." Even if the doctor was bad with names, he was describing a sailor
with a demeanor very nearly the opposite of Benjamin Spooner
Briggs's. And even though he rightly identified the salvage ship as the
Dei Gratia, Jephson also incorrectly named its captain.

There was more. The story began by quoting a Gibraltar newspaper article that Sprague and Flood knew had never been published,
and included erroneous facts from other newspaper reports. According to Jephson, the *Dei Gratia* had towed the *Marie Celeste* into

Gibraltar. He said that all of the ship's lifeboats were still slung to their davits and that its voyage had been so calm that a "bobbin of silk" was found still standing on the sewing machine. Jephson even set the time of the incident a year later, in December 1873.

The author, this Jephson, claimed to be a Harvard expert on consumption, the son of a preacher—what more upstanding character reference did one need?—and a "distinguished advocate for Abolition." He said his connection to the story began during the war, when he had fought for the Union. He was injured at Antietam and taken to a nearby home where an old slave woman named Martha recognized him as the good white man who "writes books and fights for coloured folk." Because of that, she gave him her most prized possession—a strange, black stone, smooth and very nearly round, that looked strikingly like a human ear. Jephson thought the woman a tad crazy, but accepted the amulet rather than offend her.

A decade later, Jephson wrote, happenstance placed him on the doomed ship. He had developed some trouble with his lungs and his doctor suggested that an ocean voyage would help his breathing (one of the more subtle ironies of the story). He booked passage on the *Marie Celeste,* where he was one of two passengers besides a crew of seven men, the captain, his wife, and young child. While Jephson was making his arrangements, a third passenger arrived: a mulatto with a mangled hand. His name was Septimius Goring, and he was from New Orleans. Before the ship left Boston—another inaccuracy the bureaucrats spotted—on October 16, 1873, Jephson said that two of the crewmen disappeared and were replaced by black men hanging out on the quay.

Soon after the voyage was underway, Jephson said, strange things began to occur, most involving the passenger from New Orleans. Tibbs found Goring examining the ship's chronometers in the captain's cabin; Goring was seen talking in hushed tones with the crew; he meticulously charted the ship's course on his own map. These odd incidents continued for a week. Then, on October 22, all hell broke loose.

That afternoon, Goring "accidentally" fired a revolver that he claimed to have been cleaning. The bullet impacted the wall where Jephson's head would have been had he not fortuitously gotten up to take a walk around the deck just moments earlier.

Later that same evening, Tibbs rushed into Jephson's cabin searching for his wife and child. The captain was a frightful sight, so much so that it startled the doctor.

"Even the sailors, who are generally stolid enough, were deeply affected by the sight of him as he roamed bareheaded and disheveled about the deck, searching with feverish anxiety the most impossible places, and returning to them again and again with a piteous pertinacity."

No one could find the captain's wife and child. The crew assumed they had fallen overboard while walking the deck. Jephson eventually had to calm Captain Tibbs down with opium-laced coffee.

Less than two days after his family went missing, the captain apparently committed suicide, shooting himself in the face. Jephson rushed to the captain's cabin when he heard the gunfire, noting that it must have also alarmed Goring. The mulatto was already there, leaning over the body.

"Is the ship accursed?" an excerpt from Jephson's diary read. "Was there ever a voyage which began so fairly and which changed so disastrously?"

The voyage continued with the first mate in command and Jephson, Goring, and Harton, the third passenger, left to ponder their horrible journey. Soon, another of the white crewmen was injured when one of the ship's hatches crashed down on him in the hold. If he hadn't moved quickly enough, Jephson noted, he would have been killed. As it was, the man's foot was crushed. Then, on the night of October 31, Jephson awakened to find Goring standing over him in the cabin. When the doctor was startled out of his slumber, Goring claimed that he was searching for medicine to cure a toothache.

The voyage continued on without incident for a week, with the crew expecting to reach Portugal any day. One day, Goring took interest in Jephson's ear-shaped amulet, showing it to one sailor who reacted bizarrely. But when Goring attempted to throw it overboard, the man stopped him. Jephson wrote that by then—finally—he had determined Goring was maniacal, and began to suspect that his amulet might have value beyond what he ever imagined.

"When I compare the effect produced by the stone upon the sailor, however, with the respect shown to Martha on the plantation, and the surprise of Goring on its first production, I cannot but come to the conclusion that I have really got hold of some powerful talisman which appeals to the whole dark race. I must not trust it in Goring's hands again."

On November 9, members of the crew—who had began to treat Jephson with great respect—spotted something in the sky that looked like the Peak of Tenerife, a landmark of the Canary Islands off the coast of Africa. The men were confused not only by the sight but also by the temperatures—never had the waters off Portugal seemed so *hot*.

Of course, it was Tenerife. The crew soon realized they had been lured off course because someone had tampered with the ship's instruments. But before they could correct the problem and set sail, natives from the nearby coast arrived in canoes and took the ship. The natives bound and gagged Jephson and the others, taking their orders from Goring. The man from New Orleans leaned over and spoke to Jephson.

"You will bear me witness," he said in his softest accent, "that I am no party to sparing your life. If it rested with me you would die as these other men are about to do. I have no personal grudge against either you or them, but I have devoted my life to the destruction of the white race, and you are the first that has ever been in my power and has escaped me. You may thank that stone of yours for your life. These poor fellows reverence it, and indeed if it really be what they think it is they have cause. Should it prove when we get ashore that they are mistaken, and that its shape and material is mere chance, nothing can save your life."

The natives took Jephson off the ship, loading him into a canoe for the trip ashore. As they rowed away, Jephson said he could hear the splashes of other sailors being thrown off the deck of the *Marie Celeste* and into the dark Atlantic.

Jephson was taken to the natives' village and later to a large building where many of the locals had gathered. His amulet was taken from him by a gray-haired man, who fit it perfectly onto a statue of Mohammed that had been cut from jet-black meteor stone. "The parts dovetailed together so accurately that when the old man removed his hand the ear stuck in its place for a few seconds before dropping into his open palm." Jephson had returned the missing piece of the statue and, for that, the natives treated him like a god.

Later that night, Goring explained to Jephson what had happened. The tribe was descended from Mahometans, and the statue was carved from stone thought to be from the heavens. When this tribe moved away from Mohammed and Mecca, they took half the stone with them, turning it into a statue. When a small group of the schism moved south hundreds of years earlier, one man snuck into the temple and carved off the ear for luck. Legend said that one day the ear would return, so Jephson's delivery suggested divine prophecy. For that reason, Goring could not kill him—the natives would not allow it.

Goring let Jephson go, explaining that he could never truly control the tribe while there was a courier from the heavens in their midst. But before releasing him, Goring told Jephson the secret behind his plans. He held up his mutilated hand and said, "[T]his was done by a white man's knife. My father was white, my mother was a slave. When he died she was sold again, and I, a child then, saw her lashed to death to break her of some of the little airs and graces which her late master had encouraged in her."

Goring told Jephson to carry his message of hate and revenge back to white people, and then set him adrift in a small boat. He was picked up a few days later by a British steamer.

From the day on which I found myself once more in the bosom of my family I have said little of what I have undergone. The subject is still an intensely painful one to me, and the little which I have dropped has been discredited. I now put the facts before the public as they occurred, careless how far they may be believed, and simply writing them down because my lung is growing weaker, and I feel the responsibility of holding my peace longer.

Perhaps Jephson's story spread so quickly through seaports on both sides of the Atlantic because it was the first thing resembling a clue to turn up in eleven years. Since the *Mary Celeste* was found adrift and empty, no sign of Captain Benjamin Briggs, his family or crew had shown up anywhere. Although there was no shortage of theories on how the crew met its demise, there had not been so much as a rumor suggesting anyone had found the crew's remains, or any definitive clue to their fate. There certainly had been no witnesses to come forward.

As much as he was wary of the story, Horatio Sprague was intrigued by this new wrinkle in an old case. He believed any claim, no matter how outrageous it might be, should be investigated. "I ask to myself, what motives can have prompted the writer of the article in question to refer to this mysterious affair, after the lapse of eleven years?" Sprague wrote to John Davis, the assistant secretary of state in Washington.

"As the Department cannot fail to feel a certain interest to ascertain whether there be the least suspicion of truth in any portion of what is stated in the article referred to in the *Cornhill Magazine,* I have taken the liberty to call its attention to it, especially as it may have the opportunity of examining the author of this extraordinary composition."

For some reason, the story reminded Sprague of one of the half dozen or so queries he had received in the days after the incident. Soon after reading "J. Habakuk Jephson's Statement," Sprague began to question the authenticity of a letter from T. A. Nickelsen, who had claimed to be a German official from the Island of Fohr, home of two of the *Mary Celeste* sailors. Perhaps Sprague only wanted to know if any of the ship's crew had ever turned up, or maybe the story caused him to think the letter might have been a hoax. Whichever was the case, Sprague wrote to his diplomatic counterpart in Berlin, inquiring about the identity of the man, and whether anyone had ever heard from the Lorenzen brothers.

Were there any "widows, wives or parents of seamen who were lost or supposed lost in the *Mary Celeste* in November 1872 still or lately living?"

Sprague was afraid he had missed something.

Arthur Conan Doyle was quite pleased and annoyed at the same time. Not only was his story a success—his first published in such a prestigious magazine—but also he had stirred a mystery, something that Doyle had a great respect for. Perhaps this little dustup even endeared him more to the notion of puzzles no one else could solve. Although he was unhappy with *Cornhill Magazine's* refusal to give bylines, he certainly had to admit it made the story more of a sensation than it otherwise would have been. When some people speculated Robert Louis Stevenson had written "Statement," Doyle was again pleased to be in the company, and annoyed that more people did not know he had written the talk of the town. His frustration was tempered somewhat by the payday from *Cornhill,* which was roughly the equivalent of a year's rent.

It was no accident Doyle chose the *Mary Celeste* as the subject of his breakthrough story, for the mystery had fascinated him since he was a boy. Doyle's friend, the novelist Robert Barr, said that the tale "made a powerful impression on his young mind. This mystery of the sea set the future Sherlock Holmes at work finding a solution for it."

Born in Edinburgh, Scotland in 1859, the future creator of the world's greatest detective had been an inquisitive lad who dreamed of writing, but was smart enough to hedge his bets by studying medicine. It was a fortuitous decision. In the late 1870s Doyle, studying at the University of Edinburgh Medical School, met Dr. Joseph Bell, the man who would inspire his famous character. Working on his studies and observing his mentor by day, Doyle spent his nights pursuing his real passion. He wrote countless stories, submitting them to a variety of periodicals. His first publication came in 1879, when a minor magazine printed "The Mystery of the Sasassa Valley."

Soon after that first sale, Doyle went to sea. He took a post as ship's surgeon on the Greenland whaleship *Hope* and a year later took a similar assignment on a steamer out of Liverpool. In all, the young doctor spent two years plying the oceans, providing him an ample knowledge of life aboard a sailing ship, and leaving him plenty of time to dream up mysteries and the solutions to them. Both would serve him well in the coming years.

In 1882 Doyle returned to life on land, settling in Portsmouth, and with a new cache of life experiences, the future master of the modern mystery began to write seriously. Within a year there were a couple of stories published, but nothing of note until mid-1883, when the editor of *Cornhill Magazine* accepted "J. Habakuk Jephson's Statement."

It was the coup that Doyle's career needed. *Cornhill Magazine* was the premier fiction magazine in England at the time. Founded by the publisher George Smith in 1860, the magazine's first editor had been one of Smith's better-known authors, William Makepeace Thackeray. The magazine specialized in serialized first publications of novels by some of the most famous writers of the day, but included short stories, essays and poetry from contributors such as Anthony Trollope, Harriet Beecher Stowe, Robert Browning and Alfred, Lord Tennyson. *Cornhill* had published the breakthrough novel *Far From the Madding Crowd* in 1874 by a then-unknown Thomas Hardy. The acceptance of Doyle's lengthy, 13,000-word story among such company was a tremendous boost for the young author, and not just because of the pay. It loudly proclaimed that Arthur Conan Doyle the writer had arrived.

Cornhill's strict policy was to not give bylines, sometimes leaving critics guessing who had written what. Friends said that after "Jephson's Statement" hit the newsstand, it was all the young doctor could do to restrain himself from stopping people on the street and pointing out that it was he—and not the famous Robert Louis Stevenson—who had written the story.

"What gave me great pleasure and for the first time made me realize that I was ceasing to be a hack writer and was getting into good company was when James Payne accepted my short story 'Habakuk Jephson's Statement' for *Cornhill*," Doyle wrote in his *Memories and Adventures*. "I had a reverence for this splendid magazine with its traditions from Thackeray and Stevenson and the thought that I had won my way into it pleased me even more than the cheque."

That *Cornhill* was primarily a fiction magazine evidently did not occur to either Sprague or Flood. While they didn't believe the story, they couldn't fathom the purpose of it. Like so many others, they simply took the tale at face value. They could not have realized the author had spent years poring over the details of the case, just as they had, looking for the real solution. Doyle was quickly making it his life's work to fit a complex collection of facts into a singular conclusion. And just like Flood and Sprague, Doyle found that with the *Mary Celeste* no one answer was a perfect fit.

Short of finding that one true solution, it was easy to make the story seem even more sinister. Just leaving the ship's lifeboats in place—a detail that would stick with the legend for a century—added an entirely new level to the mystery. Even the upright bobbin of silk, picked from one sensational newspaper article, found its way into a few of the allegedly factual accounts. The hot meals that some claimed were found on the galley table were not included in "Statement," but when that bit of trivia was introduced to the legend, Doyle got blamed for that as well. (A novelist named Clark Russell is now credited with that addition to the *Mary Celeste* legend, which apparently was taken from his novel based on the ghost-ship story, *Mystery of the Ocean Star*).

Doyle's story renewed interest in the *Mary Celeste,* sparking a fresh round of newspaper and magazine articles, and setting a course for the hoaxers that would follow. Today most maritime scholars agree that his story is one of the primary reasons the legend of the Ghost Ship did not die. The historian George Sand Bryan said that "Doyle had unconsciously blazed a trail that in the fullness of time would be well trod; and variant tradition, in which every tongue brings in a several tale, was all the while leading the story of the *Mary Celeste* deeper and deeper into the maze of fancy."

The Briggs family said nothing of the story publicly, but could hardly have been pleased by it. There is evidence that James and his mother avoided talking about it at all—even their descendents did not mention Doyle, a curiosity given his prominence in *Mary Celeste* lore. Perhaps that is not so strange, though. It could not have been easy to discuss even the fictional possibility of such a gruesome end for their loved ones. Most likely they resented the story for the fabrications, hoaxes and slanderous tales that it spawned.

Charles Edey Fay, the twentieth-century *Mary Celeste* scholar, correctly pointed out that Doyle was not the first to use the *Marie Celeste* name (it appeared with that spelling on some Custom House documents) but the author is certainly to blame for its subsequent widespread use. In the late nineteenth and early twentieth century, the ship's name was given as the *Marie Celeste* more often than it was correctly christened—even by the Briggs family and Solly Flood. It is just another legacy of Doyle's short story.

In 1887, a few years after "J. Habakuk Jephson's Statement" appeared, the first Sherlock Holmes story was published. *A Study in Scarlet* was an immediate hit, propelling Arthur Conan Doyle to the ranks of the most-respected and best-selling authors. Inspired in part by his old mentor Dr. Bell, the pipe-smoking, cocaine-abusing sleuth became the model for every detective hence and introduced the world to the modern mystery. Doyle took the genre a step beyond the work of Edgar Allan Poe, whom he had admired as a boy. Later, some said Sherlock Holmes should have tackled the mystery of the *Mary Celeste,* but in some ways he already had. "Jephson's Statement" included many elements of the standard Holmes story, including Doyle's (or Holmes's) theories of deductive reasoning. (Years later, another writer penned *Sherlock Holmes at Gibraltar,* a tale of Holmes and his sidekick, Dr. Watson, attempting to solve the infamous case.)

Despite his growing fame, Doyle's authorship of "J. Habakuk Jephson's Statement" remained a mystery until 1891 when the story was included in *The Captain of the Polestar and Other Stories.* Some said he even grew to regret writing the story. A few claimed that in one of his later stories, a ship called the *Sophy,* with references to rats invading its hull, was a not-so-subtle slap at people who indiscriminately spun yarns and made various charges about Captain Briggs. But by that time, it was too late.

The damage had been done.

The secretary of state's office was less than enthusiastic about an investigation and gently denied Horatio Sprague's request. John Davis told Sprague if he got any real information to please forward it, but for the time being Washington did not see any need to pursue the claim. Perhaps they recognized it as fiction, or just had little interest in an old case that had little bearing on State Department business. It would not have been out of the question for Davis to fear that perhaps Sprague was just getting old.

"The article to which you refer has been read with attention and much interest," Davis wrote. "The mystery which surrounds the fate of the master and crew and the passengers, or even the cause that induced or forced them to abandon their vessel, is in no way satisfactorily explained in that statement, and it is conceived that, from the information we now possess, no solution of the mystery has yet been presented."

Sprague had no better luck with German officials, who assured him that T. A. Nickelsen was indeed a former parish chief on the Island of Fohr. The new parish chief was R. I. Lorenzen—apparently of no relation to the *Mary Celeste* sailors—who said that Sprague was probably suspicious because of the awkward wording of Nickelsen's letters. The parish chief said neither the Lorenzen brothers nor Arian Martens, who apparently also lived on the island, had ever returned.

"The relatives know as little about the missing men as myself," Lorenzen said. "The mother of the two brethren [Volkert and Boz] is still living and she does not cease to deplore the loss of her two sons. The eldest of whom was married, his wife and daughter are still living here in poor circumstances. The younger brother was betrothed and his bride has married another seaman and also lives in this village. Arian Martens—his wife and children are likewise living in Amrum, in uneasy circumstances."

Sprague's misgivings were alleviated somewhat, for he wrote no more about the matter. If he still harbored doubts, he diplomatically kept them to himself. Having nowhere else to turn, the old consul let the matter drop.

"J. Habakuk Jephson's Statement" aroused in Frederick Solly Flood a new interest in the case. Although he denounced the tale publicly, it must have given the attorney general some satisfaction to see someone else attribute the disappearance of the ship's crew to violence. Even as an old man with little time left to live, Flood was still scheming. A year after *Cornhill Magazine* published "Jephson's Statement," the queen's proctor at Gibraltar suddenly decided that he had not been paid for his services in the 1873 salvage hearing and promptly wrote to Sprague demanding restitution from the U.S. government. The salvers and owner of the ship, he said, had never reimbursed him for the various inspections and reports done on the condition of the ship and its cargo.

Flood claimed the job of Her Majesty's Advocate General and Proctor did not pay him for suits relating to derelicts, excepting whatever the ship's owners paid. He even used the *Cornhill* story as an excuse, saying that the need for those reports and his extensive fact-gathering were only underscored when the previous year someone claiming to have been a survivor of the *"Marie" Celeste* had made false statements. He argued that his work made it possible to disprove the Jephson account. Once again, Flood proved only that he had an admirable lack of shame.

"I desire to express my unabated confidence in the honor, liberality and trustworthiness of all the American people, and that in response to this communication, means will not be found wanting to requite my arduous labors and zeal not merely for the protection of the rights of individuals, but for the advance of public justice in which the whole American people are interested," Flood wrote.

Thoughtfully, Flood even provided a bill to the United States, but the amount on that invoice has been lost. It didn't matter, it would not be paid. While writing to Flood that he had no authority to make such decisions, Sprague investigated the matter before forwarding the request to Washington along with his belief that Flood was owed absolutely nothing. Martin W. Stokes and George F. Cornwell—who had served as J. H. Winchester's attorney in the salvage hearing—told the State Department that Flood had done nothing more than his job, a job for which he received a salary from the queen.

Although Sprague continued to be cordial to Flood—he was a diplomat, after all—the veteran American consul at Gibraltar made it clear that he would not even bother Washington with any more of these claims. In the shadow of the Rock of Gibraltar, Frederick Solly Flood had become something of an old joke.

"I would beg to state confidentially that Mr. Flood is an Irish gentleman," Sprague wrote. "Although reported as being over eighty years of age, he has always been considered an individual of very vivid imagination, and to have survived, to some extent at least, the judicious application of his mental faculties; such is, I believe, the general opinion of the community at large, even among his most intimate and personal friends."

Frederick Solly Flood, a man as responsible as Doyle for the *Mary Celeste* legend, went to his grave believing that criminal wrongdoing of some nature had cost Captain Benjamin Briggs, his family and crew their lives. If those beliefs had subsided over the years, then the mysterious "J. Habakuk Jephson's Statement" certainly had rekindled them in Flood, and they would smolder for the rest of his life.

Oddly enough, Flood—who was still trying to turn a profit on the case—said nothing publicly in January 1885, when the former derelict attracted new headlines for its latest, and final, stroke of bad luck. It's puzzling, especially given the notoriety Doyle bestowed on the ship, that the news from America that winter did not excite Gibraltar more, did not spark more conspiracy theories or ghost stories.

For that very month, the *Mary Celeste*—like its former crew—simply vanished.

NINE

Dead Reckoning

"Keep her on course," the captain said.

At the helm, Ernest Berthold complied, returning to the original heading with a slight turn of the wheel. The ship's bow nudged almost imperceptibly to starboard.

He had veered off after sighting a black smudge on the horizon four or five miles away. Berthold had not been sure what it was—the bright sun on the water made it difficult to see—so as a precaution, turned to avoid it. But as soon as he did the captain waved him off. The helmsman thought little of it initially, figuring his commanding officer was quite familiar with these waters and knew what lay ahead.

As it turned out, he did. The captain knew exactly where he was going.

It was 12:30 on the afternoon of January 3, 1885, and Captain Gilman C. Parker had come on deck ten minutes earlier. The *Mary Celeste* was sailing into the Gulf of Gonâve, the expansive bay between Haiti's northern and southern peninsulas. The ship was due in Port-au-Prince by evening, and she had made fairly good time since leaving Boston on December 16. To that point, it had been an easy cruise.

To most sailors, the brigantine that sailed into Haitian waters that day would have seemed a ramshackle little boat, perhaps even pitiful. The *Mary Celeste* was in ill repair, her hull and rigging showing the signs of age and neglect, and the unforgiving wear the sea inflicts on a vessel that is not constantly tended to. The *Mary Celeste* no longer received any special care or attention—it was a money pit, and its owners pushed hard just to break even with it. There was little beauty left in her sleek lines. She was functional at best, a second-rate ship, and that was being generous.

The condition of the ship mattered little to her crew. They were simply happy to have work. The weather was an additional perk, as it was a nice day, a pleasant escape from the harsh New England winter. Berthold was at the helm on first mate Joe Howe's watch, and a couple of other sailors milled about on the forecastle. The seas and wind were mild, a little chop. The ship was not moving very quickly, making only about four knots, but then moderate conditions were a hallmark of the Caribbean winter, conditions that would make it paradise found for thousands of vacationing Americans in the coming years.

That the captain was loitering on deck at that time of day struck the helmsman as odd, but a dutiful seaman, he said nothing. Parker seemed to be waiting for something and when he spoke, breaking the silence, Berthold did as he was told. He turned the ship's bow back onto a collision course for the black object just ahead.

"Is that a fishing boat?" Berthold asked.

He did not believe that to be the case; Berthold was just making conversation or trying to extract the captain's thoughts from him. Either way, it didn't work. Parker stood silently, a satisfied look on his face as he watched the ship draw closer and closer to the dark thing ahead.

"He only smiled and told me to keep her on course," Berthold later testified.

One hour later, a sickening rumble announced the impact as the *Mary Celeste* plowed into Rochelais Reef. The ship lurched violently to a stop, the sudden cessation of momentum jerking the foremast from its stepping. The mast fell like a chopped tree, the sound of snapping rigging following it down. It hit the water with a loud thwack after splitting the deck railing and buckling hull planks.

The ship shook aggressively as the razor-sharp coral "chawed" into its underside, tearing through the hull that had been lovingly molded on the beach at Spencers Island more than two decades earlier. It sounded like paper being shredded. That noise, coupled with the crashing and breaking of equipment and cargo, ended only after the ship settled onto the reef and nudged slightly backward. Every sailor who heard the destructive symphony knew this was damage that could not be repaired.

Through the confusion of impact the crew held on admirably, some of them not realizing until too late exactly what their job on the voyage had been. Moments after the impact, a calm Parker ordered his men to cut away the foremast—it was still held to the ship by some rigging. As soon as that task was finished, Parker ordered the mainmast chopped down as well. Sometimes sailors would cut away the masts in an attempt to save a ship by lightening its load, enabling it to float a little higher in the water, but that was not the case in this instance. Parker was not interested in saving the *Mary Celeste*. He was destroying her, and doing a pretty good job of it.

With the ship foundering on the reef and its rigging cluttering the sea, Parker ordered the lifeboats launched. As an afterthought, he told his sailors to take whatever liquor they could carry—something of a bonus, prosecutors would later allege. The seven men took to the boats, abandoning the ship as Benjamin Briggs and his crew had done thirteen unlucky years earlier. They steered toward Miragoane on the southern shore of the bay, leaving the hulking wreck impaled on the craggy reef, its bowsprit reaching toward the heavens now at a violent angle. As they sailed away from the wreck, some of the men looked back at the black smudge on the water that they had made decidedly larger. The ship lay at an unnatural angle. It looked dead, a ghost ship of a different kind. The *Mary Celeste* would sail no more.

In retrospect, the decision to wreck the *Mary Celeste* followed a natural progression. The ship had been deemed unlucky going back

This model of the *Mary Celeste* by Neale Birdsall of Marion,
Massachusetts, represents the ship as it looked following its fall
1872 refit, when it was still a ship with promise. The model is on
display at the Sippican Historical Society in Marion. *Photograph
Courtesy David B. Barker*

nearly two decades, declining rapidly in its latter years. After losing
$5,000 on the ship, David Cartwright sold the *Mary Celeste* to Wesley
Gove in 1880. Gove tried everything to make the ship a success,
changing its homeport from New York to Boston, Providence and
even Brunswick, Georgia, before returning once again to Boston. For
a few months Gove owned the ship outright, but soon took on four
other investors who managed the ship with him throughout its final
days. For most of that time Captain Thomas L. Fleming commanded

her, but in August of 1884 he was replaced by Parker. Parker took the ship on one trip to the Caribbean, leaving that month and returning to Boston on November 8, a trial run for what was to come.

Just as Winchester, Cartwright and even Dewis did before him, Gove was losing money on the *Mary Celeste*. To borrow a phrase from modern-day yachters, it was a hole in the water into which he threw money. It wasn't entirely the ship's fault. There were few lucrative charters to be had for a ship of its size, as the days of sail were winding down. A small, slow cargo ship like the *Mary Celeste* was not an attractive choice for anyone but the cheapest merchants. But it seemed there was more to it. The ship was plagued by bad luck and even worse publicity. In the summer of 1884, when Gove and Parker made preparations for the first trip to Haiti, the States were still abuzz over the controversial "J. Habakuk Jephson's Statement." As if they needed any reminder of the ship's tragic past, it was suddenly news again among sailors. It had not been easy to raise a crew before; that unwanted publicity could not have helped matters.

In the trial that followed, Gove was never implicated in any crime, either because he hadn't known about the plot, or prosecutors could not find enough evidence to link him to it. Even if he wasn't involved in the scheme, he stood to benefit from it by ridding himself of the bad-luck brig. Either way, the outcome was the same. With the ship and cargo insured for $25,000, Parker sailed the *Mary Celeste* from Boston a week before Christmas of 1884, determined that it would not return.

When Parker and his crew reached the Haitian mainland, they met a man named Mitchell who was the American consul's agent in port. Parker told Mitchell there had been an accident and offered to sell him whatever cargo he could salvage from the ship for just $500. They didn't care if they lost money, Parker said, the crew just wanted to go home. An opportunist, and obviously a trusting one, Mitchell jumped at the chance, and Parker did not plan to wait around until the consul inspected his treasure. He quickly sent word of the *Mary Celeste*'s sinking back to the States and secured passage home for himself and his crew. Gove and the owners of the cargo claimed a hundred percent loss to the insurance companies.

Another *Mary* had brought Kingman N. Putnam to Haiti. Putnam, a well-known New York marine surveyor, had come to the island to investigate the recent loss of the schooner *Mary L. Phipps.* The insurance companies that held policies on the *Mary Celeste* learned Putnam was in the area and sent word requesting him to make a few inquiries. Putnam agreed to look into the matter when he finished his business in Port-au-Prince.

In Miragoane, Putnam learned from a disgruntled Mitchell that the crew of the *Mary Celeste* was already gone. The consul's agent was none too diplomatic about Parker, either. Even though Mitchell had recovered just about everything onboard the ship, which was still perched on the reef several miles out to sea, he clearly had been duped—there had been nowhere near $500 worth of merchandise on board the ship to begin with. Mitchell's office was littered with all that he had salvaged, a bunch of junk that would have been thrown overboard from most ships. One look at Mitchell's meager bounty was all Putnam needed to convince him the wreck of the *Mary Celeste* was no accident.

"I opened one case which had been shipped as cutlery and insured for $1,000. It contained dog collars worth about fifty dollars. Cases insured as boots and shoes contained shoddy rubbers worth about twenty-five cents each," Putnam recalled.

That night, Putnam secured a berth on yet another *Mary* in port, the *Mary E. Douglas.* He gave the captain money to purchase part of Mitchell's salvaged cargo and carry it back to Boston. He addressed the crates to the various insurance companies holding policies on the *Mary Celeste,* and may well have added the word "evidence." Those crates would be strong proof in the fraud case that Putnam now knew was a certainty.

It seemed to be an open-and-shut case. Putnam arrived in the States feeling he had enough evidence to have Parker indicted for conspiracy and barratry, but prosecutors wanted more evidence. The district attorney's office needed the letters to the consignees in Port-au-Prince before they would go to trial. The attorney hired the surveyor to return to Haiti, a job he took against his better judgment.

Unable to find timely passage, Putnam booked charter on the British steamer *Saxon,* where he was listed on the manifest as "chaplain" since the ship was not licensed for passengers. Putnam was carrying a subpoena to bring back Mitchell to testify about the nature of his deal with Captain Parker. Even more than crates of junk and boring documents, prosecutors wanted to go into court with a witness.

Putnam was dubious about the assignment, and with good reason. When the *Saxon* arrived in Haiti, a general from the island's military came aboard and said that Mitchell had heard about the subpoena and did not want to testify. In fact, the general said he suspected Mitchell would flee if they attempted to serve a warrant on him. Although Putnam's subpoena carried no weight of law in Haiti, the island's president, General Louis Etienne Felicite Salomon, amicably offered to send out troops to round up the consul. Putnam had to politely decline the offer, realizing the diplomatic implications of shanghaiing "an American Consul on a [British] vessel might entail some consequences which I did not care to assume."

When Putnam went ashore in an attempt to convince Mitchell to come back willingly, he found that the consul had indeed disappeared. But he had left behind the remaining cargo from the *Mary Celeste* in his office, and Putnam promptly confiscated it. This would not be a completely wasted trip.

They were not criminal masterminds by any stretch of the imagination.

It took the insurance companies little time to learn from Boston merchants that the *Mary Celeste*'s crew had bought tons of rotten fish and bottles of watered down ale just before leaving port. They evidently did not even bother to ask the merchants to keep it quiet. One of the insurance companies hired Henry M. Rogers, a Harvard-educated attorney, to track down some of Parker's crew to serve as witnesses in the case. Years later, Rogers outlined for newspapers his cat-and-mouse chase with the crew, an adventure that would rival any modern detective novel.

Rogers insinuated himself into the Boston waterfront life, attempting to find anyone who knew anything about the *Mary Celeste*. There was talk, he soon found, but nothing substantive—nothing to hang a case on. He heard tell that the first mate on the voyage had been hired only a day before the ship sailed, which was odd. He also heard that Parker had been bragging just a bit too much.

"Little by little I began to get the story. I found that the captain of the [ship] had been asked whether he was not afraid some of the crew would give him away, and that he had replied that he could buy any of them for a glass of rum," Rogers said. "The mate of the *Celeste* had been shipped only the day before she sailed. If I could get him, and get him to tell the true story, he would be my most important witness."

Joseph E. Howe had been Parker's first mate on the trip, but after returning from Haiti he quickly hired on as captain of a Boston freighter. Rogers learned which ship Howe had sailed on and soon had a general idea of when it would return from a run to Hamburg. Although he "arranged to get word as soon as she was reported from Highland Light," Rogers found out that Howe's ship had returned only after it made port. By the time he reached the docks, Howe was gone.

"Pretending to be a friend, I asked where 'Cap'n Joe' might be, and the watchman said he had gone home to East Boston, and would come back next morning for his dunnage."

Rogers struck up a conversation with the watchman, and after a few leading statements was able to find out how long Howe had been gone and get a fairly good description of him. The attorney tracked Howe to the North Ferry, followed him home, wrote down the address and went to get his "papers," apparently a subpoena. When he returned to the house, however, Howe was gone again.

Rogers searched nearby saloons until he found Howe sitting at a table by himself in the back of a dark bar. Rogers wandered up to the sailor, acting as if he'd had a few too many drinks, and began to buy rounds for Howe. Before long he was deep into a friendly conversation with the former first mate of the *Mary Celeste*. Their banter continued until Rogers thought Howe had enough liquor in him to loosen his lips a bit. Finally he said, "I want you to tell me, Joe, all you know about the . . . *Celeste.*"

"He shut up then, but I began to feed him what I already knew—that the cargo was a fake, that the ship was piled up in broad daylight on a sunny morning on the only rock anywhere near, and that the captain wasn't afraid of what he, Joe, might say because he could buy him for a glass of rum," Rogers told the *Boston Sunday Globe* as a ninety-year-old man in 1929.

Howe had no idea the insurance companies—much less prosecutors—were on to the scheme. It sounded as if they already knew everything, and he feared being found guilty by association. At the same time, he did not particularly savor the idea of ratting out the captain. Afraid that someone would overhear the conversation, Howe left the bar.

Rogers followed him out and together they went back to Howe's house, where the captain's wife helped convince her husband to tell his story. Rogers may have tipped the scale by suggesting Howe's testimony could protect him from charges of being a partner in the conspiracy. He was being offered immunity.

Reluctantly, Howe gave in and spun a yarn that matched the suspicions of prosecutors perfectly: On the voyage south, Parker had let Howe in on the plan, telling him they were going to run the *Mary Celeste* aground at Turks Island. Howe, trying to talk the captain out of it, told him it would be suicide—they would all drown if the ship went aground there. The first mate had only enough influence to make Parker reconsider the location.

Shortly after that conversation, the captain marked a rock in the middle of the Gulf of Gonâve, a reef that he no doubt knew from years of sailing into Haiti. Knowing the captain's intentions, Howe said he had asked Parker, "Do you think you can hit that rock?"

Within days of hearing Howe's story, Rogers had subpoenas for every man who had been aboard the *Mary Celeste,* and arrested them all pending trial as soon as they came in on various merchant ships. This time, the ghost ship's crew would not disappear before the trial.

On April 20, 1885, Gilman C. Parker was arraigned in a Boston courtroom. The indictment was handed down a month later and named Parker along with just about every merchant who had shipped cargo aboard the *Mary Celeste*. U.S. Attorney George P. Sanger and the grand jury foreman, William H. Fay, signed the indictment, which accused the men of being involved in a scheme to "willfully and corruptly conspire, combine, and confederate together to cast away and destroy said vessel, with intent then and there, in each of them . . . to injure, that is to say, to defraud, any person or corporation who might there afterward underwrite any policy of insurance on the sail goods on board . . ." The men each faced a $10,000 fine and ten years in prison for a conspiracy conviction.

Absent from the indictment were the names of Wesley A. Gove and the other shareholders in the ship. The Boston district attorney's office had not sought criminal charges against the owners, either from a lack of evidence or intent. In some ways, it was a matter of dollars and common sense. The majority of the $25,000 in insurance was held on the freight, which clearly did not resemble the contents listed on the ship's manifest. The government argued that the cargo was overinsured by at least tenfold, but made no such claims about the ship's insurance—it appeared to be just about right. Gove didn't stand to make an unusually large profit from the alleged accident. The owner's position was just cloudy enough to throw the entire case into doubt. The prosecutors chose instead to go with a sure thing.

There is other evidence the prosecution never suspected Gove was involved: Parker was also indicted on barratry, a maritime law charge of fraud or negligence by a ship's master against its owners. While that suggests Gove had been wronged, there is a chance the charge was trumped up as a valuable plea bargaining tool. In the late nineteenth century, barratry was a hanging offense.

When the trial began on July 20, the *Nautical Gazette* and *Boston Post* devoted considerable ink to the prosecution's argument that the

entire voyage was a ruse for hauling worthless cargo. The district attorney said the ale bottles were only partly filled, and then only with
water rinsed through empty casks. The *Gazette* reported that, according to the government's case, the conspirers paid little attention to
even the most common details.

"It was noticed that more bottles of ale were billed to a barrel than
would go in a barrel, it being known that regular shipments were so
many dozen to a flour barrel, and a dozen more for a sugar barrel," the
paper's story said.

Putnam, who appeared in court as a prosecution witness, produced evidence that a claim for fifty-four cases of women's boots was
in fact made against crates filled with a bunch of old rubber over-
shoes. The press could not get enough of the trial, which was the
greatest kind of sensationalism.

Although the papers labeled the story "remarkable," they made
only cursory mention of the *Mary Celeste*'s tragic past. It seemed the
conspiracy behind this single voyage was more than enough to sell a
few newspapers. The *Boston Post,* after reporting on the testimony re-
garding watered-down ale, ran its story under the headline "What
Kind of Beverage Did the *Mary Celeste* Take Out For the Haytiens?"

Watered-down ale was just the beginning. Investigators for the
various insurance companies ran through a laundry list of fraudulent
cargo found in the *Mary Celeste*'s hold. The fish on board was spoiled
pickled herring, and the butter was "slush," basically melted fat. Then
there were the dog collars in place of cutlery. Also, Raphael Boris had
insured 975 barrels of worthless herring for $4,875—about $50,000 in
early twenty-first-century dollars. For the day, it was a rather brazen
crime.

The defense put on quite a show. Parker's lawyers were overly an-
imated as they argued the insurance companies' attorneys had built
the entire case out of nothing for the prosecution, that the captain had
done nothing wrong. It was all hype, they argued. Henry Rogers said
it was a grand spectacle of showmanship. "The defense attorneys were
wild," he said.

While the defense could do a passable job of confusing a case built on bills of lading and insurance policy red tape, they had a bigger problem to deal with: the prosecution had witnesses.

Ernest Berthold, who had been at the helm of the *Mary Celeste* when she struck the reef, offered perhaps the most damning testimony. It should not have surprised Parker's lawyers that the crew might testify, for they otherwise stood to be indicted as accomplices. Berthold was quick to say that he was doing only as he was told.

"I was at the wheel, going on at 12:30 P.M. The captain was there—it was the mate's watch," Berthold recalled. "The captain came down beside me. I kept her on her course, but changed it when I saw the reef; that was ten minutes after the captain came up. I asked the captain if that was a fishing boat. He only smiled and told me to keep her on course."

Parker, of course, said it was a lie, even after Jacob English, another member of the *Mary Celeste*'s final crew, corroborated Berthold's testimony. The testimony of both men belied another of Captain Parker's claims, his boast that he could buy his crew for a glass of rum.

Gilman C. Parker argued that miscommunication and a simple mistake on the part of his helmsman had caused the accident. He said that Berthold had mistakenly steered hard to starboard when he had ordered hard to port. By the time Berthold tried to correct his course, Parker claimed, it was too late to change course again and the *Mary Celeste* foundered on the reef.

"I had no more intention of wrecking the vessel than I had of cutting my throat," Parker testified. "If the vessel had been put to port when I ordered it, I have no doubt we should have gone around the reef."

Parker criticized every piece of the state's evidence: the charts were wrong, the ship had not been on that course—anything he could think of to refute the charges. He said that he had thrown much of the ship's paperwork into the water because on his previous trip he had lost 30,000 feet of lumber "and because it was on the manifest, I had to pay duty on it."

Parker denied the state's contention that the former first mate had been fired because he knew too much about the conspiracy. The man,

Parker claimed, had been a drunk. As it turned out, the first mate's replacement—Howe—could hardly have been more problematic to Parker than a rummy.

Throughout the trial, Captain Joseph Howe listened to the testimony of witnesses and corrected information for the district attorney. He did not take the stand during the trial, although his wife provided one piece of evidence that greatly undermined Parker's claims of innocence. Mary Howe testified that soon after her husband arrived home from Haiti, Parker personally delivered a threatening letter reminding her husband to keep his mouth shut about the wreck. She produced the letter in court and it became a key piece of evidence:

Cap. J.E. Howe:

I would advise you not to know to much a bout cargo fer the shipers have put in their bill of Invoice to the adgestors and the Protest and Log Book as they stand is all that I want. You will be cald over to the Insurance look out you do not get in the Roung track by knoing to much.

G. C. Parker.

Prosecutors argued that Parker had "every inducement that a man could have" for committing this fraud on the insurance agencies and owners of the ship, and his illegible note proved he in fact did it. An assistant district attorney said that Parker "knew that the vessel was an old one, that she was fully insured for the amount of money that her owners would sell her for."

Even more damaging, the government showed that Parker had been sailing that route into Haiti for many years and could hardly have failed to notice Rochelais Reef on his previous trips there. Prosecutors told the jury that Gilman C. Parker had known exactly where the reef was, and knew exactly what he was doing.

The jury deadlocked.

Putnam later said it was not because the evidence was unconvincing, but that a few members of the panel had a problem with aiding the state's case for barratry, which would have sent Parker to his death. Some of the jurors thought the punishment did not fit the crime.

The jury began its deliberations on a Friday night and by the next morning reported to the judge that it could not agree. Judge Carpenter said the barratry charges would have to come in another indictment and told the jurors to disregard them, hoping it would remove the main sticking point. To an extent, it did. Later that day, the jury came back to the courtroom having voted to acquit three of the shippers. Parker and three others—including Boris, who bought the rotten fish—were found guilty on one count of fraud, but the jury was deadlocked on the other. Judge Carpenter, frustrated, dismissed the jury and announced there would be another trial.

The thought of a second trial and the possible resulting penalties were too much for most of the men. Boris pleaded guilty and paid back with interest the $4,875 he had collected on the spoiled fish. Kingman Putnam later said that another of the shipping merchants—faced with the prospects of another trial—committed suicide.

Three months later, while awaiting his new trial, Captain Gilman C. Parker died as well. What killed him was never clear, though some people speculated it was the cloud of suspicion that finally got him. His death ended the criminal investigation. On October 22, 1885, U.S. Attorney George P. Sanger filed notice with the court that the government "will not prosecute this Indictment further." The *Mary Celeste* had claimed her last victims.

When the *Mary Celeste* sank off Haiti in 1885, she had been sailing for thirteen years since the disappearance of her most famous crew. The ship and its legend were known throughout the world of the merchant marine. Stories of tragedies surrounding it were passed down to new generations of sailors on lonely bow watches in desolate stretches of the Atlantic. In the days following the Boston trial, the accounts of the *Mary Celeste*'s sinking became as muddied as every other story about it. Some people claimed the ship had sailed from New York in May of 1885, although she could scarcely muster a crew at double the normal wages. In that version, the ship was lost off Cuba, carrying barrels of water insured as molasses. Perhaps it was just sloppy reporting, for the story did not need embellishment. The truth was bizarre enough.

How long the broken hulk of the *Mary Celeste* sat perched atop Rochelais Reef, no one knows. For years, some people claimed the ship had simply disappeared, as if it might still be sailing the waters between the Old and New Worlds. But that, like so many other things, was just a myth.

At some point, men came and burned the ship to the waterline, its hull boards popping as the flames engulfed the hulk. Fire consumed the *Mary Celeste* in a brilliant funeral pyre until it slid off the rocks and into its grave in the emerald waters somewhere off the island of voodoo.

PART III

TEN

The Great *Mary Celeste* Hoaxes

At first, he mistook it for the name of a lady.

The reference was obscure, the old man on his deathbed and not making much sense. He had mentioned it while gesturing to some papers lying nearby, bequeathing them to his former boss with a weak wave of his hand.

Howard Linford said he had paid little attention to the man's rambling. He simply accepted the papers, a gumbo of documents and writings that clearly meant something to his old servant. He gathered there was something about this woman among the papers, but he did not know what. He only remembered that the dying man, whose name was Abel Fosdyk, had whispered the words as if revealing a secret: *Mary Celeste.*

Linford, the headmaster of a prominent prep school outside London, recounted the scene in the November 1913 issue of *Strand* magazine, one of the most popular and influential literary publications of the day. Linford said he had been compelled to offer his story after a July article in the magazine featured famous authors devising their own solutions to the mystery of a long-lost ghost ship. The name of the ship, Linford said, rung a bell.

Linford said that Fosdyk—who had once been a sailor of some sort—told him that among his papers was an account of the *Mary Celeste*.

"I suppose he said 'the,' but at the time I had no notion of what *Mary Celeste* meant, and imagined it was a woman," Linford wrote.

Before Fosdyk could explain any further, he died.

In that issue of *Strand,* Linford offered Fosdyk's account as a survivor's tale of what really happened on the *Mary Celeste.* He had kept the servant's papers in storage, never imagining he would look at them again. He described the author, his former employee, as a "man of exceptional reticence and self-control" who kept the diary from which the story was excerpted for more than thirty years. Linford conceded, however, that "No word on the subject was ever mentioned by the writer to me."

Linford seemed to be distancing himself from the Fosdyk story, for it was a fantastic tale of madness, tragedy and unbelievable coincidence on the high seas. It was an account unlike anything else associated with the ship's legend over the years. It also seemed remarkably well timed, and Linford's own son had thoughtfully provided illustrations. But as far-fetched as it was, people believed.

Fosdyk wrote that in the fall of 1872 he had decided to leave America, but did not say why. Not wanting to wait for official departure papers, he contacted an old acquaintance, Benjamin Briggs, and arranged passage as steward on the *Mary Celeste* when it sailed from New York.

The trip was rough, the ship sailing through one storm after another, and Briggs seemed on edge most of the way. He became, Fosdyk said, "so irritable one scarcely dared approach him." Briggs was traveling with his wife and daughter, who was called "Baby," but Fosdyk claimed was in fact a schoolgirl of about seven or eight. The girl was restless and bored, and climbed the ship's rigging like a tomboy. Early in the voyage, Briggs saw his daughter balancing on the bowsprit and, in a fit of unbridled rage, slapped her down in front of the crew. Once he calmed himself, however, Briggs ordered the ship's carpenter to build a quarterdeck around the bowsprit for Baby to sit on while she watched the waves.

Fosdyk described this quarterdeck in great detail. It was a wooden deck mounted on the front of the ship and had support beams running along both sides of the hull. Essentially, it was a large platform precariously perched before the bow.

One morning a few weeks into the voyage, Briggs berated his first mate at the breakfast table, calling him a coward for not jumping into the sea to rescue a drowning sailor on a previous voyage. The mate, whom Fosdyk called "Howard," argued in his defense that he had been fully dressed and a man couldn't swim in his clothes. The remark enraged Briggs, and he mocked the mate, repeating his claim over and over, emphasizing each word: "A—man—can't—swim—in—his—clothes."

Briggs vowed to show the mate exactly how well a man could swim in his clothes and left the cabin, headed for the main deck. His wife, who had observed the exchange, begged her husband not to dive into the cold Atlantic. She made several pleas, and came up with a number of sound reasons, but finally argued only that he would ruin his new suit. The captain would not be dissuaded. Briggs undressed and took some of the mate's clothes to wear, leaving his suit and pocket watch in the cabin.

The entire crew gathered on the bridge to watch as Briggs threw a rope over the side of the ship and climbed down. At the urging of Mrs. Briggs, two sailors joined the captain in the swells to make sure he did not drown. Briggs swam around the ship with his deckhands following closely, Fosdyk wrote. It was almost comical for a while. But as they passed near the ship's bow, a scream came from over the gunwales—one of the men was being attacked by a shark. It was a horrific scene, the gray-blue water bubbling red as the other two men tried to save the sailor. Mrs. Briggs, her daughter and the rest of the crew climbed atop the newly built quarterdeck either to watch or

help—it was never really clear which. With the weight of seven people on it, Fosdyk said, the deck collapsed, spilling them all into the
cold, unforgiving sea.

It was a slaughter.

The shark—or perhaps other predators attracted by the blood—
ate most of the crew. Some simply may have drowned, but were probably devoured later. Fosdyk said he watched the savagery while
clinging to the detached quarterdeck, which saved his life. It kept him
out of the sharks' reach, and eventually served as a raft that carried him
all the way to the African coast.

Fosdyk covered the salient points of the case so well that some
newspapers declared the mystery solved. The servant's tale cleared up
some of the more curious things about the incident: Why no one was
found on board. Why no survival gear had been taken. It explained
the strange marks found on the *Mary Celeste*'s bow—they were obviously the notches for "Baby's quarterdeck." It even related how the
crew could disappear and leave behind the lifeboats, an erroneous as-
sumption that, thanks to Arthur Conan Doyle, had become a staple of
the ship's legend.

But it was all a little too neat.

One of the more interesting aspects of the account, George S.
Bryan noted in his book *Mystery Ship,* was the casual mention of how
Briggs had come to leave his pocket watch in the first mate's quarters.
He had laid it on a table alongside the mate's own watch, according to
Fosdyk. It was a curious detail to remember, and odder still that he
found it worth mentioning in his account, which allegedly had been
written in the 1890s. It was also a mistake on someone's part, as it
completely discredited the story. The two watches found side by side
was fiction, an invention from one of the stories in the *Strand*'s July
issue—the one that Linford claimed reminded him of old Fosdyk's
papers. The July issue of *Strand* apparently sparked more than memories in the headmaster.

For a while no one noticed the slipup as the servant's tale made international news, and even the *New York Times Magazine* reported the
story within weeks of its publication. None of these news organiza-

tions had bothered to check the facts, and Fosdyk's account was rife with errors, including the size of the ship and the names of every member of the crew save for Briggs.

The discrepancies did not go unnoticed for long. In Buffalo, a librarian named Frederick J. Shepard soon denounced the story as fiction. Shepard, who studied the *Mary Celeste* as a hobby, said in a letter to the local paper that the known facts of the incident "show the impossibility of accepting this version as having any basis." Shepard practically rolled his eyes in print at the notion of a ship's company falling overboard en masse, as well as the "improbability that a survivor could have escaped."

"The story of the *Strand* writer, in spite of attempts to bolster it with footnotes and a plausible preface, is almost as fantastic as the famous one by Conan Doyle . . . It is actually clumsy."

Linford had anticipated the reaction, and attributed the errors to Fosdyk writing his account twenty years after the incident. He said that, "Of course, minute errors will always creep in when relating facts a long time after their occurrence." This alibi did little good. Shepard had released the hounds, and just as quickly as they had jumped onboard, the press attacked the servant's tale. The *Nautical Gazette* devoted an entire article to pointing out Fosdyk's inaccuracies a month after the story came out.

While people soon realized the names and dates in the story did not jibe with the facts, they managed to overlook the obvious: that Linford might be pulling another Conan Doyle. Most historians of the early twentieth century took Linford at his word. For a century, Fosdyk has been accused of writing a fictitious manuscript that he was hesitant to circulate; that he was reluctant to pull the trigger on his hoax. But Fosdyk was only an alibi.

According to most accounts, Linford was an intelligent man, highly regarded in educational circles. He was headmaster of a prestigious prep school in Hampstead, a borough of London. And six months after reading a series of stories on the *Mary Celeste*, he published a strange survivor's tale in a literary magazine that specialized in fiction from the top names in literature (including regular contributions from Doyle). No doubt the headmaster knew of the ruckus the Sherlock Holmes creator had stirred with his tale; perhaps he even entertained dreams of publishing in a prestigious magazine, of fooling the literary set in which he was so firmly ensconced. Maybe he was just having a little fun and the prank quickly got out of hand.

There is no evidence Linford actually wrote the Fosdyk tale (save, perhaps, for the detail of the two watches), but he left what might be a telling clue. In the *Strand* Linford wrote that, "I would like to emphasize the fact that I do not vouch for the truth of anything narrated."

It could be interpreted as a printed wink. But if anyone suspected Fosdyk's tale was another misleading piece of fiction, they said nothing of it publicly. Soon, the impact of the Fosdyk account would be diluted by a wave of *Mary Celeste* hoaxes, stories that would convolute and confuse the legend of the Ghost Ship forever.

In the years following Doyle's scandalous short story, a steady stream of alternate versions of the *Mary Celeste* legend appeared in magazine and newspaper articles, most of them with fewer reliable facts in them than even "J. Habakuk Jephson's Statement." These versions were offensively inaccurate, sometimes even purposely so. They stole erroneous information from each other, most notably false details of lifeboats still slung to the davits and half-eaten meals still on the galley table (in some versions the meals were still hot). Briggs was identified alternately as "Griggs" and "Triggs"; Morehouse was often referred to as "Boyce." The ghost ship was most often christened the *Marie Celeste*. That moniker flagged the most fantastic tales, and in some ways became the Ghost Ship's malevolent alter ego. While the true story remained unsolved—while the *Mary Celeste* remained a mystery ship—the *Marie Celeste* sailed through a fantasy world of increasingly unbelievable situations. Most of these stories even repeated as fact details from Doyle, even though by the 1890s the story had been exposed as fiction.

Few of the people actually involved in the incident were still around to correct the inaccuracies. Frederick Solly Flood died in the late 1880s, still awaiting payment for his invaluable services. Horatio J. Sprague died shortly after seeing the beginning of the twentieth century, and just a few years after welcoming another famous New Bedford–area sailor to Gibraltar—Joshua Slocum, who was sailing solo on his famous trip around the world. A few years later, Sprague's son took the job of American consul at Gibraltar, as his father before him had done. They became the State Department's first three-generational span of consuls.

The men of the *Dei Gratia* scattered following the salvage hearing, and outside of their own communities, few remembered their names. Even the purported factual articles on the *Mary Celeste* often failed to identify the sailors who actually found the ghost ship. Usually, they were recognized only if they mentioned sailing on the *Dei Gratia,* something most of them made a point not to do very often.

David Reed Morehouse welcomed the anonymity and in some ways even the misinformation. He was not offended that he was called "Boyce" in stories, for he wanted nothing to do with the mystery. After leaving Gibraltar in 1873, he had relinquished command of the *Dei Gratia* for a variety of reasons, but the taint of scandal had to have been among them. In later years it bothered him greatly to see the tale spin out of control. Morehouse told his wife that perhaps the saddest thing of all was that there was no mystery or malfeasance, only tragedy.

"Why, Captain Morehouse felt very badly about the whole thing," his widow claimed. "I've heard him tell the story a hundred times and shake his head and say, 'Poor Briggs! He and his wife and crew perished in that small, open yawl. There can be no other way out of it.' "

Morehouse and his wife, Desiah, eventually left Nova Scotia and retired to Cambridge, Massachusetts. In October 1904, Morehouse may have read J. L. Hornibrook's assertion in *Chambers's Journal* that a kraken—the legendary giant squid—had picked off the crew of the *Mary Celeste* one by one. It was only a hint of things to come, but Morehouse would not be around to see the worst of the stories. He died on March 4, 1905—nearly thirty-two years to the day after his long-forgotten testimony in the *Mary Celeste* salvage trial.

Oliver Deveau, the former first mate of the *Dei Gratia,* outlived his former captain by seven years. He died at the age of seventy-six, only a few years after sailing to Cuba on his last professional voyage. Like Morehouse, Deveau never escaped the shadow of the *Mary Celeste,* even though most stories failed to name him.

Not long before Deveau died, a man named Jacob Hamel tried to take his identity. The *New York Herald* reported Hamel's deathbed claims that he was first mate of the *Dei Gratia*—and that he had killed the last of the *Mary Celeste* crew. Most of the crew had died of smallpox, Hamel claimed, and only Briggs, his wife and the ship's cook were still alive when he boarded the ship. Hamel said his crew threw the survivors overboard, took a tidy sum of cash they found ($8,000) and told their captain the *Mary Celeste* was apparently a derelict.

Even if he was seldom recognized anywhere else, Deveau's hometown never forgot his greatest adventure, never mistook him for another sailor, and never entertained any notion that he had done anything wrong. In his obituary in the *Digby Courier* of September 20, 1912, it was noted that, "Captain Deveau has been interviewed by hundreds of newspaper men during the past forty years. He related the story to the editor of the *Courier* in the cabin of an old tern schooner *Xebec* of Bear River more than thirty years ago, when Captain Deveau was chief officer of that vessel, and the editor 'a small cabin boy.' "

The editor wrote that Deveau could always find some fact to debunk any theory on the loss of the *Mary Celeste*'s crew, but he still "could not account for their strange disappearance." Deveau's obituary ended not with a remembrance of the old man, who was something of a local celebrity, but of the *Mary Celeste.* It said, "We very much doubt if the mystery will ever be solved."

As the country shed its Victorian ways, the legend of the *Mary Celeste* reflected those changes, taking on a much more sinister tone. The dawning of yellow journalism was evident in new stories of the Ghost Ship, which were often cruel hoaxes hinting of lust, illicit affairs or psychotic behavior on the part of Benjamin Briggs. The family's only comfort was that, aside from Fosdyk, people almost invariably misnamed him.

Fosdyk was not even the first of the year. On several occasions in 1913 the *Mary Celeste* dominated headlines on both sides of the Atlantic. That so many grand claims and wild accusations surfaced in one year hardly could have been coincidence; clearly they were feeding off one another.

It was a strange time to contemplate forty-year-old mysteries, as the world was on the brink of war. The end of fighting in the Balkans was merely a calm before the much larger storm of World War I. In the United States, lifestyles were about to change more than anyone realized, with the sale of the first electric refrigerator in Chicago and the start-up of horseless-carriage production by a man named Henry Ford. Both his assembly-line method of mass production and his automobile, which he called the Model T, would have a major impact on the new century.

Congress kept busy changing the nation's Constitution, in the middle of a stretch that would see a total of four amendments. Just that year, Congress ratified the sixteenth amendment, establishing a nationwide income tax. Women marched on Washington demanding the right to vote, which would be accorded them a half dozen years later with an amendment that was at least more popular than its predecessor, which had the gall to outlaw liquor.

Even with all that to consume a nation—and a world—most people were instead distracted by the tragedy of the White Star Line's great ship the year before. The April 14, 1912, sinking of the *Titanic* had captivated the world, in no small part because she had been hailed as "unsinkable." Survivors regaled reporters with stories of survival in the icy waters of the North Atlantic, of the spectacle of watching the mighty ship slip below dark blue waters.

While the *Titanic* was easily the greatest maritime disaster of all time, there was never a lull between ship disasters; such is the way of the sea. But the loss of the White Star liner seemed to mark an unusually busy, and tragic, era on the water. By the end of 1913, dozens of vessels had been lost, including nineteen ships that disappeared in a fierce November storm on Lake Superior, costing Canada and the United States nearly 250 sailors in three days.

In the midst of these maritime disasters several people dredged up the *Mary Celeste*. Of course, it had never completely gone away—only gotten stranger. Just after the turn of the century, one sailor claimed to have found a skeleton clutching a message in a bottle on one of the tiny islands of St. Paul's. Inside the bottle was an account, written in German, of a steamer abducting the crew of a small, becalmed brig and later killing them. Then, a few years before the *Titanic* tragedy, a man unveiled a cryptic cipher message purporting to solve the mystery. He claimed the bizarre puzzle had been found at the offices of the *Gibraltar Chronicle*, but the editors denied it and the suspicious Ramon Alvarado of Cincinnati soon disappeared.

Scarcely a month after Fosdyk's account surfaced—in the same issue of the *Nautical Gazette* that debunked the servant's tale, in fact—someone came forward with a new account of piracy on the North Atlantic. The *Gazette* declared the tale of Demetrius a "much more likely story" than Fosdyk's.

It originally had appeared in the *Nautical Magazine* of Glasgow as a reminiscence of Captain Dmitri Lukhmanov, who was identified as an "agent of the Russian Volunteer fleet at Hong Kong." The captain wrote that in 1884 a Greek sailor named Demetrius Specioti claimed to have sailed aboard the Ghost Ship under an assumed name. After a routine trip across the Atlantic, he said the crew of the *"Marie Celeste"* was lost not far from Gibraltar when they were shanghaied by a gang of pirates.

The ship had been flying the British flag when Captain Briggs spotted it, Specioti said, and someone on the vessel signaled that they were short of provisions and starving. Briggs invited them to refresh their supplies from his stores, so the ship sent over a launch. When it came alongside, the *Marie Celeste*'s crew noticed there was only one man at the oars, and a huge tarp covered the rest of the boat. After the boat was tied up, pirates jumped from beneath the tarp and overpowered Briggs and his men. The pirates explained that they had lost much of their crew to disease and needed extra hands to man their ship. Demetrius said the pirates left the *Marie Celeste* deserted for the *Dei Gratia* to find.

The crew's demise came later, Demetrius claimed. The pirates treated the men of the *Marie Celeste* reasonably well, but the fever that had killed the ship's original crew eventually claimed Briggs, his wife and daughter. Following their captain's death, the rest of the *Marie Celeste's* crew hatched a plan to overtake their captors, but waited too long to act. That night an Italian mail steamer hit the pirate ship, sinking it and killing everyone on board except, conveniently, Demetrius. He said that in the confusion he managed to get aboard the Italian ship and secure passage to the next port.

In 1873, newspapers might have bought Demetrius's tale, but by 1913, conventional wisdom had changed. Even though there had been a few documented incidents of pirates taking ships near the African coast as recently as the 1890s, no one paid much attention to Demetrius Specioti's story.

The pattern was set.

Every new, sensational story came to light in one of two ways. Either there was a deathbed confession or someone—usually a seafaring man—told a strange tale he claimed had been related to him by another sailor on a dark, boring night at sea. It's impossible to say whether these were deliberate hoaxes or just the stories that men told to pass the time. They shared only one thing in common: nearly all the details were wrong—the spelling of the ship's name, the number of crewmen, the names of the people on board, even the port from which it sailed. It seemed no one even tried to stick to the facts. Of course, by that time the line between fact and fiction, long eroding, had all but disappeared. Even the Briggs family couldn't keep all of it straight, often calling the ship the *Marie Celeste.*

In 1924, Captain Howard Lucy told reporters a tale of mysterious treasure that he claimed had been related to him years earlier by a bo's'n mate on a voyage through the South Seas. The man, who Lucy called Triggs, said he'd been the bo's'n on the *Mary Celeste's* infamous voyage and that there was no tragedy. The ship had been only a day from the coast of Portugal when the crew spied a drifting steamer, and Captain Benjamin Briggs ordered six men to check it out. On board the deserted ship, the sailors found an iron safe filled with gold worth £3,500.

Briggs ordered the men to take the gold and scuttle the ship to cover their tracks. But worried in hindsight about the legality of what he'd done, Briggs decided he and his crew should disappear as well. He was ready to scuttle the *Mary Celeste* when a passing merchant vessel spotted them. Believing that a ship foundering on a calm day would raise eyebrows, Briggs instead chose to abandon the freighter in lifeboats—it was never clear whether "Triggs" meant the *Mary Celeste*'s yawls, or ones taken from the steamer. Either way, the name of a London schooner was painted on the boats and the entire crew set off for Cadiz, where they disappeared with the money.

Once again, the press bought it.

London newspapers proclaimed that Captain Lucy had revealed the answers sought for years. By introducing greed as a motive, the yarn played to lingering suspicions and gave it immediate credibility. Never mind that there was no record of a lost steamer matching that description, or of any such treasure disappearing, it sounded plausible: men making off with gold, however slight the amount. According to this story, Briggs orphaned his only son for a mere £1,200 worth of gold.

The most interesting aspect of the story was how it reversed the roles of Briggs and Morehouse. In this version, it is Briggs who comes across a derelict. Perhaps it seemed a tad too serendipitous. Soon, reporters sought out Lucy with additional questions, but the captain disappointed newspapers, saying he could provide no further details. Lucy told the *London Daily Express* he had heard the story forty years earlier and that Triggs was long dead. Backpedaling, Lucy said he believed Triggs had been an assumed name anyway, and suggested the man could have been one of the actual *Mary Celeste* sailors using a not-very-creative nom de plume.

Through all the years of incredible stories and unseemly accusations, the Briggs family had remained quiet, refusing to dignify such tripe with a denial. No one bothered to correct the misstatements—no matter how great the publicity—because they believed it would do no good, and could only bring painful memories to the surface. But the Triggs story, with its insinuations of theft and desertion, was more than they could bear. This time, the family could not remain quiet.

"As Captain Benjamin S. Briggs of the *Marie Celeste* [sic] was a cousin of mine and the said story reflects very unjustly upon his character, I have been appealed to, as one of the family, to set the record straight," Dr. Oliver Cobb of Easthampton, Massachusetts, wrote in the October 26, 1924, *New York Times.* "Captain Briggs was a Christian gentleman. He belonged to a family of shipmasters who lived up to the best traditions of the sea. To represent him as a criminal deserter of his ship is to desecrate his memory, and any such slanderous statement is resented by the family."

Cobb and other members of the Briggs family thought speaking out might quell the idle talk. But it was a changing world. The last whaling ships were leaving New Bedford, and the days of sail—the days of the seafaring Briggses—had passed. Truth no longer counted for much. Things that had long been thought impossible were now being proved quite possible. In a few years, in fact, a man would *fly* across the Atlantic.

By then, the legend of the Ghost Ship would be almost completely out of control.

In June 1925, *Chambers's Journal of Literature, Science and Arts* published "The Truth about the *Marie Celeste:* A Survivor's Tale," written by a man who went by the name Lee Kaye. At first glance, it only seemed to be more of the same: a secondhand story told by a sailor who had not even bothered to check his facts. But Kaye provided one element no one else had. He claimed that John Pemberton, the source of the account, was still alive.

Pemberton seemed to confirm the worst suspicions of Frederick

Solly Flood, and added even more tawdry twists. On that fateful cruise, he claimed there were tragic deaths and murders coincidental to the true purpose of the voyage, which was insurance scam.

Pemberton said he had joined the *Marie Celeste* as ship's cook in 1870, before Benjamin Briggs took over as captain. The crew that Briggs commanded in 1872 was shorthanded, Pemberton recalled, because he could find few sailors who wanted to sail with whale oil as cargo. Perhaps that is why Briggs had to hire a "sad bully" named Hullock as his mate. According to Pemberton, Hullock and Briggs did not like each other because the mate had once asked for Sarah Briggs's hand in marriage. She refused, and Hullock blamed Briggs for keeping him away from the woman he loved.

Pemberton said Briggs also was in cahoots with the *Dei Gratia's* captain—named "Moorhouse" in this account—to carry the *Marie Celeste's* excess cargo. In exchange for giving him a piece of the charter, Moorhouse allowed Briggs to use some of his men. They would meet off the Azores to transfer sailors and cargo, but Pemberton implied there were more sinister shenanigans in the works.

The trouble began long before the two ships could rendezvous. One day early in the voyage, Mrs. Briggs—who did not have her baby with her—was playing the piano in her cabin during a storm when the lines securing it snapped. The piano thrust forward, slamming Sarah Briggs against the bulkhead, crushing her internal organs. Within a day, she was dead.

Briggs went mad. He accused Hullock of sabotaging the rope, insinuating that it was revenge for Sarah's rebuff. Soon he believed the entire crew was in on the murder, and ordered the steersman thrown overboard. The crew ignored the request, but tossed the piano into the Atlantic in an attempt to pacify the captain's rage. Later that same night Briggs disappeared. When the crew could not find him, Hullock chillingly told one sailor that the captain "went after the piano."

By the end of November, another sailor had been lost overboard in a brawl, and two others deserted in a lifeboat. When the *Dei Gratia* met up with the ship near the Azores and Moorhouse realized only three of his sailors and Pemberton were left on board, he decided to increase his profits. He salvaged the ship, telling the courts he had found the *Marie Celeste* abandoned.

Although the story contained more than its share of factual errors, it found an audience by offering a healthy dose of lascivious details. Elements of unrequited love and jealously made the other stories seem dull by comparison, and the notion that Pemberton was still alive gave the claim extra credibility. The chorus began again: some newspapers immediately hailed this as the answer to the mystery (proving once again an almost infinite gullibility among the press). The family, as it had done with the Triggs story a few years earlier, quickly condemned the tale and denounced it as a cruel fraud.

"To us and many other friends and relatives who waited long for news of these dear ones, and who still mourn their unreturning feet, their story is no fraud or romance, but a great sorrowful tragedy," Oliver Cobb wrote.

But this story would not go away so easily.

Three years later, Pemberton's tale resurfaced in a book titled *The Great* Mary Celeste *Hoax*. The author of the book was Laurence J. Keating which, if for no other reason than his initials, people correctly assumed was Lee Kaye. In his introduction, Keating claimed the noble intention of putting "on record an exact and accurate account of what really did happen on board the vessel during her famous and magical voyage, to explain why and how she was abandoned, and to reveal what became of the crew."

Keating claimed to have interviewed "survivors" and referenced a number of official papers to expose the long-standing mystery, but offered no clue as to where the answers had lay hidden for half a century.

"It would not be possible nor appropriate, in a book of the present dimensions, to include *in extenso* all the reports and documents which have been examined for the purpose of this work, or to recount in detail the complete narratives of the men who have knowledge of the separate phases of the mystery of the *Mary Celeste*," he wrote.

Keating—or Kaye—had corrected some of the most outlandish errors from his magazine article (the result of having so many of them pointed out in reviews and editorials) but still managed to make a mess of things. Stretched out to full-length form, his story was so full of implausible plotlines that it was very nearly nonsensical. But published by reputable houses in both London and New York, the Pemberton story garnered serious attention and reviews in major newspapers around the world. As a result, it became the most successful book on the ghost ship.

At the time *The Great* Mary Celeste *Hoax* appeared, the country was on the brink of the Depression and a little more wary. After an initial round of laudatory reviews, Pemberton was attacked by Cobb, the *New Bedford Standard-Times,* the New York media and Frederick J. Shepard, the librarian in Buffalo. In the *Buffalo News,* Shepard said the book had "scarcely a correctly stated fact in it." Even the painting of the ship in the front of the book looked nothing like the real *Mary Celeste,* Shepard noted. Cooper Gaw, writing in the *New Bedford Standard-Times,* said that *The Great* Mary Celeste *Hoax* was appropriately named, "but not in the sense that the author intended."

The critics were astonished mostly by Keating's flagrant disregard for the well-established facts in the case, and took him to task for it. Eventually the book was almost universally panned, and later reporters—most likely tired of being duped—began to dig into the story. Shepard searched for a "Capt. Penny" of Connecticut who Keating thanked for having done research for the book, but could find no such man. Gaw, who was in touch with the Briggs family, learned that no one had ever heard of a Hullock courting the former Sarah Cobb. Other reporters, meanwhile, searched for bigger fish.

The reaction to *The Great* Mary Celeste *Hoax* was not surprising. Of all the lies told about the *Mary Celeste* over the years, Keating's was undoubtedly the one that made Benjamin Briggs look the worst. Pemberton portrayed Briggs as a hothead drunkard who was scheming to pull off insurance fraud. In short, a man of questionable morals, exactly the opposite of how he had been regarded his entire life. The allegations were so hurtful, so outrageous to the family that Arthur Briggs—Benjamin's son—was compelled to speak publicly about the *Mary Celeste* for the first time in his life.

For years, Arthur Briggs had refused every request for an interview about the *Mary Celeste* incident. He had tried to lead a quiet, digni-fied life after moving back to New Bedford as an adult. There, he be-came a bookkeeper and banker, married and settled down. Normalcy was his refuge.

Even as an old man, the mystery consumed him, which was un-derstandable—it had changed his life. Arthur still had many of the things found on the *Mary Celeste,* but despite the constant reminder of these artifacts, he felt no compulsion to speak out about the inci-dent. Like his father, Arthur was a reticent, reserved man. But when Laurence Keating told Pemberton's story, Arthur Briggs could keep quiet no longer. The frustration was evident in his comments, the words of a sixty-year-old man who had lived with a lifetime of sor-row. Arthur told the *Boston Post:*

> *Why, the man has his facts wrong. It was very easy to prove that his yarn is untrue. In the first place Pemberton wasn't even a member of the crew of the* Mary Celeste. *Another thing—the* Mary Celeste *did not carry a piano. My mother had a melodeon aboard and it was found intact, despite what Pemberton says. The melodeon was returned to my family, along with other things belonging to my mother and father, and we still have it.*
>
> *The cargo of the brig was not oil and lumber as Pemberton would have it, but 1,700 barrels of alcohol.*
>
> *There are other mistakes in Pemberton's story, but why go into them? The fellow's explanation of the mystery is just like a hundred or so other vague yarns that have been advanced; it doesn't jibe with the facts.*

They were Arthur's first—and last—words on the subject.

Arthur Briggs did not live to see his father vindicated. In 1931, at the age of sixty-six, heart disease claimed Benjamin Briggs's only son. He died in New Bedford on October 31, which would have been his little sister's birthday.

Keating did not allow criticism—even from Arthur Briggs—to stop him. He stood by his story and artfully dodged attempts by reporters to interview Pemberton. In 1929, after *The Great* Mary Celeste *Hoax* was published, one reporter traveled to Liverpool for an interview with the man who had unveiled the truth about the great ghost ship. But Keating said the former *Mary Celeste* cook was too sick to talk and refused to grant the reporter an audience. Soon after that, Keating reported that Pemberton had died in a nursing home. A photo of the man ran with the obituary, which seemed to deaden the whiff of scandal, although some of the most ardent followers of the *Mary Celeste* mystery continued to debunk the tale. Ultimately, Keating's account became just another controversial chapter in the legend of the Ghost Ship—some believed it while others denounced it.

Aside from Sir Arthur Conan Doyle, Laurence Keating had the greatest impact on the legend of the *Mary Celeste*. If the details of the story were forgotten, the malevolent overtones the dubious journalist attributed to the mystery would stick. In 1935, a British horror film titled *The Mystery of the* Mary Celeste (released in the United States as *Phantom Ship*) borrowed some of his themes to create a suspenseful melodrama. In the first minutes of the film, Benjamin Briggs proposes to Sarah Cobb, who also has been courted by Captain Morehouse. Sarah agrees to marry Briggs and sail with him on the *Mary Celeste,* but before they can leave Briggs and Morehouse meet and exchange strong words, the *Dei Gratia*'s captain accusing Briggs of stealing the woman he loves. When Briggs has the audacity to later ask Morehouse to borrow one of the *Dei Gratia*'s sailors, his rival agrees, but secretly pays the man to make sure tragedy befalls Briggs on the voyage.

The star of the film was famed horror actor Bela Lugosi, who played Anton Lorenzen, a last-minute addition to the *Mary Celeste*'s crew. For reasons initially left unsaid, Lorenzen sailed under the fictitious name of Gottlieb. Not long into the voyage crewmen begin to die or disappear mysteriously. One man tries to rape Sarah, but is killed by Lorenzen. As the crew is picked off, Briggs becomes increasingly suspicious of mutiny or some other plot. Soon he and Sarah disappear.

With only the first mate, Toby Bilson, Lorenzen and one other sailor left on board the ship, there is the inevitable showdown. Bilson and the other sailor fight, each believing the other is the killer. When the first mate triumphs, he tells Lorenzen they should steal the *Mary Celeste* and sell it in some port—the Azores or Gibraltar. Lorenzen then reveals his identity. He reminds Bilson that six years before he had been shanghaied on the *Mary Celeste,* forced to sail by the mate himself. He then kills Bilson, but, a religious man, Lorenzen either forgets or regrets his actions, running though the ship calling out for Briggs before throwing himself overboard in a storm.

It was Hollywood's first take on the mystery, and although not a particularly well-known film, it only solidified Keating's incarnation of the legend.

More than twenty years later, Macdonald Hastings, the British writer and one-time editor of the *Strand,* made some inquiries about Laurence Keating. While seeking information on the elusive journalist he received a letter from another old ship captain who had met Keating. A mutual friend of the captain and Hastings declared Keating a fake.

Aside from all the other proof that people had compiled over the years to dismiss *The Great* Mary Celeste *Hoax,* the best clue came from this former friend of the journalist. He noted that an *Evening Standard* article from years earlier proved the hoax outright, because the photo of the man purported to be the *Mary Celeste*'s cook "John Pemberton" was no such person.

It was Keating's father.

ELEVEN

Into the Mystic

On the afternoon of December 5, 1945, five Grumman torpedo bombers took off from the naval air station at Fort Lauderdale and banked east over the Atlantic. The planes, called Avengers, flew in tight formation toward the Bahamas, where the crews were scheduled to go through a series of detailed exercises before returning to Florida. It was an advanced lesson in navigation for pilots nearing the end of their apprenticeship. Although World War II had ended just three months earlier, the U.S. military had not become lackadaisical in its training.

The planes had been ordered to fly nearly sixty miles off the coast to the Hen and Chicken Shoals, do some low-level bombing, then change course three more times before returning to base. Even though most of the fourteen men on the five planes were still technically trainees, it wasn't considered a particularly arduous task or difficult flight pattern. It was basically a triangular route.

Flight 19 was supposed to be gone for two hours.

The events of that afternoon would become infamous in part simply because Flight 19's disappearance sparked the largest ocean search and rescue mission to date. The Navy, Coast Guard and scores of private ships combed the Atlantic for five days, but never found a trace of the missing men or their airplanes—not a piece of debris, a lifeboat, or an oil slick. But the most intriguing thing about Flight 19 was the bizarre radio transmissions between the fighters and the base, the way the pilots sounded so disoriented, and so lost. There's also the fact that a search plane sent to find the men went missing as well, and that no one ever learned exactly what happened. Flight 19 became such a frustrating mystery that some historians and journalists called it the *Mary Celeste* of aviation.

Aside from the obvious enigmatic similarities, the two stories had much in common. The circumstances surrounding the disappearance of the Avengers didn't neatly fit one answer. Some of the facts seemed completely contradictory, which led to a series of wildly divergent and outlandish theories. Countless inaccurate facts emerged, often compounded in each succeeding version of the story. Flight 19 took on greater prominence and mythic proportions as the years passed, and its similarities to the Ghost Ship took hold in the minds of people looking for otherworldly solutions to unsolved riddles. Ultimately, stories of the lost squadron and the *Mary Celeste*'s missing crew would form the crux of a new mythology.

Just off the east coast of the United States is one of the busiest shipping lanes in the world, a trade route established by sailors centuries ago, long before European freighters skirted the coast delivering their wares to colonial seaports such as Charleston and Savannah. It can be a treacherous stretch of water. The Gulf Stream courses north less than a hundred miles off the coast in most places, serving as a runway for tropical weather systems that barrel up the eastern seaboard most of the year.

It should come as no surprise that the convergence of a busy shipping lane and consistently unpredictable weather would result in a fair number of disasters at sea—it is the very recipe for trouble. But in the years following the loss of Flight 19, some people began to see a troubling pattern in the Atlantic. One area in particular was the site of dozens of bizarre incidents. Steamers disappeared without so much as a distress call, untended sailboats were found adrift. And it wasn't just water traffic. It seemed that an unusually high number of aircraft also disappeared between San Juan, Miami and Bermuda. In one way or another, many of these disasters evoked the spirit of the *Mary Celeste.*

In January of 1880, a British training ship called the *Atalanta* sailed from Bermuda with nearly 300 people onboard. Shortly after she was listed overdue, London papers began to speculate on the ship's fate, alternately attributing the loss to storms, icebergs or fire. No trace of the *Atalanta* was ever found. In 1918, the USS *Cyclops* disappeared after leaving Barbados bound for the Chesapeake Bay. The ship, also carrying nearly 300 sailors, didn't make a radio transmission after leaving Barbados and never sent a distress signal. Some officials suspected the ship hit a mine, while others blamed the weather.

A few years later, in January 1921, the schooner *Carroll A. Deering* was found deserted on the Diamond Shoals in the legendary Graveyard of the Atlantic. The ship was headed home to Portland, Maine, after a long trip to South America. The *Deering* had appeared to be fine earlier that day when it was spotted passing Cape Lookout at the southern tip of the Outer Banks. But that night, the ship ran aground with its sails set, not far from Cape Hatteras.

Rescue teams fought their way to the shoals to help the crew, but the *Carroll A. Deering* was empty. Its lifeboats were gone, and there was no sign of anyone onboard. Some people said the sailors tried to abandon ship after it ran aground and their lifeboats were swamped. Dredging up the theories associated with the *Mary Celeste,* others blamed piracy, mutiny and insurance fraud. Some accounts included the familiar—and erroneous—detail of hot meals on the galley table.

In 1944, the Coast Guard ran upon a similar situation when the Cuban cargo ship *Rubicon* was found drifting off the coast of south Florida. The *Rubicon* seemed to be in good condition, but was missing a lifeboat and had a mooring line hanging over its bow. A dog was found onboard, but the crew had vanished. In a United Press International story in the *New York Times,* the discovery was called "a maritime mystery reminiscent of that which for a long time involved the *Marie Celeste* [sic]."

While the mid-Atlantic has always been dangerous water for ships, until Flight 19 the area claimed no prominence in aviation lore. That changed shortly after 4 P.M. on December 5, 1945, when the Avengers should have been making their approach to Fort Lauderdale. Lieutenant Robert F. Cox, a trainer at the naval air station, was flying near the base when he picked up some disturbing chatter between two pilots. They sounded confused.

"I don't know where we are. We must have got lost after that last turn," one of the voices said.

After trying for several minutes to reach the men, Cox made radio contact with Lieutenant Charles Taylor, Flight 19's leader. Taylor was a combat veteran with more than 2,500 hours of flying time, who had recently transferred to the Fort Lauderdale base from Miami. Taylor should have known the territory well, but instead told Cox that both of his plane's compasses were "out" and that he didn't know where he was. Taylor said he thought they were flying over the Florida Keys, which, if true, was a major navigational error on the squadron's part.

Cox said that if the planes were flying over the Keys, Taylor needed only to put the sun off his port wing and fly north until he reached Miami. Meanwhile, he would try to intercept the squadron and guide them in. Taylor told him not to bother.

"I know where I am now. I'm at 2,300 feet. Don't come after me."

A few minutes later, Taylor was back on the radio, announcing that he had just flown over a small island and that there was no other land in sight. Clearly, he wasn't in the Keys.

Navy officials were perplexed by the squadron's confusion, but were convinced the planes were flying over the Bahamas. Air-traffic controllers told Taylor to turn his planes west, toward the sun, until they hit land, but he apparently believed the order had come from another plane and ignored it. Transcripts of the radio transmissions show dissension among the squadron. There was no consensus on exactly where they were.

At 5:15, long after the planes were listed as overdue, Taylor announced that they would fly 270 degrees—west, basically—until "we hit the beach or run out of gas." Less than an hour later, however, he turned the planes east. Taylor had decided they were somewhere over the Gulf of Mexico. The squadron was flying in circles. And wherever they were, one thing was apparent: soon the Avengers would run out of fuel and have to ditch. The rescue team would have to move fast, but they had no idea where to begin. Worse still, conditions were deteriorating fast. At Palm Beach, just north of the base, there were reports of foul weather just offshore. Over the Bahamas, there were showers diluting visibility. Whitecaps churned a nasty winter sea. The Atlantic was becoming quite inhospitable.

Long after the planes should have run out of fuel, the control tower was still picking up chatter among Flight 19 pilots. Taylor refused to go to emergency channels, fearing one of his planes wouldn't make the switch and they would lose contact. The trainer was trying to keep his students together. He was recorded telling the other pilots to fly in close formation.

"We'll have to ditch unless landfall . . . when the first plane drops below ten gallons, we all go down together."

Soon after that, there was nothing else from the darkening skies. A short time later, at 7:30, one of the first search planes reported that it was airborne. It was never heard from again.

Flight 19 became a legend every bit as sensational as the loss of the *Mary Celeste*'s crew had been in its day. Postwar America was spellbound, ready to turn its attention from historic—and horrific—events to the distraction of a good mystery. With the coming of radio and television, the world seemed a much smaller place, a place where things didn't just disappear. And unlike their ancestors, twentieth-century Americans were not willing to write off anything as unexplained. Unsolved mysteries were a vacuum abhorred in the modern age. Lacking answers, people soon began to devise their own explanation, and they came up with a solution more fantastic than anything ever blamed for the loss of the Ghost Ship's crew.

The Bermuda Triangle was not actually named until 1964, nearly twenty years after the Avengers vanished. A writer named Vincent Gaddis used the term in an *Argosy* magazine article on the "triangle of death," as some people had taken to calling it. By then, writers had been chronicling the strange disappearances for nearly a decade. In the seven years after Flight 19, a half dozen other planes were lost over the Atlantic, some in similarly peculiar accidents. It seemed there was a pattern to it, and in the early 1950s occult magazines such as *Fate* began speculating on the strange forces at work, sowing the seeds of legend. If nothing else, the pulps had great material to work with between the *Mary Celeste* and Flight 19. The solution that soon evolved was a whopper. Notions of pirates and mutiny—sensational in the *Mary Celeste*'s day—seemed quaint compared to twentieth-century tales of magnetic anomalies in the Earth's crust, Atlantis, UFOs and even dimensional vortexes.

To be sure, there was some dissension among believers. People not only disagreed on why ships and planes disappeared in the "triangle of death," they couldn't even agree on how big it was. Some said it included the Caribbean, others insisted it didn't. The most accepted northern boundary was Bermuda, but others said that it reached all the way up the East Coast of the United States. A few argued that the Triangle extended east all the way to the Azores, neatly folding the site of the *Mary Celeste* incident—and just about every other accident on the Atlantic—into its borders.

It seemed unfathomable that there wasn't something to it all. The sheer number of unexplained disappearances—more than fifty ships and twenty airplanes lost, or their crews missing—was proof enough for many of the landlocked masses that something strange was indeed happening out there. Throughout the 1960s and 1970s the Bermuda Triangle, or the Devil's Triangle in the most sensational accounts, attracted the attention of newspapers, filmmakers and television shows, peaking with Charles Berlitz's best-selling book, *The Bermuda Triangle*. Berlitz's book eventually sold more than 2 million copies—roughly the same as a Stephen King novel would sell a decade later. People have always loved a good, scary story with a healthy dose of the supernatural.

Science has offered a few explanations for why so many shipwrecks might occur in the nebulous boundaries of the Triangle, most of them fairly simple and decidedly unsensational. In recent years, meteorologists have said waterspouts and freak storms that dodge radar are to blame. Bad weather can force—or knock—a crew off a ship as easily as sinking it. Clearly that was the case in some instances, but when facts didn't jibe they were sometimes omitted from the legend. Some of the more titillating Bermuda Triangle accounts neglect to mention the storm damage ships have suffered.

Perhaps the most interesting theory offered by scientists is that ships and planes might get lost because their compasses go haywire, which may have happened to Flight 19. The notion of upset or nonoperational compasses is an element of several Triangle tales, and may be attributed to a natural occurrence. In a 1974 issue of *Sealift* magazine, Howard L. Rosenberg said that spinning or malfunctioning compasses could be a symptom of ships and planes crossing the eightieth meridian, along which "true north and magnetic north are in perfect alignment and compass variation is unnecessary."

Compasses point to a magnetic north near Prince of Wales Island above Canada, but most people navigate using charts that call the North Pole "true north." Depending on where a ship or plane is, the compass variation between the two can be significant. In the Azores, for instance, the difference between "true" and "magnetic" north is 20 percent. Just off the coast of Florida, the variation is nil in some places where the two are in perfect alignment. Oddly enough, the only other place this alignment occurs is in the Pacific Ocean east of Japan, an area that sailors—perhaps not coincidentally—call the "Devil Sea" for its high incidence of disappearing ships. Some scientists say that in both these areas compass deviation may cause some people to wander off course and into trouble.

Critics of that theory and people who believe something far more insidious occurs in the Triangle say the explanation is ludicrous, and they have a point. The compass variation happens only along the eightieth meridian—a relatively small area—and nowhere near where many ships and planes disappear. There are charts that most navigators use to correct for the phenomenon and few, if any, credible accounts of compasses spinning on the meridian line. Not everyone who has fallen victim to the Triangle has been a bumbling incompetent.

The Bermuda Triangle quickly became a melting pot for just about every maritime myth and natural occurrence ever encountered or imagined—mermaids, Atlantis and UFOs. Even sea monsters, which were once blamed for the loss of the *Mary Celeste* crew, were not outside of the realm of possibility. In 1904, the British author J. L. Hornibrook claimed that a giant squid ate the Ghost Ship's sailors. Calling the beast an octopus, Hornibrook speculated that one of its elongated arms first took the helmsman. As he yelled, others came on deck where they too were eventually pulled into the ocean.

While it seems like a tale straight out of Jules Verne, most sailors believe there are a number of these beasts in the ocean. Herman Melville was moved to write of the giant squid in *Moby-Dick,* calling it perhaps an even more sinister creature than the white whale. In Melville's book, the *Pequod's* crew launched their boats at the sight of what they thought was a whale. Coming upon the creature, however, they found "the most wondrous phenomenon which the secret seas have hitherto revealed to mankind. A vast pulpy mass, furlongs in length and breadth, of a glancing cream-color, lay floating on the water, innumerable arms radiating from its centre, and curling and twisting like a nest of anacondas, as if blindly to catch any hapless object within its reach."

Gazing upon the creature, with no "perceptible face," the men of the *Pequod* decided they would sooner fight Moby-Dick than this "white ghost."

The kraken has been a staple of maritime legend for centuries, but it is one fish story that may not be much of an exaggeration. Classic paintings of squid the size of sailing vessels, their tentacles reaching the highest points on a mast, are not as unbelievable as they might seem. Increasingly larger squid—or at least their partial remains—are found nearly every year. There are so many modern accounts of squid attacking ships that it is hard to dismiss them. In the 1930s, the crew of a Norwegian Navy ship claimed they were attacked three times by a giant squid. The beast, at least fifty feet long by the crew's estimate, followed the same pattern each time: it swam alongside the ship, passed it and then lunged onto the bow, tentacles wagging menacingly. Eventually the squid let go, was sucked into the propeller, and came out calamari.

In the 1970s, the USS *Stein* had to be put in dry dock when its sonar suddenly went haywire. Workers inspecting the sonar dome said it was scratched up as if something had clawed it. Embedded in the rubber coating protecting the dome they found giant claws identical to those found on squid tentacles.

The giant-squid theory may have been linked to the *Mary Celeste* solely on the basis of the "strange markings" found on its bow. Even though such creatures may exist, it still was an almost nonsensical solution: Would a crew allow themselves to be plucked off the ship one by one instead of just retreating below deck? But it did not matter that these tales defied logic, for common sense and facts mattered little in some stories. At one point—probably around 1912—one man even claimed that the *Mary Celeste*'s crew abandoned ship because they were on a collision course with an iceberg. Never mind that no icebergs have ever been found as far south as the Azores and Portugal, it was a popular notion in the days after the *Titanic* sank.

A staple of Triangle mythology is the idea that vanishing ships and planes move into another dimension, and may even be in suspended animation waiting to return. This theory supposes there is a vortex leading to this other dimension somewhere in the Triangle, and only ships and planes that cross directly through it disappear. The rest sail or fly on unmolested. Sometimes, according to this logic, a crew may pass through the vortex, but not the ship.

Similar ideas come into play when Atlantis is blamed for the Triangle. As early as 1926, the *British Journal of Astrology* speculated that the *Mary Celeste*'s crew simply dematerialized when the ship sailed over the resting place of the Lost Continent. Although the authors were unclear about the reason, they suspected the Great Pyramids of Egypt were involved. The American psychic Edgar Cayce believed Atlanteans possessed the power of lasers channeled through giant crystals. His theory would become one of the more popular Bermuda Triangle explanations.

The *Mary Celeste* may have been linked to Atlantis by arguments over the fabled city's location. Some say it was in the middle of the Atlantic, others argue it was near Crete or even western Turkey. But some have suggested Atlantis was near the Azores, the spiky island chain that lies in one of the deepest parts of the Atlantic—and is the last documented location of the *Mary Celeste*'s crew. Cayce believed Atlantis to be farther south, and predicted it would rise again in 1968 near Bimini. That year, long after Cayce had died, a pilot discovered a wall of uniformly cut stones in the ocean floor off the island. The Bimini Road, as it is called today, is still considered by some to be the remains of streets or a wall surrounding Atlantis. It is also, incidentally, near the flight path of Flight 19.

For some people, this is all too much to be coincidence.

Although elements of the Bermuda Triangle mystery seem to defy explanation, there have been some inconsistencies in the story, and at times, a few deliberate hoaxes. Much like later versions of the *Mary Celeste* legend, many stories in Triangle lore bear little resemblance to what actually happened. One famous shipwreck attributed to the Triangle was a French sailing vessel called *Rosalie*. In 1840, the ship was allegedly found near Nassau in a condition that, if it happened, foreshadowed the *Mary Celeste* incident: it was cruising with its sails set and without a crew, there was no appreciable damage to the boat, and most versions of the story say the cargo included wine. But the accounts are wildly conflicting. Some say Bahamian officials helped the crew off the ship when it ran aground, and it later floated away. Others insist the ship never even existed.

Flight 19 has been fictionalized about as well as Sir Arthur Conan Doyle could have managed. The first mistakes may even have been unintentional, but by the 1960s the story of the lost Avengers had been stretched so much it barely resembled the actual incident. When interest in the Triangle was at its apex, the most common version of the legend held that the Avengers were flying a routine patrol on a sunny day with a crew of experienced pilots, details that took away the possibilities of an inexperienced crew or bad weather. Vaguely disconcerting quotes often were attributed to the Avenger pilots, such as "Even the ocean doesn't look as it should." Some reports claimed that Taylor had said his compasses were spinning.

Comments from the pilots were sometimes twisted to sound stranger than they actually were. Taylor's innocent remark to Cox—"Don't come after me"—translated in some versions to "Don't come after us," the implication being that aliens or some other malevolent force had them. That reference came just as interest in UFOs was beginning to supplant the Triangle's allure. Eventually, speculation that aliens were behind Triangle disappearances became so common that Steven Spielberg worked it into *Close Encounters of the Third Kind*. At the beginning of the film, the five Avenger planes are returned as sort of an olive branch from the aliens. At the end of the movie, the Flight 19 pilots are returned to, of all places, Wyoming.

The UFO mythology was born in the same era as the "triangle of death" stories that sold tons of pulp magazines in the 1950s. With the first modern UFO sighting in 1947—and a rash of others following soon after—some argued that aliens had visited the Earth for years and we were just catching on. Strange incidents from the past—such as presumably primitive Egyptians building massive pyramids—were soon attributed to UFOs and their pilots. In 1955, a Michigan astronomer named Morris K. Jessup also suggested aliens took the *Mary Celeste*'s crew.

Jessup's speculation on flying saucers, now legendary in the field, is the basis for much of modern UFO mythology. His theory on magnetism (which can make compasses spin) as the possible source of propulsion for flying saucers is still a popular idea. His ideas of alien abduction preceded the twentieth-century rash of reported extraterrestrial kidnappings by at least a decade.

Jessup claimed no particular knowledge or proof of anything that occurred on the *Mary Celeste,* he simply attributed almost everything to aliens, whom he suspected lived somewhere between the Earth and the moon. An entire chapter in his book, *The Case for the UFO,* is devoted to lost ships and crews that may have been taken off the planet (the Flight 19 pilots were victims, too, Jessup said). While ridiculing the idea that a giant octopus ate the *Mary Celeste*'s crew, Jessup nevertheless conceded that, "it cannot be denied that a malignant curse enshrouded this unhappy vessel."

In his book, Jessup recited a remarkably accurate history of the Ghost Ship from its construction to its loss, but doesn't argue that aliens were responsible for all the ship's misfortunes—just its most famous one.

"There are several facts we must stress," Jessup wrote. "First, the upper rigging of the ship was slightly damaged, as if some unusual accident or activity took place there. Then, the compass was damaged. Aside from these, there was no note or disarray or struggle. Life had departed from the ship instantly, apparently with all the routine activities interrupted and no preparations made: log book on the table, clothing in order, sails set, galley undisturbed—but no records in the log anywhere!"

Jessup credited aliens with extraordinary skills in science and engineering, but obviously didn't believe they were perfect. He suggested the people aboard the *Mary Celeste* were teleported by aliens who could navigate the galaxy, but weren't real good in tight spots: they apparently clipped the ship's masts while hovering overhead.

Jessup offered no reason why aliens might abduct anyone, let alone the crew of a tiny nineteenth-century merchant ship. He believed aliens, who had visited Earth throughout history, might only be checking on the progress of man. The crew of the *Mary Celeste* may have just been in the right place at the wrong time.

"There is always the possibility that the open seas provide an easy *catching place,*" Jessup wrote, adding the italics.

Jessup is at least partially responsible for two elements of the ongoing mythology of a widespread UFO cover-up. Not long after *The*

Case for the UFO was published, legend has it, a marked-up copy of the book found its way into government hands. Notes in the margins purported to be a synopsis of something called "The Philadelphia Experiment"—an alleged 1943 incident in which the U.S. Navy teleported one of its destroyers from the docks of the Pennsylvania port to Norfolk, Virginia, in a matter of seconds. Jessup claimed he knew nothing of the matter, but the government—according to the story—pressed the case and he eventually agreed to help them discover who had written the notes.

Near the end of the 1950s, Jessup's friends reported a change in him, as he began to fear his investigations were hitting too close to home. He had written a new book on UFOs and gave copies of the manuscripts to a few close friends "just in case." A few days later, he was found dead in his car in Florida. It was ruled a suicide, but some believe that Jessup was one of the first victims of a shadow organization with links to UFOs known as the Men in Black.

Although the *Mary Celeste* has been drawn into the mystical world that it helped create, it remains a mystery that attracts scientists, historians and sailors who want a more terrestrial answer to the century-old maritime riddle. In the mid-twentieth century, some people found a surprising number of alternative explanations to the puzzle, solutions that had nothing to do with the supernatural. One of the more interesting stories surfaced in 1948, when a former British intelligence agent named Dod Osborne told of being stranded on a vanishing island in the North Atlantic.

It happened in the 1930s near the Arguin Banks, where Osborne had been sailing on the *Girl Pat,* a sixty-eight-footer powered by diesel and sail. The ship was about a hundred miles off French West Africa headed for Dakar when it suddenly appeared that the *Girl Pat,* which had been making fourteen knots, wasn't moving. The boat also seemed to be listing slightly to windward. When the sailors took a sounding, they discovered the boat, which had a ten-foot draft, was in eight feet of water. They had run aground.

Within thirty minutes, all the water beneath the boat had disappeared and the *Girl Pat* sat high and dry on a sand island. It was particularly odd given how far out to sea the ship was. Not only should the ocean have been hundreds of feet deep in the area, but also, tides that close to the equator are not dramatic enough to have such a swing. Osborne said that it "seemed as if a giant hand had grasped the bottom of the boat and lifted her firmly, but very carefully, out of the water. She felt as if she had been placed tenderly on a cushion."

The crew argued whether they should row for the mainland in a lifeboat or even get out and walk around on the sand. Ultimately, they chose to stay on board, perplexed by their predicament. Osborne said, "I noticed that in the excitement none of us had thought to stow the sails."

The next day, the *Girl Pat* sat on an island one mile around and three feet above sea level. In the distance, Osborne could see similar banks rising up out of the Atlantic, one disappearing only hours after it had appeared. The crew of the *Girl Pat* considered striking out for the African coast in a lifeboat, but after seeing the other island sink, they opted to wait. That night, Osborne awoke to the familiar rocking of a floating ship. The island beneath them was disappearing fast— eight feet below the surface one minute, fourteen feet the next. Using the anchor as a winch, they pulled the boat off the sand but were soon stuck on another bank, where they spotted an ominous sight: the ribs of a rusted steamship hull protruding from the sand. Luckily, the ship didn't stay stuck for long this time. By nightfall, the *Girl Pat* was free again.

The sand banks were known to Africans as the Phantom Islands, Osborne learned. French scientists of the day believed the islands were formed by a great underground river flowing beneath the Sahara Desert. The river deposits sand from the desert between sixty and one hundred miles out to sea. When the outlet of the river clogs, pressure eventually builds up, causing the mounds of sand to belch out of the ocean.

Osborne said that while the *Girl Pat* was grounded 600 miles south of the coordinates where the *Dei Gratia* crew found the *Mary*

Celeste, he believed the Ghost Ship had sailed to that spot empty after it was released from one of these disappearing islands.

Because Briggs most likely sailed using dead reckoning, it would not have been uncommon for the *Mary Celeste* to be off course by several hundred miles, Osborne said—and the *Girl Pat* had not been at the northern extreme of the Phantom Islands. By that reasoning, Briggs and company could have been stuck much closer to the spot where the *Dei Gratia*'s crew found the ship.

"If a steamship can err 20 miles in an 80-mile trip, it would be easy for a sailing ship to err 600 miles in a 3,000-mile crossing of the Atlantic—and they frequently did," Osborne said. Storms in the Azores that fall could have pushed the *Mary Celeste* far enough south to run into the Phantom Islands.

"The rest is easy to imagine: the captain and his wife and child and the crew crowding into the lifeboat and rowing away from the island, as my men wanted to do; the journey to the mainland and the terrible, final ordeal on the hot sands of the desert. Their chances of survival in the desert in 1872 were smaller than ours would have been in 1936," Osborne wrote, unveiling his theory in *Life* magazine.

After that, the *Mary Celeste* would have been released from its perch and prevailing winds and currents would have pushed it back to the northwest, where it was found.

There are other natural phenomena that have been blamed for the disappearance of the *Mary Celeste*'s crew, occurrences rare enough to startle even a veteran mariner such as Benjamin Briggs, but not so far outside the realm of possibility as to be easily dismissed. As it turned out, one of those ideas in particular would fittingly turn up as an explanation for lost ships in the Bermuda Triangle.

In 1966, a former New England sailor and veteran of the Navy's Hydrographic Office concluded that Benjamin Briggs and his crew were most likely scared off the *Mary Celeste* during an encounter with a waterspout. Gershom Bradford offered several examples of the fury of waterspouts in the form of testimonials from survivors: how waterspouts spawn winds capable of ripping sails and flooding crew quar-

Abandoned ship manned by ghost crew

The same marine tradition that shaped Atlantic's insurance protection for the *Mary Celeste* produces better business insurance for you today

When the spanking brigantine *Mary Celeste* cleared New York Harbor in November of 1872, her destination was Genoa, Italy. But the 10 souls aboard sailed only into oblivion, and tragic fame.

Nearly a month after her departure she was sighted in the mid-Atlantic, sailing on the starboard tack, ghost-like out of the mist. Weather was not severe, and she appeared to be making normal progress.

But there was an alarming quiet about her. When she was hailed, no one answered. When she was boarded, not a person was found. There was ample food and water. The cargo was intact. The ship was absolutely sound. To this day, no one has ever unraveled the mystery of why the passengers and crew of the *Mary Celeste* vanished without a trace.

Five American companies carried the insurance on the *Mary Celeste* on that fateful voyage. Only one survives today—the Atlantic. As a marine insurer, Atlantic's philosophy of protection has always been to write sound, quality coverage for all insurable risks—and pay claims promptly, fairly and ungrudgingly. This broad-minded approach of always doing what's best for the policyholder has guided Atlantic for 123 years.

What does this mean to you today? Simply this. When you insure your business, your home, your car or your boat with the Atlantic Companies, you can rely not only on the best insurance protection, but you may also expect your claims to be settled in the true tradition of the marine insurer—promptly, fairly and ungrudgingly.

And since we believe that an independent insurance agent or broker serves you best, that's the *only* way Atlantic sells its quality protection.

THE ATLANTIC COMPANIES
ATLANTIC MUTUAL · CENTENNIAL · 45 Wall Street, New York

This 1965 magazine advertisement from Atlantic Mutual depicts the moment the *Dei Gratia* sailors spotted the *Mary Celeste* abandoned at sea. The ad illustrates the pop-culture appeal of the Ghost Ship legend. Atlantic Mutual held a policy on the ship's cargo on its infamous voyage. *Permission and license to use the photograph is granted by the Atlantic Mutual Insurance Company* ters with water; how the damage, like that of a tornado, can be erratic, tearing one thing to shreds while a few yards away something else is left undisturbed.

It is one of the more intriguing theories, but Bradford had to defend it from the normal question: why, in such weather, would Briggs abandon a hundred-foot ship for a yawl? Bradford said the crew of the *Mary Celeste* didn't abandon ship—at least not initially. The crew survived the encounter, Bradford speculated, but while checking their damage in the "vacuum-like" condition they had just been through, found six feet of water in the hold where there had been little or none minutes before. Believing the *Mary Celeste* was sinking, the crew then abandoned ship. Bradford said the weather conditions could have drawn more water into the sounding pipes than there really was in the hold, rightfully alarming the crew.

Once the crew left the ship, Bradford said, Briggs most likely noticed the *Mary Celeste* was riding fine in the water; that it was not sinking at all. But catching up to the brig was not an option. Headwinds, and the ship's greater length and speed, soon put them out of reach, and the entire crew perished later in another gale.

Bradford had no proof of waterspouts in the Atlantic on that day, and there would have been no way to prove that even then. Still, his idea is considered one of the better theories of Briggs's disappearance. Whether he is right or not, Bradford at least may have come close to uncovering the final moments of the *Mary Celeste*'s crew, something more likely than sea monsters, the Triangle and little green men.

Something even more frightening.

TWELVE

Without a Soul

In later years, the Ghost Ship haunted his dreams.

The sea had taken many people Oliver Cobb loved and admired, but the *Mary Celeste* had done something worse. It tainted them. As he grew older, it became a dark presence overshadowing precious memories of a world long since passed. The ship had become to him the personification of the Briggs family tragedy.

Perhaps it was Cobb's decision to write a memoir that stirred his preoccupation with the mystery, or it could have been the string of cruel hoaxes that besmirched his lost cousin's name. With the death of the last Briggses who remembered Benjamin and Sarah, he may have considered himself the only survivor of the seafaring clan. And while his elders had been reticent to speak of the tragedy, Cobb wasn't. He thought it was time to turn the tide.

Born in 1858, Cobb was twenty-three years younger than Benjamin Briggs but in some ways felt as close to him as a brother. Cobb lived at Rose Cottage periodically while growing up, and in fact his fondest childhood memory was spending the fall of 1867 in the grand home. He remembered doing daily chores at the direction of Captain

Nathan Briggs and, in the evenings, listening to the old salt and his
friends recount their days before the mast. Because they were most
often away on their own journeys, Cobb saw the Briggs boys infrequently (although he would eventually ship out once with Oliver). In
his memoir, *Rose Cottage,* Cobb wrote with wonder about those rare
festive occasions when the entire Briggs family gathered. It was the
very portrait of the New England seafaring life. At one dinner when
most of the brothers were home, Cobb recalled, the family had
brewis—a dish of fish and hardtack that, being standard shipboard
fare, was one of Mother Briggs's specialties. James took so much that
Oliver teased him by asking, "James, will you please pass the platter?"

Mother Briggs scolded her son, "Why, Oliver, that is his plate."

"Oh, excuse me," Oliver said, "I mistook it for the platter."

Such light moments were scarce for the doomed family. Within a
few years of that Sunday dinner, Cobb noted, most of the people at
the table were dead.

Cobb had witnessed the end of an era, the end of the days of sail,
and the end of a family. He was there in the winter that the last of the
family's seafaring men disappeared, and the fall prior to it, when Benjamin and Sarah Briggs had made their plans to sail on the *Mary Celeste.*

"They expected to be very comfortable," Cobb recalled. "I well
remember plans for this voyage. Captain Ben told Sarah that Mr.
Richardson was going with him as mate; he had been with Captain
Briggs before this."

At the time, it had seemed both exotic and routine—just another
transatlantic trip. But young Oliver Cobb's ideals were destroyed a few
months later when word reached Rose Cottage that Benjamin
Briggs, Sarah and Sophy had gone missing.

Cobb first spoke publicly about the *Mary Celeste* after Benjamin
Briggs was accused of lurid behavior and criminal scheming by one
hoaxer. For years, he had been struggling to find his own solution to
the mystery, something that might have given his cousin reason to
leave the ship. Casual conversations with sailors, his own experiences

at sea, and years of thought had steered him to a single conclusion. During the Pemberton controversy in 1926 Cobb told the *Boston Post* that, "Undoubtedly the crew of the *Mary Celeste* abandoned their vessel because they feared an explosion."

Cobb said the decision to desert ship was most likely prompted by a rumbling in the hold, which—as it had been explained to him—sometimes happened on vessels that carried alcohol if the hold wasn't vented properly. Cobb believed building pressure in the watertight belly of the ship greatly concerned Briggs, who had never hauled alcohol before and was overly cautious with his family aboard.

Although the crew attempted to take in sail before launching the lifeboat, Cobb speculated that accumulating gases blew the ship's fore hatch into the air, where it landed upside down on the deck. That frightened the men so badly that they fled without bothering to finish furling the sails or lashing the wheel.

"In their haste, they neglected to attach a line to the vessel by which they could be towed," Cobb said. "That was a mistake, but an understandable one."

When the crew realized the *Mary Celeste* was not going to explode, Cobb said, it was too late to catch up to the ship. Benjamin Briggs, his family and crew perished sometime later, either because the lifeboat capsized or they ran out of provisions before reaching land.

Cobb had weighed this scenario for years, and ultimately found it preferable to James Briggs's idea that his brother deserted because he feared the becalmed *Mary Celeste* was drifting too close to the rocky shore of St. Mary's. Cobb believed his theory fit the facts better. Soon he began to correspond with other men also drawn to the Ghost Ship, notably an Atlantic Mutual executive named Charles Edey Fay. The two men traded information and ideas and, over time, Cobb's theory evolved. By 1940, when he was eighty-two, Cobb published his solution in *Yachting* magazine. His basic premise was unchanged from a dozen years earlier, only the details tweaked.

"I think that, the cargo of alcohol having been loaded in cold weather at New York early in November and the vessel having crossed the Gulf Stream and being now in comparatively warm weather, there may have been some leakage and gas may have accumulated in the hold," Cobb wrote in *Yachting*. "The captain, having care for his wife and daughter, was probably unjustifiably alarmed and, fearing a fire or an explosion, determined to take his people in the boat from the vessel until the immediate danger should pass."

In the intervening years, Cobb had made one noticeable change to his theory. He now suspected that Benjamin Briggs had taken the mainsail halyard as a towline for the lifeboat. But before the crew could make it back to their ship, the towline snapped.

Cobb's theory was endorsed by Fay, who at the time was finishing one of the most comprehensive accounts of the *Mary Celeste* mystery. The idea also seemed plausible in the maritime industry. Insurance agents of the day considered exploding alcohol a common danger on cargo ships. Sailors had reported that "the escaping gases from kegs of alcohol, in a warm climate and in the hold of a pitching ship, might make heavy rumbling noises, and even cause a spontaneous explosion of the gases, sufficient to blow off the hatch without actually setting off the entire cargo."

Either because of Cobb's ties to the Briggses or Fay's endorsement, the idea of a pressure-cooker cargo hold on the *Mary Celeste* became the most widely accepted explanation for what caused Benjamin Briggs and his crew to abandon his ship in the fall of 1872. For people with little interest in the more supernatural or fantastic theories, it has stood for more than sixty years as the most reasonable scenario.

The problem is, it could not have happened that way.

On November 7, 1872, after suffering two days of battering winds and rain in New York Harbor, the *Mary Celeste* sailed from its anchorage off Staten Island. A harbor pilot guided the ship to the open water beyond Sandy Hook, where Benjamin Briggs, his family and crew disappeared over the horizon.

It is possible to reconstruct their next two weeks with a fair degree of accuracy. The *Mary Celeste* sailed a course that on a map would appear to arc north toward Newfoundland and, in fact, it did. The Great Circle route, which takes into account the curvature of the Earth, was the shortest path to Europe—a 3,000-mile trek from New York. Along this busy trade route they might have passed within sight of several ships over the course of the voyage, although no one ever reported talking to the *Mary Celeste*'s crew.

For nearly the entire trip, the weather was almost unbearably rough. The December 7, 1872, issue of the *Shipping and Commercial List* of New York said that "The present year has been rather more than unusually fruitful of tempestuous weather and gales on both sides of the Atlantic, and the percentage of marine disasters must have been above the average."

Anecdotes from sailors supported that claim. In late November, sailors on the steamer *Baltic* arrived in New York telling of a two-day gale on November 18 and 19 that must have played havoc on every ship in the vicinity. The following day, in fact, the *Baltic* crew had to rescue the men of one ship that sank during the blow. Several other vessels mentioned encountering the same storm. The *Mary Celeste*—in the same vicinity—most likely ran afoul of the same weather.

Sailing through those storms the entire crew worked very nearly around the clock to keep the brigantine on course and afloat. On a normal cruise, there would have been two watches: Briggs would have taken three men, Richardson the others. Working four-hour shifts allowed half the sailors to rest while the others worked. But based on the reports of other ships sailing through the North Atlantic in November 1872, the crew of the *Mary Celeste* did not have that luxury. The dangerous blows barely let up on them for the entire voyage.

On November 24, the ship closed to within a hundred miles of the Azores, where it skirted a storm with winds of nearly forty miles per hour that must have kept the crew nervous throughout the night. No doubt the sailors were exhausted, punchy—perhaps not even thinking clearly. The rain didn't help matters.

Sometime in the predawn hours of the next morning, the rain and wind stopped. The *Mary Celeste* was sailing southeast past the Azores, keeping the chain to port. The light weather was a welcome relief and gave the crew a chance to retire to their bunks for some rest. At 5 A.M., the man on watch spotted Santa Maria—St. Mary's, southern-most of the Azores. Three hours later, at 8 A.M., the *Mary Celeste* sailed six miles southeast of the island on an east by south heading.

Shortly after that, something went horribly wrong.

In Sir Arthur Conan Doyle's *The Sign of the Four,* Sherlock Holmes said that "when you have eliminated the impossible, whatever re-mains, *however improbable,* must be the truth . . ." Applying that logic to the *Mary Celeste,* it is possible to exclude nearly every theory about the crew's disappearance. Had Doyle been privy to the information now available, J. Habakuk Jephson may have made a very different statement.

Over the years, the most credible solutions to the *Mary Celeste* mystery have centered on natural phenomena—violent storms, water-spouts, even shifting islands. While they are plausible theories, they are also impossible to verify. A waterspout could have chased the crew off the *Mary Celeste*—and there is some evidence that might suggest it—but there is nothing that proves it. In fact, it's unlikely that any of these things would make Benjamin Briggs leave his vessel. Unless the deck was awash, the entire crew would not abandon ship because they be-lieved that it *might* sink. To do otherwise would have been suicidal, for in such horrible conditions a damaged hundred-foot ship would still be better than a twenty-foot lifeboat. The fact that the ship survived proves it didn't see weather that was too severe.

Every scenario offered over the years has hinged on sudden trauma—a catastrophe that unfolded so quickly Briggs and his crew did not have time to read the situation correctly, react properly or col-lect their belongings. But there is no real sign of panic in the sparse clues left behind. For 130 years, the most obvious solution has been overlooked. The evidence that is available suggests an altogether dif-ferent end for the crew.

Meteorological reports show that just after passing the Azores the *Mary Celeste* sailed into a patch of calm weather with almost no wind. Even though the lack of breeze brought the voyage to a stop, it was a welcome relief after the stormy weather. It gave the crew a chance to relax for a bit, and Benjamin Briggs an opportunity to do something he'd been forced to put off for more than two weeks. Becalmed, he finally had the chance to ventilate his hold.

The weather on the Atlantic had been so bad that month the *Dei Gratia* crew had not opened their ship's main hatch for more than an hour in three weeks. It was not an ideal situation as the *Dei Gratia* carried a hold full of petroleum—cargo that definitely needed to air out occasionally. Briggs had the same problem with his alcohol, but fighting the same weather, probably had not had the chance to open his hatches either.

According to a report from the American consul at Genoa, nine barrels of alcohol in the *Mary Celeste*'s hold had busted open at some point in the voyage—most likely between the time the ship left New York and when it was found derelict, which is when it encountered the worst weather. That means at some point while Briggs and his crew were still onboard, 450 gallons of the chemical spilled into the ship's bilge. Lighter than water, the alcohol floated on top of whatever was already in there.

For years, most people assumed the alcohol the *Mary Celeste* hauled was whiskey, rum or even denatured, "raw" spirits being exported to fortify Italian wine. The bills of lading for the voyage have been lost, so there is no way to know for certain. Contemporary to the event, however, some people claimed the alcohol was not potable, an argument used to refute the drunken-crew theory. The few clues and descriptions of the cargo that survive support that idea, and suggest that on its most famous voyage the *Mary Celeste* carried some sort of industrial alcohol.

According to Oliver Deveau's testimony, the wooden casks in the ship's hold were stamped with the generic word "alcohol." Several years before the *Mary Celeste* sailed from New York, in the 1860s, the United States government began to tax liquor. If the ship had carried distilled spirits of some sort, the barrels should have been covered with tax stamps and descriptions of what variety of drink—whiskey, rum or brandy—was inside. Most distillers printed not only the type of liquor on these barrels, but also included their brand names. A barrel with the generic notation of "alcohol" was more likely some sort of industrial or medical chemical, a methanol or even formaldehyde ("medical" alcohol has been listed in some accounts of the mystery, in fact). It would not have been out of the ordinary for the *Mary Celeste* to carry such a cargo. The United States was routinely shipping various industrial alcohols to Europe in the mid-nineteenth century for use both as fuel and solvents. In Deveau's court testimony, he specifically said there were no spirits on board the ship.

As with everything in the case, there are contradictory facts. The U.S. consul in Genoa listed the alcohol as having a specific gravity of 0.815, and declared it 93.95 proof. While the specific gravity (which refers to weight; the alcohol was lighter than water) is consistent with various alcohols—including methanol—the proof suggests a distilled spirit. But the consul could have made a mistake. Proof is a number derived by doubling the alcohol by volume content (a whiskey that is 90 proof is actually 45 percent alcohol by volume). For a layman, it is an easy statistic to confuse. The 93.95 could have represented either the alcohol by volume or its purity, which would beyond a doubt be some kind of industrial alcohol. The oddest thing about the consul's statistics is that 93.95 percent is an extremely unusual proof designation for a distilled spirit, according to experts in the industry. But alcohol that is nearly 94 percent pure would be consistent with methanol used for industrial purposes.

The most telling clue survives in the Maritime Register. According to New York Harbor records, the *Mary Celeste* spent a week at Hunter's Point just before it sailed. The register lists the ship at Manhattan's Pier 44 on October 16, 1872, and Hunter's Point on October 23. By October 30, the ship was back in the city, this time moored at Pier 50. Hunter's Point is in Queens (across the East River from the United Nations building) and in 1872, it was a veritable industrial park in Long Island City, home to several refineries and factories. The area became so overrun with chemical plants making such things as varnish and solvents that by 1890 residents were complaining of the toxic mess in the water. If the *Mary Celeste* was picking up cargo there—as it undoubtedly was in the week before it sailed—it was probably taking on some sort of industrial chemical.

If there had been distilled spirits in those barrels, it is practically impossible that there was a "rumbling" in the hold as Cobb and other sailors contended. There was nowhere near enough heat to make any kind of alcohol volatile enough to threaten explosion. Cobb attributed the alcohol problems to the weather: He said the *Mary Celeste* left New York in cold weather, crossed the warming waters of the Gulf Stream and ran into trouble off the notoriously moderate Azores. In fact, the temperatures in New York the week Briggs sailed hovered around the forties and fifties. The Azores got no warmer than the sixties, a differential that would have had no impact on alcohol. The temperature in the hold would have to exceed 200 degrees Fahrenheit to have any effect on the barrels.

Instead, the problem came from the alcohol that seeped from those barrels.

The American consul in Genoa reported that nine barrels were empty, but there was never any accounting for the lost chemicals. If 450 gallons of distilled spirits had spilled into the *Mary Celeste*'s bilge, the captain and crew would not have noticed until the ship was unloaded. No whiskey, bourbon or rum would give off fumes potent enough to even make a person dizzy. But if 450 gallons of methanol or formaldehyde were poured into the ship's hold, it could have had serious physiological effects on the crew. It could have caused them to become light-headed or nauseous. A potent enough whiff of certain kinds of methanol could even cause hallucinations. Because it is lighter than water, the alcohol would have stayed in the bilge, floating on top of any seawater, until the hold was pumped completely dry. (It is unlikely there was much water in the bilge when Briggs and his crew were onboard, anyway. The 3½ feet of water found by the *Dei Gratia*'s crew undoubtedly accumulated during the ten days the *Mary Celeste* sailed with her hatches open.)

Depending on the type of alcohol, the stench alone would have been enough to force the crew to seek fresh air, as some industrial alcohols are about as tolerable as ammonia. The men of the *Dei Gratia* did not mention encountering a foul stench on the ship when they found it, but by then the ship had sailed for ten days through winds strong enough to tatter its foresails. Perhaps the sailors, already numb to the chemical smells on their own ship, just didn't notice whatever faint trace was left. There are unsubstantiated accounts of people mentioning the ship's rank smell when it was moored in Gibraltar, but there is better evidence that something foul had infested the *Mary Celeste*. In their court testimony, the *Dei Gratia*'s sailors described a ship that had all its hatches, doors, skylight and many of its windows left open.

A ship that had been left to air out.

Briggs was in a dilemma. He had the vapors of an industrial chemical seeping from the hold and no breeze to stir the air. At least in his mind—if not in truth—sealing the hold could be dangerous. But if the hatches were left open, the crew might pass out or be sickened by the fumes. With the ship becalmed, the vapors hung in the air, as suffocating as a wet blanket. There was little they could do for relief but get off the ship until it passed. Briggs may have realized what happened and had the men pump out the bilge, which is why the *Dei Gratia*'s crew found the sounding rods and other pump equipment lying about on deck. But even after the chemicals were drained from the bilge, the fumes would have hung in the air for a while. To ventilate the ship, they would have left the pumps off the sounding pipes that reached from the bilge to the deck. Left unobstructed, the pipes offered a measure of ventilation. The crew also would have opened every hatch, door and window they could before departing, not taking the time to unseal the portholes nailed shut or covered with canvas during the storms.

That is why the ship was so *wet*.

Sailors learn quickly that on the ocean it is unwise to leave a ship unbuttoned. Left open, everything onboard invariably gets drenched—not so much from sudden squalls as the waves that invariably break over the bow. It is the same principle that dictates sailors more often than not wear foul-weather gear. But the *Mary Celeste* was left almost completely opened. The testimony of the *Dei Gratia* sailors differs slightly on the position of the hatches when they found the ship. Some of them said only the lazaret and fore hatches were open, while others said "all" hatches were. If the main hatch was not completely uncovered, it was only because they could not get to it until they removed the lifeboat strapped over the opening. Regardless, there are only two reasons to leave a ship as vulnerable to the weather as the *Mary Celeste:* to scuttle it—or air it out.

The clues found on the ship fit the scenario perfectly: Everything was wet because the *Mary Celeste* had been opened up to allow a breeze to pass through. The men weren't wearing their foul-weather gear because it was a clear, moderate day. They were not carrying their pipes because, with the fumes wafting through the ship, no one dared light a smoke. Then there are the things they left behind. If they had thought the ship was sinking, the crew would have taken important papers, navigational equipment and the logbook. Over the years, dozens of people dreamed up wild stories about why the *Mary Celeste* sailors left all their clothes, their valuables and the rest of their belongings onboard without concluding the most obvious: *because they expected to come back.*

In his salvage hearing testimony, *Mary Celeste* owner James H. Winchester makes it clear that neither Briggs nor Richardson would have deserted the ship unless they thought it was sinking, or it was the only way to save their own lives. In fact, neither man had to make the choice. On the morning of November 25, the crew believed they were simply getting off the ship temporarily. There was no immediate danger to the ship—just the crew—so they weren't going through a normal checklist. They didn't take the ship's important papers or any of their belongings. They likely did not carry much, if any, food. They saw no need to do so. In the open ocean, there was no question they would stick close by.

With the mainsail down, it was a fairly simple matter to use the peak halyard—the rope that drew the sail up the mainmast—as a towline for the lifeboat, just as Oliver Cobb speculated. There was no question they needed to remain attached to the ship. Without a towline, the lifeboat would drift away from the ship with no way to catch up again. During the salvage hearing, Deveau made a point of noting there had been no towline on the *Mary Celeste,* but he didn't stop to think the crew had used the main peak halyard.

He did note that the halyard, hanging over the side, was broken.

Benjamin Briggs was a veteran of twenty years at sea, and he did not survive that long by being a fool. He knew it was dangerous to get off a ship at sea and would not have done so without a lifeline. It is a cliché among sailors that if you don't like the weather at sea, give it a minute—it'll change. So, as any experienced captain would have done, he tied his lifeboat to the ship. He took the peak halyard of the mainsail and fastened it to the front of the launch. If the wind picked up or the seas got too heavy, the crew could simply use the rope to draw the small boat back to the *Mary Celeste.* It was a fine idea, and should have worked. But two small mistakes, coupled with a tragic coincidence, led to their doom.

Either because they didn't see the need or because the smell was driving them from the deck, the crew did not bother hauling in all the sails. The sails left unfurled were on the foremast (save for the jib). To tie up those sails the men had to go aloft and, dizzy from the fumes, they might have found it difficult, if not impossible, to climb the ratlines.

The ship's wheel is harder to explain. The crew either neglected or chose not to tie off the wheel hard to port or starboard. Normally, when a ship's wheel was left unattended, sailors looped a rope around one of its pegs to hold the rudder where they wanted it. Briggs may have told one of the men to do this and he forgot, or the captain was tending to his family and never gave the order. Most likely, no one thought to bother because the ship wasn't moving.

Even if they hadn't been dog-tired from two weeks of fighting the weather, the crew of the *Mary Celeste* might have failed to finish these tasks of basic seamanship because they were either in a hurry to escape a foul stench or they were already light-headed. Taken together, these oversights would not necessarily have doomed the crew, but they had another problem. The main peak halyard was an old, frayed rope.

If toxic fumes were driving the crew from the *Mary Celeste,* the main peak halyard was the best towline to use. It was a heavy line—it hauled the biggest sheet on the ship—and with a diameter of nearly three inches it should have been one of the strongest. The halyard had another benefit: It would have been one of the longest lines, if not *the* longest line, onboard. The peak halyard would have allowed the crew to drift 200 or more feet away from the *Mary Celeste.* It put a lot of sea between the ship and the lifeboat.

Once the crew scrambled into the yawl, they drifted away from the ship for a precious breath of fresh air. For a moment, the crew may have felt they had found a fine solution to their problem: they were attached to the ship with a heavy lifeline and, finally, they could breathe. But as soon as Briggs cleared his head, he realized he had worked himself into an unattractive situation. While they needed a good breeze to air out the ship, too much wind would be trouble. With four foresails still set, the right gust could conceivably set them off on a dangerously fast sail at the end of the towline. Nervous, there was nothing he could do at that point but wait.

It was an uncomfortable predicament in more ways than one. The *Mary Celeste's* sole boat was likely a small yawl—cramped quarters for nine adults and a two-year-old who probably did not appreciate the merits of sitting still. It's impossible to say how long the crew drifted at the end of the tether, how long they planned to let the ship air out. But sometime later that afternoon, they felt the first puff of breeze. It may have been almost comforting at first, bathing them in fresh sea air.

Overhead, a new weather pattern stirred.

On the afternoon of November 25, conditions over the Azores changed quickly and dramatically. After the calm morning, a gale blew in unexpectedly and churned the North Atlantic into a healthy storm. If they saw the foul weather on the horizon, the crew of the *Mary Celeste* might have tried to pull themselves closer to the ship using the towline, a woven lifeline only a few inches in diameter. That is, if they'd seen it coming in time.

When the blow came, the *Mary Celeste* caught the wind in the few sails that were set. The canvas drew taut, there was a slight tug at the mast and slowly the ship lurched forward. It began to pick up speed.

Benjamin Briggs, who lived between the two largest whaling communities in the world, may have been reminded of what the whalers called a Nantucket sleigh ride. In the moments after a whale is harpooned, the beast instinctively swims away in an attempt to escape what is hurting him. With the harpoon tied to the boat, whalers are taken on a fast trip across choppy water, practically skimming over the waves. Briggs would have realized that, like whalers on a sleigh ride, he was in a dangerous situation. As soon as they felt the movement, the crew of the *Mary Celeste* would have begun a tug of war to draw their lifeboat back to the ship. It would have been difficult to make headway on even moderate seas. For a while, they struggled with the lifeboat rocking violently on increasingly rough water, waves breaking over the bow, drenching the men who had left their foul weather gear on the ship. The struggle might have gone on for close to an hour, maybe even longer. Perhaps at some point they were almost within reach of the ship, but not quite close enough.

And at some point, the halyard broke.

The remaining piece of the halyard found hanging over the *Mary Celeste*'s gunwales was a well-worn rope, later reports said, in dire need of replacement. Clearly, the ship had not gotten *all* new rigging during its refit two months earlier. When the men of the *Dei Gratia* pulled the line aboard the *Mary Celeste,* they noted only that it was "snapped" and they had to splice it to rerig the mainsail. They claimed there was no towline because they didn't realize they had repaired it.

After the halyard broke, the rest happened quickly. The crew immediately realized they were in trouble and paddled frantically to try to reach the *Mary Celeste.* But they knew it was no use—there was no chance they could catch up. Benjamin Spooner Briggs may have thought about all his lost siblings for a moment, recognizing the cruel truth before anyone: He was following family tradition. He was lost at sea.

Sometime later, the *Mary Celeste* disappeared over the horizon, leaving eight men, a mother and her child to fend off the ocean in a tiny lifeboat. No one would ever know if they were crushed beneath a wave or simply succumbed from a lack of food, water and shelter. All that's certain is that they drifted to their deaths, leaving behind a world that for more than a century would ponder their fate. Men would blame pirates, tidal waves and shifting plates in the Earth's crust; invent tales of voodoo, malevolent aliens and other things that nineteenth-century seafarers could not have imagined. But none of those fantastic stories could match the true terror those ten people felt in the single moment they realized they had been left to die by their own ship.

When they watched, helplessly, as the Ghost Ship sailed away without a soul on board.

Off the Island of Voodoo

The diver swam in a lazy search pattern, gliding through impossibly blue Caribbean water like a shark trolling for its next meal.

Below him, a jagged mountain range of dark coral jutted out of the white blanket of sand. Fluorescent fish darted in and out of the reef, dodging hundreds of souvenir-sized conch shells littering the seabed. Above, two local fishermen in hollowed-out canoes watched with momentary curiosity.

More accustomed to diving in the Great Lakes than the tropics, Mike Fletcher felt like he was swimming through a poster in a travel agent's office. This undersea vista seemed a place more suited for vacation than archaeology, a more likely setting for lost treasure, gold doubloons, and wrecked Spanish galleons than the grave of the world's most notorious ghost ship.

Still, Fletcher and the rest of the NUMA team felt that it had to be here somewhere. Years of research into the final days of the cursed merchant ship pointed to this isolated spot: Rochelais Reef, a lonely outcropping of coral in the giant bay between the northern and southern peninsulas of Haiti. On this reef, according to surviving historical accounts, the *Mary Celeste* finally met its end.

By the spring of 2001, when NUMA began its search for the *Mary Celeste,* the ship had been mostly forgotten. It had become a footnote in maritime history, its name appearing only occasionally in the pop culture of the occult—featured on a few errant websites, an episode of the television show *In Search Of,* perhaps co-opted as a phantom ship in a cartoon. The ship had drifted out of the American consciousness, its once-infamous name only vaguely familiar. Clive Cussler's National Underwater & Marine Agency wanted to reverse that trend and restore the ship to its rightful prominence as the sea's greatest mystery.

The best way to do that was to find its remains.

Locating shipwrecks is never easy, but in the case of the *Mary Celeste* researchers and divers at least had something to go on. When the ship was intentionally wrecked in 1885, the trial that followed offered promising leads. In most cases, NUMA divers do their work in deep water far offshore, often in near-zero visibility. So they were pleasantly surprised to learn that, if nothing else, they would be searching in clear, shallow—and warm—water. The *Mary Celeste* had done them the courtesy of sinking in paradise.

Ignoring the tourism bureau scenery, Fletcher concentrated on the sticklike instrument he held in front of him. Most beachcombers would have called it a metal detector, and technically it was. The magnetometer could measure slight changes in the earth's magnetic field, which are usually caused by the presence of metal. Fletcher used the portable device to explore areas too shallow for the NUMA boat to search with its own equipment. Unsurprisingly, much of the water around the reef was too shallow to accommodate the draft of the fifty-four-foot charter boat, so Fletcher was on his own.

Although he was looking for a wooden sailing vessel, Fletcher knew there should be ample metal to register a signal: nails, hull sheathing, perhaps even blocks and tackle. As he swept the magnetometer across the sand, Fletcher hunted for other signs of a wrecked sailing vessel. It was hard to make out any shapes on the bottom, where the fish and conch shells mixed, creating the strange illusion of a leaf-covered lawn. Aside from metal, Fletcher was searching for wood or any other corroded piece of debris that suggested a nineteenth-century ship had sunk in the area. He didn't dare dream of finding anything as obvious as the ship's bell or an artifact engraved with its name; Fletcher knew better than to harbor such high hopes. He knew they would be lucky to find anything. Clive Cussler, novelist and founder of NUMA, always said, "Shipwrecks are never where they are supposed to be."

But then, on April 5, 2001, as Fletcher swam near an island made entirely of conch shells, the magnetometer signaled that there was something down there, just below him. Through darting schools of fish, he tried to spot what it had picked up. In the sand at the base of the reef, he found it. Buried beneath a veneer of coral growth, Mike Fletcher saw the unmistakable glint of metal.

Clive Cussler could certainly appreciate a good sea mystery, and he had always considered the *Mary Celeste* one of the best. A lifelong student of the sea and a pioneer of sport diving, Cussler had sailed onto the literary scene thirty years earlier with a series of adventure novels featuring a handsome, cunning diver named Dirk Pitt, a sort of tanned James Bond. The marine archaeologist worked for a fictional government outfit called the National Underwater and Marine Agency, and his adventures in the deep were testament to Cussler's lifelong fascination with shipwrecks. The Dirk Pitt novels, which included *Raise the Titanic!* and *Sahara,* were so successful that Cussler soon had the means to bankroll his own, real-life NUMA. With the nonprofit agency incorporated, and a handful of professional divers signed on, the author made plans to look for all the lost ships he'd read about as a child.

By the late 1970s, Cussler and his growing band of sea hunters were circling the globe searching for shipwrecks. NUMA took no souvenirs or artifacts for itself, never laid claim to the ships or tried to raise them. Cussler considered finding the wrecks the fun part, and said he just wanted to promote interest in maritime history. Given the success of his novels and the discoveries of NUMA, he'd succeeded. Cussler's team got credit for dozens of shipwreck finds, some of them long-forgotten old steamers, others famous ships such as the *Carpathia,* the luxury liner that rescued *Titanic* survivors and was later torpedoed off Ireland. Outside Charleston Harbor, a NUMA dive team in 1995 uncovered the lost Confederate fish boat *H. L. Hunley*— the first submarine to sink an enemy warship in battle.

In 2001, Cussler decided it was time to hunt down the infamous ghost ship. He had asked a NUMA researcher to look into the *Mary Celeste*'s possible whereabouts twenty years earlier, but had never turned his full attention to it—a case of too many ships, too little time. But by the dawn of the new century, Cussler couldn't ignore it any longer. When NUMA found a ship, Cussler had a model of it built for his office. Looking over the great variety of warships, luxury liners and square-riggers lining the room, he felt the *Mary Celeste* would be a perfect fit for the collection.

It was like something out of one of his novels.

NUMA chartered the *Ella Warley II* for the search, and Cussler met up with the ship off the coast of Haiti in the spring of 2001. Already on board were the ship's captain, Allan Gardner, and two divers from Eco-Nova. The team had sailed to the Caribbean island from Ft. Lauderdale, Florida, ready to tape any discovery they might make. The Halifax, Nova Scotia–based Eco-Nova team produced a documentary series on NUMA's work called "The Sea Hunters." The show, one real-life Dirk Pitt adventure after another, was televised regularly in nearly every country in the world except, oddly enough, the United States. The divers, John Davis and Mike Fletcher, had several reasons to be interested in the search for the *Mary Celeste*. Not only would it make a great "Sea Hunters" episode but, because the ship had been built in their backyard, there was still much local interest in it.

As plans for the expedition came together, Eco-Nova helped research the final days of the *Mary Celeste*. The group studied records in the U.S. and Haiti going back more than a century, looking for charts that marked wrecks and hazards to navigation. The site where the ship allegedly went down was notoriously desolate. Their paper chase found only one ship that was ever recorded lost on Rochelais Reef, and it was the *Mary Celeste*. That meant if they found anything around that reef, there was a fair chance it would be their ghost ship. All they had to do was find the reef, and look on its windward side. But experience told them it was never that easy.

Soon after making Haiti, they set a course for what they believed was Rochelais, a partially exposed reef in the Gulf of Gonâve. The huge bay between the island's peninsulas is a turquoise expanse of water. In the gulf, the hazy, mountainous landscape of Haiti looms in the distance, an unsettling presence on the horizon. It is a mysterious place to most Americans, one of the largest islands in the West Indies, but the one that attracts the fewest tourists because of the country's political unrest. For the entire time the group was in the gulf, only Cussler and Davis would travel into the country.

The trip across the gulf took hours. As the boat drew closer to the spot they had marked on their map, a small dot just south of Gonâve Island, the NUMA team realized they weren't heading for a reef. They had found another island.

The men were puzzled, not knowing whether they had discovered an uncharted island or were just off course. As the others looked over the maps, Cussler tried to pick out the reef with his binoculars. When his line of sight crossed the tiny island, which was no bigger than a parking lot, he was surprised.

"Those look like huts," he said.

In the twentieth century, Rochelais Reef saw dramatic changes that went unnoticed by most of the world. Eighty years earlier, two brothers had moved onto the exposed coral to be closer to the conchs they harvested for a living. Over time, the reef was built up with discarded shells until the mass formed an island. Soon other families joined the brothers on this spit of "land," desperate to escape impoverished conditions in mainland Haiti, one of the poorest nations in the world. The islanders harvested the abundant conchs, eating what they needed and selling the rest to support themselves. By 2001, about 120 people lived on the island in shanties made of whatever flotsam or jetsam they could find. The manmade island had eluded most nautical charts for years. It was abject poverty with a million-dollar Caribbean view.

The NUMA divers collectively winced when they got a closer look at the huts, wondering if any of the stray boards holding them up were from the *Mary Celeste*. Using the ship's raft, Davis and Fletcher went ashore to investigate.

On the island, the divers were greeted amicably, but none of the locals knew anything about a shipwreck in the area. That wasn't good news—if there were a wreck nearby these fishermen certainly should have known about it. But all they could pick up from the awkward gumbo of Creole and Spanish words was something about an old, crusty anchor. One of the older fishermen told them it was a little ways off the reef and that he'd take them to it for $1,000 U.S. The sea hunters didn't bite. They had a boatload of swag that seemed all the more impressive in the third world, so they bartered. After some negotiation, the fisherman settled for a couple of cases of Coke and some gas for his outboard. It was just as well—the anchor turned out to be twentieth-century junk, lost off a ship that sailed long after the *Mary Celeste*.

Despite the islanders' claims that there were no other shipwrecks in the area, the *Ella Warley*'s magnetometer was picking up signals all around them. The faint readings made it appear there was something stretching almost onto the banks of the manmade island, but the ship couldn't get in close enough to get an accurate recording. For the second time on the trip, they worried that the island may have played a hand in the ship's disappearance: What if the fishermen had built their island on top of the wreck? Fletcher, a master diver, was sent to find out if that was what had happened. He suited up in full wetsuit and yellow gloves and went over the side of the boat into the sapphire water.

A Caribbean dive was a luxury for Fletcher. He'd been diving since he was a teenager and had made a living at it since 1977, mostly working on construction sites, building bridge pilings and such. Most of his early diving experience came in the Great Lakes, and although not initially involved in maritime archaeology, he learned early on about the gold-rush mentality of shipwrecks. In 1984, he discovered a sunken side-wheeler in Lake Erie called the *Atlantic,* in 160 feet of water off Long Point. The *Atlantic* went down in 1852, and men tried to salvage it unsuccessfully in the late nineteenth century, but ultimately its location was lost. After Fletcher found the ship, he notified authorities and a row over salvage rights broke out between the United States and Canada. Later an American salvage team tried to horn in on the wreck. Fletcher found himself spending an inordinate amount of his time fending off amateur and professional salvers who wanted a piece of the historic old ship.

As a result of the *Atlantic* fiasco, Fletcher formed very solid opinions about the value of shipwrecks and the politics behind them. His fight to protect the wreck also impressed a number of people in the business, including both Cussler and Eco-Nova. A decade later, Fletcher found himself hired to dive on important shipwrecks all over the world.

Fletcher and his boss, John Davis, had worked with Cussler on the *Carpathia* dive off the southern coast of Ireland, but this was their first extended trip with the author. As Cussler recounted the strange tale of the *Mary Celeste* on the deck of the *Ella Warley II,* and listed various theories on the crew's fate, Fletcher noted that if the ship were here, it was strange serendipity.

"It's fitting that it would end its days in the land of voodoo," he said.

Like so much of the Ghost Ship's history, its final resting place had an ironic twist to it. In "J. Habakuk Jephson's Statement," Arthur Conan Doyle attributes the loss of the ship's crew to voodoo-practicing African natives. Less than a century later, voodoo—carried across the Atlantic by captured African slaves—had become the dominant religion of Haiti. Given western stereotypes of voodoo and general sailor superstitions, nobody would have blamed the NUMA team if they had been wary of their target. But Fletcher gave it little thought while searching the Caribbean seabed. When he was on the job, he was desensitized, and didn't allow himself to get excited about anything he found. He knew that emotions get in the way of science and can jeopardize an entire hunt, as the search of hundreds of shipwrecks over the years has proven time and again.

As such, Fletcher was calm on April 5 when he found the first spikes and metal sheathing embedded in the coral. It was a good sign. Thin metal had been fitted to the *Mary Celeste*'s hull below the waterline to stop shipworms from eating through the wood, a common practice of the era. By themselves, the scraps weren't proof of anything. Still, Fletcher couldn't help but grow a little more confident when he came across a scattering of round stones that he noted were "totally out of place geographically." The stones obviously had come from a river. They were, Fletcher knew, most likely ballast from an old wooden sailing vessel.

As he sifted through the debris, he never allowed himself to consider that he might be touching pieces of the *Mary Celeste,* that he might have found the long-lost Ghost Ship.

The artifacts that Fletcher found were enough to convince the NUMA team that they might be on to something. Soon Cussler and Davis joined Fletcher in the water and searched the reef for more remains. It seemed there were pieces of ship scattered everywhere. Some were found half buried under the coral; others were just below the seabed. Davis found charred wood—actually two planks melded into one—that suggested whatever ship was there had been burned to the waterline.

Over the next few days, the NUMA team mapped out a grid for their shipwreck. The front of the wreck appeared to be about 200 to 300 feet from the conch island in 12 feet of water. It stretched back about 100 feet in a path that suggested to some of the divers the ship had cut a trench in the reef as it ran aground (a trench that the islanders used to launch their boats). In all, the field of artifacts almost perfectly matched the dimensions of the *Mary Celeste.*

Despite hundreds of pieces of a wooden ship and a handful of other clues, the NUMA team left Haiti unsure of what they had found. It could be the *Mary Celeste,* they knew, but they needed something

This discreet monument serves as a headstone for Benjamin, Sarah and Sophia Briggs in Evergreen Cemetery, Marion, Massachusetts. It stands, mostly unnoticed, beside the tombstone for Captain Nathan Briggs, patriarch of a great seafaring family. *Photograph Courtesy Brian Hicks*

more reassuring than an absence of other recorded shipwrecks in the area. That came a few months later. Scientists in Nova Scotia and James Delgado, NUMA's Vancouver-based archaeologist and historian, examined the artifacts and found a bounty of evidence to support their theory and, better yet, nothing that contradicted it. The stones were from a river in New York, near where the *Mary Celeste* underwent its refit—and where Yankee shipbuilders routinely got ballast for their ships in the nineteenth century.

Some of the wood the team found was indigenous to Nova Scotia, where the ship was built, and the copper sheathing dated back to the 1860s. It was circumstantial evidence, but pretty solid still. Taken together, the clues overwhelmingly pointed in a single direction. In the late summer of 2001, NUMA announced its find. The *Mary Celeste,* Cussler said, was entombed in a coral reef ten miles off the coast of the Island of Voodoo. Once again, the Ghost Ship had defied conventional maritime wisdom.

"It's the only one I've ever found that was where it was supposed to be," Cussler said.

Of course, NUMA only found her bones.

By the time the wreck of the *Mary Celeste* slipped beneath the Caribbean in the waning years of the nineteenth century, it was already much more than an assemblage of wood planking, canvas and rigging. It had become one of the sea's greatest legends, a simple tragedy that by chance sailed into immortality. All this, from a simple ship built on a quiet beach in the Nova Scotia countryside nearly 150 years ago.

In some ways the *Mary Celeste* left her skeleton on that reef while its spirit slipped away, as local lore held for so long, doomed to sail the earth forever, haunting sailors like the dark ghost ship in Coleridge's verse.

A marker to its captain, Benjamin Spooner Briggs, his wife, and daughter stands today in Evergreen Cemetery just outside of Marion, Massachusetts. The obelisk, nearly six feet high, lists only their names, birth dates, and the short, sad explanation for their absence: "Lost in Brig *Mary Celeste* Nov. 1872."

The monument stands next to the tombstone of Captain Nathan Briggs, patriarch of a great seafaring family. But their true graves are out beyond the horizon, somewhere in the deep blue, hidden forever or, as Sir Arthur Conan Doyle wrote in "J. Habakuk Jephson's Statement," at least until "the great day when the sea shall give up its dead."

Notes

My first encounter with the *Mary Celeste* came nearly thirty years ago, when I was still in grade school. My mother, who encouraged any inclination to read, bought me a paperback anthology of the "world's greatest" unsolved mysteries in a secondhand shop. There was an elaborate UFO on the cover but at that time the strange tale of the Ghost Ship—and the world of the nineteenth century— seemed just about as alien to me. Of course my mother had stumbled onto one of the more egregious versions of the legend: the lifeboats were left behind, there was an abandoned cat onboard, the meals on the galley table were still hot. At least that's the way I remember it—and the way most people who recall this story nowadays do, too.

After that introduction, I crossed paths with the ship infrequently—while reading books on the Bermuda Triangle as a teenager, when catching an episode of Leonard Nimoy's *In Search Of* at my grandmother's house. It was one of those stories that always intrigued me, but because there were so few full-length treatments, and none that I found in my hometown, I never learned much about it (the versions in sea anthologies invariably rehash the same mistakes).

The idea for *Ghost Ship* was born as I was finishing *Raising the Hunley,* a book on the Confederate submarine that I wrote with my friend and colleague Schuyler Kropf. A mutual friend of mine and Clive Cussler's mentioned he had been down in Haiti on NUMA business, and naturally I pestered him until he let me in on the secret—the announcement was still months off. In the epilogue to *Raising the Hunley,* released nearly a year later, I wrote that Cussler and his NUMA team had just found "the legendary ghost ship *Mary Celeste* off Haiti." I didn't realize it, but I had not only picked my next project, I had named it.

Diving into this mystery I discovered a story much more complex and tragic than I felt had been related before. The more traces of these people I found, the greater respect and empathy I came to have for Benjamin Spooner Briggs. He did his duty while weathering a job and profession that he longed to give up— if that's not a man who would not desert his post, I don't know what is. I became further convinced of that belief by learning about the family that shaped his character and convictions. The seafaring Briggses fascinate me, and I think that if the Ghost Ship didn't overshadow them so much, they would be worthy of a book unto themselves. Ultimately, I felt that including the family's history not only made this story more compelling, but also provided a context for the life and times in which the *Mary Celeste* sailed. Also, as I read Benjamin's scant remaining letters, I began to pick up on the great sorrow in his life. As the years passed, his desire to give up sailing grew stronger and stronger. One cold, rainy morning in November of 2002, I sat in the Peabody Essex Museum in Salem, reading a letter Benjamin had written to his mother more than 130 years earlier. When I saw the closing line in his own handwriting, in which he quoted the lyrics to "Home, Sweet, Home," I knew I had found a theme.

The hard part, of course, was making sense of the mystery. Finding one completely accurate account of the story proved almost impossible. In large part, the Vice Admiralty Court's transcript of the *Mary Celeste* salvage hearing is the basis for the crux of the book, although I'm not sure the *Dei Gratia* sailors weren't exaggerating some of what they claimed to have found. It would not have been above them to stretch the truth to buy sympathy—and hopefully a larger salvage award—from the court. But their words are all we have to go on, and we have to assume they were mostly describing everything as they remembered it. Beyond the transcript, the records of the State Department housed in the National Archives offer the most complete official account of the hearing and the subsequent fallout. For a while, the ship was such a popular topic among researchers that longtime Archives employee Kathryn M. Murphy kept a "finder" on the ship (it was later updated by Angie S. VanDereedt). The finder helped me immeasurably.

Charles Edey Fay's 1942 limited edition book on the *Mary Celeste* is a great source for most of the documentation on the ship, including maritime registers of the day, but George S. Bryan's *Mystery Ship,* also published in 1942, offers a better narrative of the events. Both books contain accounts from sources that no longer exist, making them irreplaceable resources. In addition, James Franklin

Briggs's *In the Wake of the* Mary Celeste, a chapbook published in the 1944 by the Old Dartmouth Historical Society, is packed with many otherwise unpublished gems, and Oliver Cobb's memoir of the Briggses, *Rose Cottage,* rounded out the story of the family.

Newspaper and magazine accounts vary greatly, and I didn't take facts from any of them at face value unless I felt confident in their sourcing. I believe the *Boston Post*'s interview with Arthur Briggs is credible, for instance, and trust the interview with Captain Morehouse's wife to an extent—in the narrative, I offer her account, with conditions. That's not because I think she was lying or the newspaper made a mistake, but because I have some questions about her memory fifty years after the fact. The rest of the newspaper accounts, conversely, are good only for documenting the growth of a legend—most of them are laughably inaccurate. As for my theory of what happened to the *Mary Celeste*'s crew, it developed as I researched and wrote the book. Even though I didn't have much faith in the rumbling-cargo-hold story, I was suspicious of alcohol fumes because the ship had been left completely unbuttoned. The theory presented in Chapter Twelve seemed the simplest, most logical solution. I kept waiting for one fact to stand out, to contradict my idea, but nothing ever did. Everything seems to point in that one direction.

The quotes included in the narrative come from letters or court testimony; I did not put words into anyone's mouth. Their thoughts also came from letters, except in those instances when it was so obvious what they would have been thinking that I could safely infer. I have added nothing to the *Mary Celeste*'s story. There has been enough of that already.

Prologue: December 4, 1872

3 *The ship drifted:* This account of the *Dei Gratia*'s crew first spying the *Mary Celeste* was crafted from the testimony of the sailors at the Gibraltar salvage hearing as reproduced in *The* Mary Celeste*: Judge's notes on evidence, Vice Admiralty Court of Gibraltar December 1872* (Marion: Sippican Historical Society, n.d.).

7 *A nautical mythology:* George S. Bryan, *Mystery Ship: The* Mary Celeste *in Fancy and in Fact* (New York: J. B. Lippincott, 1942): 5.

11 *One man, interested:* James Franklin Briggs, *In the Wake of the* Mary Celeste (New Bedford: Old Dartmouth Historical Society, 1944): 29.

11 *The sad way of orphans:* Macdonald Hastings, Mary Celeste*: A Centenary Record* (London: Michael Joseph Ltd, 1972): 12.

Chapter One: A Simple, Handsome Ship

15 *For as long:* George Spicer's account of carrying the body of Captain Robert McLellan home after the first voyage of *Amazon* survives only because

of a charming Nova Scotia travel book that managed to preserve an important episode in the Ghost Ship's history. Shortly before he died in 1937, Spicer recounted this tale for Clara Dennis to use in her book *More About Nova Scotia: My Own, My Native Land* (Toronto: Ryerson Press, 1937): 63–64.

17 *With the* Amazon: The story of the ship's construction, and Joshua Dewis's career as a shipwright, is documented by Stanley T. Spicer, *The Saga of the* Mary Celeste*: An Ill-Fated Mystery Ship* (Hantsport, Nova Scotia: Lancelot Press, 1994): 13–19.

18 *The crew resumed:* James Franklin Briggs provides several interesting details of the latter stages of the ship's construction in his *In the Wake of the* Mary Celeste: 8–9.

19 *The brig straddled:* Maritime historians disagree on the true designation for the *Amazon/Mary Celeste* sail plan, but it seems like much ado about nothing. Most definitions of a brigantine are nebulous. In their dictionary, John V. Noel Jr. and Edward L. Beach, both retired U.S. Navy captains, write that a brigantine is a "[s]ailing vessel with two masts, the fore-mast square-rigged and the mainmast fore-and-aft rigged. Same as a hermaphrodite brig, except that a square topsail might be carried on the mainmast, well above the normal position for a topsail." *Naval Terms Dictionary* (Annapolis: Naval Institute Press, 1978 fourth edition): 49.

20 *This craft seemed:* Bryan, *Mystery Ship:* 18.

21 *It was easy:* The Nova Scotia legends of the *Baltimore* and the Maiden's Cave are recounted by Roland H. Sherwood, *Maritime Mysteries: Haunting Tales from Atlantic Canada* (Windsor, Nova Scotia: Lancelot Press, 1976): 24–29, 98–101.

22 *Robert Dewis, another:* Dewis's account of the *Amazon*'s disastrous first voyage is quoted by Spicer, *The Saga of the* Mary Celeste*:* 23–24.

23 *Captain Parker commissioned:* Briggs, *In the Wake of the* Mary Celeste*:* 10.

23 *A few months later:* For years, the painting drifted from one Canadian museum to the next, and was reproduced in some early works on the *Mary Celeste*. I tracked it to the Canadian Park Service, but found no one there who could locate it for inclusion in this book. It's probably either in storage or hanging anonymously in some New Brunswick museum today.

24 *Spicer first heard:* The details of George Spicer's early days before the mast and aboard the *Amazon* are culled from Stanley T. Spicer's *Captain from Fundy: The Life and Times of George D. Spicer, Master of Square-Rigged Windjammers* (Hantsport, Nova Scotia: Lancelot Press, 1988); Dennis, *More About Nova Scotia:* 63; and Spicer, *The Saga of the* Mary Celeste*:* 24.

24 *When Dewis's new captain:* Spicer, *The Saga of the* Mary Celeste*:* 24–25.

25 *A new registry:* For years, writers have suggested some scandal with the wreck of the *Amazon* in 1867. It could be a case of confusing paperwork, as there

certainly was no shortage of that in the late nineteenth century. George S. Bryan points out the *Amazon* still showed up in some maritime directories as late as 1885, the year the ship, by then the *Mary Celeste,* was scuttled. "[A] phantom craft indeed," he wrote. Bryan, *Mystery Ship:* 28–32.

26 *Richard W. Haines bought it:* Letter from the Secretary of the Treasury to the Collector of Customs, New York, National Archives (Record Group 36, Records of the U.S. Customs Service, New York, Letters to the Collector, vol. 29).

26 *He reflagged the ship:* Briggs, *In the Wake of the* Mary Celeste: 11.

Chapter Two: The Seafaring Life

27 *Benjamin Spooner Briggs:* Most of the information used to reconstruct the Briggs family history came from accounts in Oliver W. Cobb's *Rose Cottage* (New Bedford: Reynold-DeWalt, 1968); the unpublished biographies of Nathan Briggs and James C. Briggs on file at the Elizabeth Taber Library in Marion, Massachusetts; the Briggs family letters at the Peabody Essex Museum in Salem, Massachusetts; and James Franklin Briggs's *In the Wake of the* Mary Celeste.

28 *Still, on Saturday:* Charles Edey Fay, Mary Celeste: *The Odyssey of an Abandoned Ship* (Salem: Peabody Museum, 1942): 3.

29 *Benjamin's younger brother:* James C. Briggs, *Autobiography* (unpublished manuscript from 1912): 19.

29 *While he was home:* Fay, Mary Celeste: 22.

29 *With its strategic location:* This portrait of Marion in the late nineteenth century was compiled from exhibits in the Sippican Historical Society museum and from the wonderful book by Judith Westlund Rosbe, *Marion, Massachusetts* (Charleston: Arcadia Publishing, 2000): 7–8.

31 *The future mariner:* James Franklin Briggs, *In the Wake of the* Mary Celeste: 13.

32 *At fifteen, he became:* Oliver W. Cobb, *Rose Cottage:* 11.

32 *If this be all:* Ibid: 16.

33 *On September 4, 1828:* Ibid: 18.

34 *Spooner Briggs was lost:* Ibid: 25.

34 *The Briggs family lived:* Briggs, *Autobiography:* 2, 34–35.

34 *In 1844:* Ibid: 1–2.

35 *On that voyage:* Briggs, *In the Wake of the Mary Celeste:* 13.

37 *On September 9, 1862:* Benjamin and Sarah Briggs wedding invitation, Benjamin Spooner Briggs papers, Peabody Essex Museum (MSS# MH 48, Series IV, Box 1, Folder 4).

37 *"We had a fine chance":* Letter of Benjamin Briggs to his brother-in-law, William Cobb, May 19, 1863, Benjamin Spooner Briggs papers, Peabody Essex Museum (MSS# MH 48, Series I, Box 1, Folder 1).

37 *While touring the Union gunboat:* Ibid.

38 *"Gentlemen, I have carried":* Cobb, *Rose Cottage:* 58.

39 *In 1865, Briggs returned:* Ibid, 73.

39 *"[He] called him Oli":* Letter of Sarah Briggs to William Cobb, February 8, 1868, Benjamin Spooner Briggs papers, Peabody Essex Museum (MSS# MH 48, Series I, Box 1, Folder 1).

39 *"What a trial":* Letter of Benjamin Briggs to his mother, Sophia Briggs, April 17, 1868, Benjamin Spooner Briggs papers, Peabody Essex Museum (MSS# MH 48, Series I, Box 1, Folder 1).

40 *He and his brothers had met:* Briggs, *Autobiography:* 18, 19.

40 *"Dear Arthur":* Letter of Benjamin Briggs to Arthur Briggs, n.d., Benjamin Spooner Briggs papers, Peabody Essex Museum (MSS# MH 48, Series I, Box 1, Folder 1).

41 *In 1855, Nathan H. Briggs:* The accidents that befell the Briggs children are recounted similarly both in James C. Brigg's *Autobiography* and Cobb's *Rose Cottage:* 51, 62.

42 *The most crippling blow:* Ibid: 63.

42 *A year earlier:* Ibid: 65–66.

43 *He financed the purchase:* Fay, Mary Celeste: 91, 97.

Chapter Three: The New World

45–46 *The picture that is presented:* L. E. Bond, *Statue of Liberty: Beacon of Promise* (Santa Barbara: Albion Publishing Group, 1999): 10–11.

46 *He had business:* Charles Edey Fay, Mary Celeste: 165.

47 *Recalling this sight:* Benjamin Briggs's final letter to his mother was reprinted in its entirety by Oliver W. Cobb in *Rose Cottage:* 66–67.

47 *Metal sheathing had been attached:* The description of the *Mary Celeste's* refit comes from newspaper articles in which James H. Winchester defends the ship's insured value. Those articles can be found in the records of Atlantic Mutual Insurance: Fay, *Mary Celeste:* 3, 58, 59. The advertisement mentioning the ship's capacity as 3,500 barrels is referenced in George S. Bryan, *Mystery Ship:* 53. A few of the other details come from James Franklin Briggs, *In the Wake of the Mary Celeste:* 12.

49 *"I hope we shall have":* Cobb, *Rose Cottage:* 67.

49 *In the past year:* Fay, Mary Celeste: 183.

50 *The troublesome little brig:* Ibid: 57–59.

51 *When Winchester visited: The* Mary Celeste, *Judge's notes:* 32–33.

51 *The accident left the crew:* Winchester's account of the lifeboat discussion is recounted in Captain Myron W. Tracy's account of the *Mary Celeste* incident, which is among his papers in the G. W. Blunt White Library at the Mystic Seaport Museum (Myron W. Tracy papers, ca. 1936, VFM 1587).

52 *When he heard:* Cobb, *Rose Cottage:* 74.

53 *The second mate was:* Crew list of the *Mary Celeste,* National Archives (Records Group 36, Records of the U.S. Customs Service, New York, Shipping Articles), and a copy of a translated German communication to the German consul, Ferdinand Schott, National Archives (Records Group 59, Consular Dispatches, Gibraltar, vol. 12).

53 *"Benj. thinks":* Cobb, *Rose Cottage:* 68.

53 *On Sunday, October 27:* The account of the Briggs family reunion was culled from family letters collected in Briggs, *In the Wake of the* Mary Celeste, 13–14.

56 *Sarah Cobb was:* Biographical information on Sarah Cobb and her marriage to Benjamin Briggs comes from Cobb, *Rose Cottage:* 65; and James C. Briggs *Autobiography:* 24.

56 *"I never heard Arthur":* Letter of Sarah Briggs to Benjamin Briggs April 11, 1872, Benjamin Spooner Briggs papers, Peabody Essex Museum (MSS# MH 48, Series I, Box 1, Folder 1).

57 *A horse disease:* Bryan, *Mystery Ship:* 53.

58 *Sarah finally got her trip:* The Central Park trip was recounted in a letter from Sarah Briggs to her sister Mary Scribner Cobb, excerpted in Briggs, *In the Wake of the* Mary Celeste: 14.

59 *That Saturday night:* Benjamin Briggs letter to his mother, Cobb, *Rose Cottage:* 66–67.

59 *Briggs did not even allow:* Ibid: 13.

60 *That Monday, Briggs:* Shipping Articles of the *Mary Celeste,* National Archives, (Record Group 36, New York, Shipping Articles).

61 *In the note, Briggs:* Cobb, *Rose Cottage:* 66–67.

61 *Morehouse commanded:* The account of Benjamin Briggs and David Reed Morehouse meeting and dining together in New York City in November 1872 is taken from an interview with Desiah Foster Morehouse, the widow of the *Dei Gratia*'s captain, published in *The Literary Digest,* Sept. 12, 1926: 44.

63 *Dear Mother Briggs:* Fay, Mary Celeste: 11–12.

64 *Sarah's final letter:* Bryan, *Mystery Ship:* 56.

64 *The* Julia A. Hallock *sailed:* Cobb, *Rose Cottage:* 69.

65 *Arthur Briggs would hear:* Briggs, *In the Wake of the* Mary Celeste: 24.

Chapter 4: The Silence of the Sea

This chapter was based almost exclusively on the testimony of the *Dei Gratia* sailors in the *Mary Celeste* salvage hearing in Gibraltar between December 1872 and March 1873, as reproduced in *The* Mary Celeste, *Judge's notes.* Certain sailors were given more credibility than others; Oliver Deveau's account, being the most thorough, provides the greatest amount of detail and Captain David Reed Morehouse's is accepted as the most accurate in regard to the time they spotted the *Mary Celeste,* the direction it was sailing and the decision to salvage the ship.

79 *In the last line:* This intriguing fact is probably just a red herring in the mystery. Most likely, Albert Richardson—who would have filled out the log slate a good bit of the time—was just doodling when he wrote this affectionate salutation to his wife. He could even have been drafting a letter on the slate. If he was writing some sort of a good-bye letter, there's no proof of it. No one made much of the notation at the trial or at the stories that followed. It's just another facet of the mystery that will never be cleared up completely.

85 *More than fifty years after:* The actions of Captain David Reed Morehouse were recounted by his widow, Desiah Foster Morehouse, to a *Boston Post* reporter and reprinted in *The Literary Digest,* September 12, 1926: 44.

Chapter Five: News from Overseas

92 *Morehouse's cryptic note:* Charles Edey Fay, Mary Celeste: 32.

94 *In one seven-year stretch:* Stanley T. Spicer, *The Saga of the* Mary Celeste: 12.

94 *Sailing the* Mary Celeste *into Gibraltar:* The account of the *Mary Celeste's* trip into the English port comes from the testimony of Oliver Deveau and Augustus Anderson, *The* Mary Celeste, *Judge's notes:* 10, 28.

95–96 *Morehouse greeted Deveau:* Ibid: 49, 50.

97 *Deveau remained optimistic:* James Franklin Briggs, *In the Wake of the* Mary Celeste: 18–19.

98 *The Master of the* Dei Gratia: Letter of Horatio Sprague to the Assistant Secretary of State, Washington, D.C., National Archives (Records Group 59, Consular Dispatches, Gibraltar, vol. 10).

98 *The State Department:* Information on the history and role of consuls, and Sprague's tenure, was found on the U.S. State Department's website, *http://www.state.gov.* Sprague's friendship with Benjamin Briggs is referenced in Sprague's letter of August 12, 1873 to James C. Briggs, National Archives (Records Group 84, Consular Post, Gibraltar, Correspondences Sent, vol. E).

99–107 *The salvage hearing began:* The account of the *Mary Celeste* salvage hearing is taken entirely from *The* Mary Celeste, *Judge's notes.* Although the transcript does not provide the exact question from the court, I summarized the likely questions asked based on the responses the men of the *Dei Gratia* gave. Anything in quotation was taken directly from the transcript, without correction beyond spelling and punctuation errors. The words of the witnesses have not been changed.

107 *For a persnickety bureaucrat:* Some of the colorful biographical information on Frederick Solly Flood was found on the website *http://www.sole.org.uk/solflood.htm,* which reprinted information from a November 1999 article in *Soul Search, the Journal of The Sole Society* by Bob Solly.

108 *Just before Christmas:* George S. Bryan, *Mystery Ship:* 62.

109 *"Apprehensions of foul play":* Ibid: 62.

109 *"For your information":* Letter of Horatio Sprague to F. Solly Flood, December 31, 1872, National Archives (Record Group 84, Gibraltar Consular Post, Correspondences Sent, vol. D).

110–111 *Morehouse sent the* Dei Gratia: Fay, Mary Celeste: 84.

111 *Oliver Briggs celebrated:* The loss of the *Julia A. Hallock* and Oliver Briggs's last days are recounted by Cobb, *Rose Cottage:* 71; and Bryan, *Mystery Ship:* 68.

112 *"Tell him not to come":* Bryan, *Mystery Ship:* 68.

Chapter Six: "A Moment of Panic"

113 *The Austin report provides:* A handwritten copy of Austin's thirty-two-page report is filed at the National Archives (Record Group 59, Notes from the British Legation, vol. 94).

115 *It had not run aground:* The affidavit of Ricardo Portunato is recorded at the National Archives (Record Group 59, Notes from the British Legation, vol. 94).

116 *Flood later reported:* Frederick Solly Flood's long letter to the English Marine Department's Board of Trade on January 22, 1873, is perhaps the best evidence of the suspicions harbored by Gibraltar officials in the weeks after the *Mary Celeste* arrived in port. Flood was not shy with his opinions. The letter is reprinted in Fay, Mary Celeste: 78–81.

118 *James H. Winchester felt:* George S. Bryan, *Mystery Ship:* 69.

118 *At that point:* The Winchester family legend of his salvage court testimony is recounted in James Franklin Briggs, *In the Wake of the* Mary Celeste: 20–21.

119 *Flood subjected Winchester:* The Mary Celeste, Judge's notes. 30–41.

121 *There are certain matters:* Ibid: 43.

122 *Sitting idly by:* Fay, Mary Celeste: 88.

122 *"A gentleman came to me":* Briggs, *In the Wake of the* Mary Celeste: 21–22.

123 *"I am of the opinion":* Letter of Captain R. W. Shufeldt to Horatio Sprague, February 6, 1873, National Archives (Record Group 84, Gibraltar Consular Post, Correspondence Received, vol. 1866–1875).

125 *In his report, Dr. J. Patron:* A copy of Patron's report is filed at the National Archives (Record Group 59, Consular Dispatches, Gibraltar, vol. 13).

125 *Vecchio had completed a new search:* Fay, Mary Celeste, 105–106.

125 *In a cable:* A cable from Horatio Sprague to the assistant secretary of state in Washington, February 25, 1873, National Archives (Record Group 59, Consular Dispatches, Gibraltar, vol. 10).

126 *Captain Blatchford was still trying:* Briggs, *In the Wake of the* Mary Celeste*:* 23.

128 *On March 3: The* Mary Celeste, *Judge's notes:* 44.

128 *In court, following:* Ibid: 44.

130 *Morehouse's testimony:* Ibid: 47–55.

132 *"There was nothing remarkable":* Ibid: 57–58.

132 *Flood was infuriated:* Ibid: 58.

133 *"For the present":* Bryan, *Mystery Ship:* 80.

134 *"The vessel was": The* Mary Celeste, *Judge's notes:* 66.

134 *The day before:* Briggs, *In the Wake of the* Mary Celeste*:* 23.

135 *Oliver Deveau left:* Ibid: 23.

135 *In his brief statement:* Fay, Mary Celeste: 117.

136 *The Judge further thought it:* Stanley T. Spicer, *The Saga of the* Mary Celeste*:* 42–43.

Chapter Seven: In the Wake of Misfortune

140 *After escaping Gibraltar:* The *Mary Celeste's* trip to Genoa and back to Boston is documented in Charles Edey Fay, *Mary Celeste:* 137. Information on the condition of the ship's cargo is in an April 26, 1873, letter from O. M. Spencer, the U.S. consul in Genoa, to Horatio Sprague in the National Archives (Record Group 84, Consular Posts, Gibraltar, Correspondence Received, vol. 1866–1875).

141 *Winchester did not have the appetite:* Winchester & Co.'s efforts to sell the *Mary Celeste* were recounted in an interview that has been reprinted by James Franklin Briggs, *In the Wake of the* Mary Celeste*:* 29.

141 *Some of the more eloquent sailors:* Ibid: 25–27.

142 *Dabney told his bosses:* George S. Bryan, *Mystery Ship:* 240.

144 *In the nineteenth century, mutiny:* Several of the motives behind mutiny were gleaned from reading Leonard F. Guttridge's *Mutiny: A History of Naval Insurrection* (Annapolis: Naval Institute Press, 1992). The "inborn readiness to flout authority" comes from Guttridge, *Mutiny:* 1.

144 *The USS* Somers *was:* The account of the *Somers* was taken largely from the fabulous maritime history book *America and the Sea: A Maritime History* (Mystic: Mystic Seaport, 1998), by Benjamin W. Labaree, William M. Fowler, Jr., Edward W. Sloan, John B. Hattendorf, Jeffrey J. Safford, and Andrew W. German: 333.

146 *"In their own practical interests":* Guttridge, *Mutiny:* 8.

147 *Captain R.W. Shufeldt, who:* Letter of Captain R.W. Shufeldt to Horatio Sprague, February 6, 1873, National Archives (Record Group 84, Gibraltar Consular Post, Correspondence Received, vol. 1866–1875).

148 *James wrote admiringly:* James C. Briggs, *Autobiography:* 7.

148 *Into the 1890s:* Macdonald Hastings, Mary Celeste: *A Centenary Record:* 146.

149 *An unnamed source:* The feud between James H. Winchester and the *New York Sun* is recounted, and both articles reprinted in Fay, Mary Celeste: 57–59.

153 *The* Dei Gratia *sailors:* All of the crewmen who sailed on the *Mary Celeste* said that bad weather had forced or scared the crew to abandon ship, some of them perhaps parroting the opinion of Oliver Deveau, their senior officer. Their references to this theory are throughout *The* Mary Celeste: *Judge's notes.*

154 *One letter came:* Letter of N.W. Bingham to Horatio Sprague, Mar. 7, 1873, National Archives (Record Group 84, Consular Post, Gibraltar, Correspondence Received, vol. 1866–1875).

155 *"The missing master":* Letter of Horatio Sprague to N.W. Bingham, April 3, 1873, National Archives (Record Group 84, Consular Post, Gibraltar, Correspondence Sent, vol. D).

156 *Sprague was more intrigued:* Letter of T.A. Nickelsen to Horatio Sprague, March 24, 1873, National Archives (Record Group 84, Consular Post, Gibraltar, Correspondence Received, vol. 1866–1875).

156 *"The general opinion is":* Letter of Horatio Sprague to T.A. Nickelsen, April 4, 1873, National Archives (Record Group 84, Consular Post, Gibraltar, Correspondence Sent, vol. D).

156 *That May, Sprague forwarded:* Letter of Horatio Sprague to O.M. Spencer, May 2, 1873, National Archives (Record Group 84, Consular Post, Gibraltar, Correspondence Sent, vol. D).

156 *He received a sad note:* Letter of Emma J. Head to Horatio Sprague, July 31, 1873, National Archives (Record Group 84, Consular Post, Gibraltar, Correspondence Received, vol. 1866–1875).

157 *It was hard to avoid:* The only remaining account of Arthur Briggs's year following the disappearance of his family is from James Franklin Briggs, *In the Wake of the* Mary Celeste: 24–25. Oddly enough, Oliver Cobb wrote nothing of Arthur's troubled times, which is stranger still given the fact that they were the same age, and according to some accounts, friends.

157 *James, who was initially appointed:* Letter of James C. Briggs to Horatio Sprague, July 19, 1873, National Archives (Record Group 84, Consular Post, Gibraltar, Correspondence Received, vol. 1866–1875).

157 *I am the last:* Ibid.

158 *Eventually the family:* Cobb, *Rose Cottage:* 71–72.

158 *Winchester had no better luck:* Briggs, *In the Wake of the* Mary Celeste*:* 29.

158 *After the sale:* Ibid: 29.

158 *David Cartwright put:* Ibid: 29.

159 *"Do I remember":* Ibid: 29.

160 *During those last miserable days:* The account of George Spicer's accidental reunion with his old ship is recounted by his grandson and biographer, Stanley T. Spicer, in *The Saga of the* Mary Celeste*:* 50–51.

Chapter Eight: Conan Doyle's Statement

164 *The story was:* George S. Bryan, *Mystery Ship:* 127.

164 *There was more:* The summation of "J. Habakuk Jephson's Statement" is taken from Arthur Conan Doyle's original text, as printed in *The Conan Doyle Stories* (Leicester, England: Galley Press, 1988): 386–422.

169 *"I ask to myself":* Letter of Horatio Sprague to John Davis, assistant secretary of state, January 12, 1884, National Archives (Record Group 59, Consular Dispatches, Gibraltar, vol. 12).

169 *Sprague began to question:* Letter of Horatio Sprague to M. S. Brewer, January 16, 1884, National Archives (Record Group 59, Consular Dispatches, Gibraltar, vol. 12).

170 *Were there any "widows":* Ibid.

170 *Arthur Conan Doyle was quite pleased:* Doyle's reaction to the reception of "Jephson's Statement" is recorded in Martin Booth, *The Doctor and the Detective: A Biography of Sir Arthur Conan Doyle* (New York: Thomas Dunne, 1997): 102–103; and Bryan, *Mystery Ship:* 124–125.

170 *the tale "made a powerful impression":* Bryan, *Mystery Ship:* 85.

170 *Born in Edinburgh:* Biographical background of Arthur Conan Doyle comes from both Martin Booth's *The Doctor and the Detective,* and John Dickson Carr's *The Life of Sir Arthur Conan Doyle* (New York: Carroll & Graf, 1987).

171 *"What gave me great pleasure":* Bryan, *Mystery Ship:* 125.

172 *The historian George:* Ibid: 127.

174 *"The article to which you refer":* Letter of John Davis, assistant secretary of state, to Horatio Sprague, April 2, 1884, National Archives (Record Group 84, Consular Post, Gibraltar, Instructions Received from the Department of State, vol. II).

174 *"The relatives know as little":* Fay, Mary Celeste: 242–244.

175 *Flood claimed:* Letter of Frederick Solly Flood to Horatio Sprague, January 9, 1885, National Archives (Record Group 84, Consular Post, Gibraltar, Correspondence Received, vol. 1885–1890).

175 *"I desire to express"*: Ibid.

176 *"I would beg to state"*: Letter of Horatio Sprague to John Davis, March 4, 1885, National Archives (Record Group 59, Consular Dispatches, Gibraltar, vol. 12).

Chapter Nine: Dead Reckoning

177 *"Keep her on course"*: The dialog of the *Mary Celeste*'s final crew is culled from the testimony of the 1885 barratry trial in Boston against Captain Gilman C. Parker. George S. Bryan, *Mystery Ship*: 275.

177 *He had veered*: Ibid.

177 *The ship was due*: Stanley T. Spicer, *The Saga of the* Mary Celeste: 52.

178 *"Is that a fishing boat"*: Bryan, *Mystery Ship*: 275.

179 *The ship shook*: Ibid: 275.

180 *After losing $5,000*: Briggs, *In the Wake of the* Mary Celeste: 29–30.

180 *Gove tried everything*: Based on the Digest of Certificates of Registry compiled by Charles Edey Fay, Mary Celeste: 201.

181 *With the ship and cargo insured*: Briggs, *In the Wake of the* Mary Celeste: 30.

181 *When Parker and his crew*: The account of the final *Mary Celeste* crew's brief stay in Haiti was recounted years after the incident by the marine surveyor Kingman N. Putnam. His story is quoted in Briggs, *In the Wake of the* Mary Celeste: 31–32.

182 *"I opened one case"*: Ibid: 31.

183 *Unable to find timely passage*: Bryan, *Mystery Ship*: 268.

183 *"an American consul on a [British] vessel"*: Briggs, *In the Wake of the* Mary Celeste: 32.

184 *"Little by little"*: Henry Rogers's story of cracking the *Mary Celeste* insurance scam case was originally published in the *Boston Sunday Globe* on January 6, 1929, and has been used to reconstruct the investigation. The article is excerpted in Briggs, *In the Wake of the* Mary Celeste: 32–34.

186 *On April 20, 1885*: Fay, Mary Celeste: 139.

186 *The indictment*: The entire text of the indictment against Parker and the merchants who were shipping fraudulent goods is reprinted in Bryan, *Mystery Ship*: 271–273.

187 *"It was noticed"*: Ibid: 276.

187 *The* Boston Post: Ibid: 276.

187 *The fish on board*: Ibid: 277.

187 *"The defense attorneys"*: Briggs, *In the Wake of the* Mary Celeste: 34.

188 *"I was at the wheel"*: Bryan, *Mystery Ship*: 275.

188 *"I had no more intention"*: Ibid: 275.

189 *Mary Howe testified*: Briggs, *In the Wake of the* Mary Celeste: 34.

189   *Prosecutors argued:* Bryan, *Mystery Ship:* 278.

190   *Kingman Putnam later said:* Briggs, *In the Wake of the* Mary Celeste*:* 35.

190   *On October 22, 1885:* Bryan, *Mystery Ship:* 283.

Chapter Ten: The Great Mary Celeste Hoaxes

195   *At first:* The servant's tale, as Abel Fosdyk's story came to be called, is recounted by Macdonald Hastings in Mary Celeste: 72–75.

196   *"I suppose he said":* Ibid: 73.

196   *"No word":* Ibid: 74.

196   *"so irritable one":* George S. Bryan, *Mystery Ship:* 146.

197   *"A—man—can't":* Ibid: 147.

198   *One of the more interesting:* Ibid: 151–152.

199   *In Buffalo:* Frederick J. Shepard, *The Buffalo Express,* December 14, 1913, collected in "The *Mary Celeste,* a sea mystery, the facts of which have been clouded by the romancers," (Collection of clippings in the Buffalo Public Library).

199   *"The story of the* Strand": Ibid.

199   *"Of course, minute errors":* Hastings, Mary Celeste: 74.

199   *The* Nautical Gazette: *Nautical Gazette,* December 17, 1913, collected in Shepard, *Mary Celeste:* 8.

200   *"I would like to emphasize":* Hastings, Mary Celeste: 74.

200   *Frederick Solly Flood died:* Flood's death is recorded on the website *http://www.sole.org.uk/solflood.htm.*

200   *Horatio J. Sprague died:* U.S. State Department website, *http://www.state.gov.*

200   *just a few years after welcoming:* Captain Joshua Slocum, *Sailing Alone Around the World* (New York: Dover Publications, 1956): 49.

201   *"Why, Captain Morehouse":* The Literary Digest, April 8, 1926, collected in Shepard, Mary Celeste: 28.

201   *Morehouse and his wife:* The last years of the former *Dei Gratia* captain are chronicled by Inez Manzer Sypher Morehouse in *330 Years of Morehouse Genealogy 1640–1970, Volume I* (Hantsport, Nova Scotia: Lancelot Press, 1978): 260–261.

202   *Not long before Deveau:* Bryan, *Mystery Ship:* 231.

202   *In his obituary:* Fay, Mary Celeste: 121–122.

204   *a skeleton clutching a message:* Hastings, Mary Celeste: 121.

204   *The* Gazette *declared:* The pirate tale of Demetrius is collected in Bryan, *Mystery Ship:* 152–154.

205   *In 1924, Captain Howard Lucy:* Ibid: 155–160.

207   *"As Captain Benjamin S. Briggs":* The New York Times, October 26, 1924, collected in Shepard, *Mary Celeste:* 9.

207 *In June 1925:* The Lee Kaye version of the Pemberton story is recounted in Bryan, *Mystery Ship:* 160–165.

209 *"To us and many":* Ibid: 166.

209 *Three years later:* Laurence J. Keating, *The Great* Mary Celeste *Hoax: A Famous Sea Mystery Exposed* (Boston: Houghton Mifflin, 1929).

209 *"It would not be possible":* Ibid: 17.

210 *In the* Buffalo News: The *Buffalo News,* August 8, 1929, collected in Shepard, Mary Celeste: 3.

210 *Cooper Gaw:* Ibid: 4.

210 *For years, Arthur Briggs:* The *Literary Digest,* September 18, 1926: 40.

211 *"Why, the man has his facts wrong":* Ibid.

211 *Arthur Briggs did not live:* Arthur's death certificate is on file in the New Bedford City Clerk's office.

211 *one reporter traveled:* Hastings, Mary Celeste: 94, 110.

213 *More than twenty years later:* Macdonald Hastings uncovered the final bit of proof needed to debunk Keating and Pemberton, a fact that has eluded some writers over the years. Hastings, Mary Celeste: 111–113.

Chapter Eleven: Into the Mystic

215 *On the afternoon:* One of the best accounts of the Flight 19 incident is "Lost Patrol" by Michael McDonnell in *Naval Aviation News,* June 1973: 8–16, available on the Naval Historical Center website, *www.history.navy.mil.*

217 *In January of 1880:* Charles Berlitz, *The Bermuda Triangle* (New York: Avon Books, 1975): 64.

217 *the schooner* Carroll A. Deering: Larry Kusche, *The Bermuda Triangle Mystery Solved* (Amherst: Prometheus Books, 1995): 65–73.

217 *The* Rubicon *seemed:* Ibid: 95.

218 *"I don't know where":* McDonnell's article "Lost Patrol" is the source of this account of the events of December 5, 1945. McDonnell took most of his information from official transcripts of the transmissions sent and received from the Ft. Lauderdale air base's control tower that day.

219 *The Bermuda Triangle:* Howard L. Rosenberg, "Exorcizing the Devil's Triangle" in *Sealift* No. 6 (June 1974): 11–15, as posted on the Naval Historical Center's website, *www.history.navy.mil.*

220 *The sheer number:* Ibid.

221 *Science has offered:* Ibid.

221 *Compasses point:* Ibid.

222 *In 1904, the British author:* George S. Bryan, *Mystery Ship:* 186.

222 *Coming upon the creature:* Herman Melville, *Moby-Dick* (Norwalk: Easton Press, 1977): 296.

222 *In the 1930s:* This giant squid tale comes from *http://nm.essortment.com/ squidgiantlarg_rehq.htm.*

223 *In the 1970s:* The story of the USS *Stein* is recounted on *www.angelfire. com/biz3/mostlyharmless/giantsquid.html.*

223 *At one point:* Fay, Mary Celeste: 128.

223 *As early as 1926:* Hastings, Mary Celeste: 122–123.

223 *The American psychic:* Berlitz, *The Bermuda Triangle:* 13–14.

224 *One famous shipwreck:* Kusche, *The Bermuda Triangle Mystery Solved:* 24–27.

225 *"Even the ocean":* McDonnell, "Lost Patrol," 9.

226 *While ridiculing the idea:* M. K. Jessup, *The Case for the UFO* (New York: The Citadel Press, 1955): 119.

226 *"There are several facts":* Ibid: 125.

226 *"There is always the possibility":* Ibid.

227 *Near the Arguin Banks:* This account of Dod Osborne's experiences off the coast of Africa was taken from his article, "The Phantom Islands," published in *Life* magazine, December 6, 1948.

229 *In 1966, a former New England sailor:* Gershom Bradford, *The Secret of Mary Celeste and Other Sea Fare* (Barre: Barre Publishing Co., 1966): 1–34.

Chapter Twelve: Without a Soul

233 *He remembered:* Cobb, *Rose Cottage:* 59.

234 *At one dinner:* Ibid: 61–62.

234 *"They expected":* Ibid: 74.

235 *"Undoubtedly the crew":* "New Light on the *Mary Celeste* Mystery," The *Literary Digest,* September 18, 1926: 42.

235 *"In their haste":* Ibid: 42.

235 *"I think that":* Cobb, *Rose Cottage:* 77.

236 *He now suspected:* Ibid: 78.

236 *"the escaping gases":* "New Light on the *Mary Celeste* Mystery," The *Literary Digest,* 42.

237 The Shipping and Commercial List: George S. Bryan, *Mystery Ship:* 57.

237 *Sailors on the steamer* Baltic: Ibid: 58.

237 *On November 24:* The weather conditions and position of the *Mary Celeste* during the last hours Benjamin Briggs and his crew were onboard are taken from a copy of the ship's log slate in the National Archives (Record Group 49, Notes from British Legation, vol. 94).

238 *Meteorological reports show:* The weather conditions around the Azores that day were recorded in a letter from the *Servico Meteorologico dos Azores* to Charles Edey Fay in 1940 and reproduced in his Mary Celeste: 251.

239 *The weather on the Atlantic:* The rough weather the *Dei Gratia* encountered, and the amount of time her hatches were opened, comes from the testimony of Oliver Deveau, *The* Mary Celeste: *Judge's notes:* 7.

239 *According to a report:* Letter of O. M. Spencer to Horatio Sprague, April 26, 1873, National Archives (Record Group 84, Consular Posts, Gibraltar, Correspondence Received, vol. 1866–1875).

239 *According to Oliver: The* Mary Celeste: *Judge's notes:* 5.

239 *Several years before:* Information on the history of alcohol in chemical applications and as a distilled spirit comes from an interview with Chris Morris, master distiller with Brown-Forman in Kentucky. Morris points out that most whiskey, rum or brandy was marked as such and that the 93.95 "proof" was an odd designation, and suggests that it could have been meant to denote its purity. Morris responded to questions about the situation, the statistics and the outcome, and only offered his opinion about the plausibility of the theory in this chapter. In other words, if you disagree with this solution, don't criticize him.

240 *The most telling clue:* The *Mary Celeste*'s movements in October 1872 are recorded in the Maritime Register that is reproduced in Fay, Mary Celeste: 165. For years, stories have alternated whether the ship was moored at Pier 44 or Pier 50. In fact, it was at both, but went to Hunter's Point in Queens for a week in between, a fact that has been ignored in practically every version of the story.

241 *If there had been distilled:* Morris interview.

241 *But if 450 gallons of methanol:* Ibid.

243 *The testimony of the* Dei Gratia *sailors:* Deveau said that "[T]he skylight was not off but open, the hatches were off . . ." At another point he says the hatch on the lazaret and the fore hatch was opened. Most of the other sailors either said "hatches" or mentioned the fore hatch and lazeret particularly. *The* Mary Celeste: *Judge's notes:* 2, 4, 16, 22, 25.

243 *In his salvage hearing testimony:* Ibid: 34.

244 *The halyard, hanging over the side:* Ibid: 7.

245 *On the afternoon of November 25:* Fay, Mary Celeste: 251.

246 *The remaining piece:* Affidavit of John Austin, surveyor of shipping at Gibraltar, National Archives (Record Group 59, Notes from the British Legation, vol. 94).

Epilogue: Off the Island of Voodoo

The account of NUMA's discovery of the *Mary Celeste* wreckage is taken from interviews with Clive Cussler, Mike Fletcher, *The Sea Hunters* episode on the expedition, NUMA press releases, and from Cussler and Craig Dirgo's book *The Sea Hunters II: More True Adventures with Famous Shipwrecks* (New York: G.P. Putnam's Sons, 2002): 195–234.

Selected Bibliography

Berlitz, Charles. *The Bermuda Triangle.* New York: Avon Books, 1975.

Booth, Martin. *The Doctor and the Detective: A Biography of Sir Arthur Conan Doyle.* New York: Thomas Dunne, 1997.

Bradford, Gershom. *The Secret of* Mary Celeste *and Other Sea Fare.* Barre: Barre Publishing Co., 1966.

Briggs, James Franklin. *In the Wake of the* Mary Celeste. New Bedford: Old Dartmouth Historical Society, 1944.

Bryan, George S. *Mystery Ship: The* Mary Celeste *in Fancy and in Fact.* New York: J.B. Lippincott, 1942.

Carr, John Dickson. *The Life of Sir Arthur Conan Doyle.* New York: Carroll & Graf, 1987.

Cobb, Oliver W. "The Mystery of the *Mary Celeste.*" *Yachting Monthly,* August 1925: 253–254.

———. *Rose Cottage.* New Bedford: Reynold-DeWalt, 1968.

Cosgrove, John N., ed. *Gray Days and Gold: A Character Sketch of Atlantic Mutual Insurance Company.* Privately printed for the Atlantic Companies, 1967.

Cussler, Clive and Craig Dirgo. *The Sea Hunters II: More True Adventures with Famous Shipwrecks.* New York: G.P. Putnam's Sons, 2002.

———. *The Sea Hunters: True Adventures with Famous Shipwrecks.* New York: Simon & Schuster, 1996.

Dennis, Clara. *More About Nova Scotia: My Own, My Native Land*. Toronto: Ryerson Press, 1937.

Fay, Charles Edey. Mary Celeste: *The Odyssey of an Abandoned Ship.* Salem: Peabody Museum, 1942.

Furneaux, Rupert. "The Truth About the *Mary Celeste.*" *Fate* magazine, December 1981: 40–50.

Gibson, Gregory. *Demon of the Waters: The True Story of the Mutiny on the Whaleship* Globe. Boston: Little, Brown & Co., 2002.

Guttridge, Leonard F. *Mutiny: A History of Naval Insurrection*. Annapolis: Naval Institute Press, 1992.

Hastings, Macdonald. Mary Celeste: *A Centenary Record.* London: Michael Joseph Ltd, 1972.

Hoehling, A. A. *Lost at Sea.* Nashville: Rutledge Hill Press, 1999.

Jessup, M.K. *The Case for the UFO.* New York: The Citadel Press, 1955.

Keating, Laurence J. *The Great* Mary Celeste *Hoax: A Famous Sea Mystery Exposed.* Boston: Houghton Mifflin, 1929.

Kusche, Larry. *The Bermuda Triangle Mystery Solved*. Amherst: Prometheus Books, 1995.

Labaree, Benjamin W.; William M. Fowler, Jr.; Edward W. Sloan; John B. Hattendorf; Jeffrey J. Safford; and Andrew W. German. *America and the Sea: A Maritime History.* Mystic: Mystic Seaport, 1998.

Lafitte, John. "New Light on the *Mary Celeste* Mystery." The *Literary Digest,* September 18, 1926.

Lockhart, J.G. *The* Mary Celeste *and Other Strange Tales of the Sea.* London: Rupert Hart-Davis, 1958.

Low, Kenneth de Courcy. "The Odyssey of the *Mary Celeste.*" *Sea Classics* magazine, October 1986: 18–19, 78–81.

The Mary Celeste: *Judge's notes on evidence, Vice Admiralty Court of Gibraltar December 1872.* Marion: Sippican Historical Society, n.d.

McDonnell, Michael. "Lost Patrol." *Naval Aviation News,* June 1973, 8–16. Naval Historical Center website.

Miller, Stanley. *The* Mary Celeste: *A Survivor's Tale.* New York: St. Martin's Press, 1980.

Morehouse, Inez Manzer Sypher. *330 Years of Morehouse Genealogy 1640–1970: Volume I.* Hantsport, Nova Scotia: Lancelot Press, 1978.

Osborne, Dod. "The Phantom Islands." *Life* magazine, December 6, 1948.

Packard, Robert F. "The Briggses of Sippican." *Cape Cod Independent,* August 1, 1973.

Poe, Edgar Allan. *Complete Tales & Poems.* New York: Vintage Books, 1975.

Powell, Edward W. *Red Skies . . . Morning and Night: A History of the Atlantic Mutual Companies.* Privately printed for the Atlantic Mutual Companies, 1992.

Rees, Richard. *The Shadow of the Mary Celeste.* London: Robert Hale, 1995.

Robinson, Burton. "Question Mark of the Sea." *The Canadian Magazine,* May 1936, 16, 34.

Rosbe, Judith Westlund. *Marion, Massachusetts.* Charleston: Arcadia Publishing, 2000.

―――. *Maritime Marion Massachusetts.* Charleston: Arcadia Publishing, 2002.

Rosenberg, Howard L. "Exorcizing the Devil's Triangle." *Sealift* magazine, June 1974, 11–15. Naval Historical Center website.

Ryder, Alice A. "Sea Tragedies of Old Rochester." *Lands of Sippican on Buzzards Bay.* New Bedford: Reynolds Printing, 1934.

Sherwood, Roland H. *Maritime Mysteries: Haunting Tales from Atlantic Canada.* Windsor, Nova Scotia: Lancelot Press, 1976.

Snow, Edward Rowe. *Mysterious Tales of the New England Coast.* New York: Dodd, Mead & Co., 1961.

Spicer, Stanley T. *Captain from Fundy: The Life and Times of George D. Spicer, Master of Square-Rigged Windjammers.* Hantsport, Nova Scotia: Lancelot Press, 1988.

―――. *The Saga of the* Mary Celeste: *An Ill-Fated Mystery Ship.* Hantsport, Nova Scotia: Lancelot Press, 1994.

Sullivan, Robert. "Darkest Mystery of the Atlantic." *New York Sunday News,* September 27, 1942.

Woodward, Kathleen. "Mystery of the *Marie Celeste.*" *The New York Times Magazine,* October 12, 1924: 2.

Index